D1613009

THE DAIMLER TRADITION

THE
DAIMLER TRADITION

BRIAN E. SMITH

TRANSPORT BOOKMAN PUBLICATIONS

©1972 Transport Bookman Publications
524-530 High Road, Chiswick
London W4 5RG

ISBN 0 85184 004 4

*Designed and printed in England by
W. S. Cowell Limited at the Butter Market, Ipswich*

Foreword by
Sir William Lyons, Chairman and Chief Executive
The Daimler Company Limited

Maintenance of tradition is of prime importance to the individuality of any marque. The particular traditions of Daimler (and of Lanchester) cars are of outstanding engineering and workmanship; this is as it should be, for Daimler were the first British 'series-production' manufacturers, whilst the Lanchester of 1895 was Britain's very first petrol-driven four-wheeled motor car. The Daimler and Lanchester Owners' Club of today contributes to these traditions by the enthusiasm of its members, and I am happy to share with Mrs George Lanchester the honour of being patron of this club; and it is through the diligence of the club's official historian that 1971 – the 75th anniversary of Daimler – is being marked by the publication of this record of the many varied types of Daimler cars which have been produced down through the years.

Acknowledgements

A number of people have kindly contributed to this work, in large or small measure. First, I am greatly obliged to Sir William Lyons for his Foreword and then my sincere thanks are due to Messrs R. E. Berry, Andrew Whyte, J. Smith and others of The Daimler Co or within the Jaguar organization for their invaluable assistance.

To Mr Osmond Rivers, former Chief Designer and Director of Hooper & Co (Coachbuilders) Ltd I must pay special tribute. Over the course of several years he has devoted much time and effort in providing me with a wealth of detail and information without which Part II would be sadly deficient as regards specialist coachwork. Mr C. M. Simpson, formerly Chief Engineer of The Daimler Co is another who has willingly advised on technical and historical matters. The task of research was much facilitated by the co-operation received from Mr J. A. Lee and the Library staff at I P C Transport Press Ltd (proprietors of *The Motor* and *The Autocar*) and to them I am also most grateful for allowing me to quote from their journals, to use extracts from Road Tests and to reproduce their pictures appearing on pp. 7, 11, 13, 79, 87, 96, 169 and 222.

Other pictures and illustrations have been kindly provided as follows:

On p. 109 and the centre picture on p. 244 by Mr Gordon Asbury, Sales Director of Stratstone Ltd; on pp. 95 and 113 by Mr R. S. Crouch of Daimler Transport Vehicles Ltd; on pp. 23, 30, 31, 32, 35, 38 and 85 by The Daimler & Lanchester Owners' Club; on p. 252 by Mr J. N. A. Fletcher; the lower picture on p. 77 by The Radio Times Hulton Picture Library; and the lower picture on p. 70 by Mr C. M. Walker.

The proprietors of *Motor Sport* have also kindly given permission for me to quote from that renowned journal.

I am honoured to be able to record my sincere gratitude to members of Her Majesty's Household for privileges granted and assistance rendered. I was also given much help by The Institute of British Carriage & Automobile Manufacturers, The Society of Motor Manufacturers and Traders, the Coventry Museum and Mr Philip Sumner, Curator and the staff of the Science Museum, London, Mr E. Roland Fox, Managing Director and Mr H. J. Beshaw, Technical Director, Vanden Plas division of British Leyland. Mr L. A. Blake, Managing Director of Hooper Motor Services Ltd gave me additional information concerning the activities and products of Hooper & Co; a similar contribution in respect of Windovers was made by Mr Malcolm of Greenford, in respect of Freestone & Webb by Mr Knott of Wood & Piggott Ltd; and by Mr J. O. H. Norris as regards J. Cockshoot & Co; Mr P. Howman kindly verified my data concerning Daimler Hire Ltd.

Messrs J. Whitbourne and Eric Chase both have my gratitude for their help with particular aspects of the photographic work. Within The Daimler & Lanchester Owners' Club there have been many who have proffered help and advice. Special mention must be made of Messrs C. Bromfield, B. Mason, Alec Norman, I. Venables and particularly H. Duncan Saunders, General Secretary of the Club – who encouraged me to compile this record and who then gladly assumed the unenviable task of reading and checking the result. Without the co-operation and special efforts of my publishers and the printers this work would not of course have reached fruition. To each and all of those mentioned and to any inadvertently overlooked, my very sincere thanks.

B.E.S.

CONTENTS

Preface

TEN MONTHS before it became lawful to drive a self-propelled vehicle on the highways of England (except under near impossible conditions), The Daimler Motor Co Ltd was formed with the principal objective of manufacturing motor vehicles; that was in January 1896. It was thus one of the very first manufacturers to be established in this country and within the first decade of its existence, the Company (by then re-constituted), had gained for itself a fine reputation for producing vehicles of sound design and construction and dependability.

The acquisition in 1896 of premises in Coventry may justly be regarded as the laying of the foundation stone of the British motor industry in which the Company occupied a pre-eminent position for so long.

From the beginning of the era, Daimler was the Royal car and throughout three-quarters of a century, Daimler cars have been prominent at State functions, on Royal tours both at home and abroad, and in numerous other notable events. Throughout successive reigns, the most distinguished families of Great Britain made Daimler an intimate part of their daily lives. Surely this was the most cogent testimony that could ever be paid a motor car.

It was not, however, merely a matter of patronage or prestige upon which the reputation was founded and sustained. The Company was never reluctant to consider the novel or to investigate the unorthodox and through its long and eventful history Daimlers can claim many 'firsts'. The painstaking care given in research and to every aspect of design, the use of the very best quality materials, and the employment of the highest degree of craftsmanship combined to justify the maker's assertion that Daimlers were 'Supreme among the world's best cars.'

To mark the occasion of its 50th anniversary in 1946, The Daimler Company commissioned that doyen of motoring writers, the late St John C. Nixon to write a complete and authoritative history of the Company. Needless to say, he performed his task in an erudite manner and commendably tackled every salient event and development concerning the Company and its activities. In the preface to that work ('Daimler 1896–1946' – G. T. Foulis & Co Ltd), Nixon referred to the general difficulties he had encountered in collating reliable information about the early Daimler cars and contemporary events and in particular he noted the sad loss to the Company of the greater part of its records through enemy action during the Coventry blitz. The problem has been exacerbated not only by the passage of another quarter century but also by reason of the fact that within that period the Company, very happily, has been far from inactive. Moreover, to chronicle all the events and to describe and illustrate all the multitude of Daimler cars produced in seventy-five years would, if practicable, produce a voluminous result. In consequence some sacrifice and compromise was imperative if this present book were to be kept to manageable proportions.

In Part I, by way of an amplified introduction to the main work comprised in the second part, the early history of The Daimler Company is briefly re-told with illustrations and details of the more important and interesting vehicles produced during the first fifty years and then in Part II an attempt has been made to record all the post-war production chassis-types and to describe in considerable detail the coachwork of the period whether emanating from the Company's works or from the coachbuilders, and whether of standard design or of the 'special' or 'one-off' variety. Several examples are known to the writer which have not been included and there are no doubt others in existence. It is, however, thought that most of the significant and outstanding styles actually produced receive an appropriate mention.

It is gratifying that notwithstanding many intervening events of great impact, the Company remains after its 75th anniversary year a producer of buses, saloon cars and limousines true to the Daimler tradition.

PART I

The Daimler Tradition – from embryo to maturity

ON THE 17th March 1834 Gottlieb Daimler was born in Schorndorf, a village in Wurttenberg, Germany. He was to become one of the great pioneers in the development of the motor car.

He was apprenticed to a gunsmith and later studied engineering at Stuttgart Polytechnic College and he subsequently spent time working in Coventry and Birmingham, England. During these years Daimler devoted much thought to the internal combustion engine but it was not until 1872 when he commenced employment as Technical Director with Doktor N. A. Otto that Daimler had an opportunity for implementing some of his ideas. By reason of his position, Daimler was able to engage the services of Wilhelm Maybach – an outstanding engineer who then became Otto's Chief Designer. Following a year's absence in Russia, Daimler returned in 1882 to Cannstatt, Germany where he acquired a small workshop and was later joined by Maybach. There the two of them successfully designed and built stationary petrol engines the ignition for which was of a novel design involving a 'hot tube'. The motors were put to a number of uses. An engine had been successfully installed in a cycle, a fire engine pump, and boats and an attempt had been made to provide power for an airship! In 1886 Daimler's first motorized carriage was completed and in the same year a friend was appointed to handle Daimler's patents. Unfortunately, this friend died within a short space of time and his widow subsequently married Emile Levassor. It was he who carried out much research work during the period 1890 to 1895 in the development of motor vehicles fitted with Daimler's engines.

Another of Daimler's experiments concerned a passenger trolley car designed to run on rails and powered by a small vertical internal combustion engine built by the inventor himself. The complete trolley was shown at an International Exhibition held at Bremen in 1890. Fortuitously, there was in attendance a young engineer named Frederick Richard Simms from Warwickshire, England. This young engineer possessed great talent and perception and was himself an exhibitor – showing an aerial cableway for passenger transport.

Simms was obviously much impressed by Daimler's engine which was of the four-stroke single cylinder type with the aforesaid 'tube' ignition. This tube of platinum extended into the combustion chamber but the closed end protruded beyond the head where intense heat by bunsen burner was applied. On the compression stroke some of the mixture was forced within the tube causing it

Gottlieb Daimler's first car of 1886, driven by Wilhelm Maybach. Sitting next to him is Daimler's son, Paul

to explode. The cylinder dimensions were 70×120 mm and the speed was controlled by a centrifugal governor allowing a maximum of about 750–800 rpm. On the descent of the piston the inlet valve opened from the resultant suction and closure was effected by the application of a light spring positioned immediately above the exhaust valve which in turn was actuated by a rod in contact with the outer face of one of the flywheels.

To facilitate the discharge of the exhaust gases, a third valve was fitted to the piston top and at the lowest point of the stroke a projection in the basechamber made contact with the lower end of the valve stem causing it to open. The consequent release of pressurized air from the crankcase coinciding with the opening of the principal exhaust valve provided a boost to the discharge process.

As a culmination to the number of early visits that Simms made to Germany, an agreement was concluded by virtue of which Simms acquired all Daimler engine patents for the United Kingdom and Colonies (except Canada). That was in 1890 at which time there was in England a general disinclination to take seriously the petrol engine and in any event development of the engine for the purpose of propelling a road vehicle would not have been commercially practicable because of the restrictive provisions of the Highways and Locomotive Act 1878. The roads had fallen into a deplorable state of repair and there were still many who held the Elizabethan view that to ride in a coach or carriage was effeminate and possibly injurious to one's physical well being!

Daimler-Motoren-Gesellschaft CANNSTATT

3

Notwithstanding such unfavourable conditions, Simms was quite enthusiastic about the Daimler engine and its potential and was anxious to popularize it in every conceivable way. He intended to use the engine at the German exhibition in London but in the event was precluded from so doing – largely, it appears because of the misapprehension of the organizers who imagined that there would be a very real danger of the 'thing' exploding. However on the 16th May 1891 the first Daimler engine ever to enter England arrived accompanied by a Daimler engined motor boat loaned to Simms for the purpose of demonstration. After encountering problems concerning a suitable venue, Simms was finally allowed to demonstrate the boat on the Thames. The boat was moored at Putney Bridge and a number of successful trips were accomplished between Charing Cross and Westminster bridges. Over the next two years Simms carried out development work and applied Daimler engines to a number of purposes and following the success of the Thames demonstrations, a number of boats were sold fitted with Daimler power units. Thus encouraged Simms concluded that it would be expedient to incorporate a private company for the further exploitation of the Daimler patents and with the hope and object of utilizing the engines in horseless carriages as soon as the stringent legislative provisions were abrogated. The vending agreement provided that the assets of Simms and Company, including the benefits of all contracts, agreements, selling rights, patents and other property should be transferred to the newly formed Daimler Motor Syndicate Limited. The capital of the new concern was £6,000 and rented premises were acquired by the Company in an arch at Putney Bridge Railway Station. After another two years – more precisely on the 7th June 1895 the Syndicate's board met and adopted a resolution authorizing Mr Simms 'to take all necessary steps in the face of good prospects . . . for preparing everything towards the formation of the DAIMLER MOTOR COMPANY LIMITED with a capital of £50 to £100,000 as may be decided later on, for the purpose of acquiring the British Daimler patents and the manufacturing of the said motors in this country.' At a board meeting held on the 19th July 1895 it was noted in the minutes that the Hon. Evelyn Ellis and Mr Simms had successfully completed their first trip in a Daimler motor carriage in this country. It was further noted that as a result of this, many enquiries and orders had been received. Steps had already been taken to implement the decision to form a new company when they were abruptly halted by the intervention of a speculator by the name of Harry J. Lawson. Whatever else may have been said and written about Law son – his perception and foresight were quite outstanding. At the conclusion of negotiations it was agreed that for £35,000 all the assets of The Daimler Motor Syndicate Ltd, should be transferred to The British Motor Syndicate Ltd, in which Lawson had a controlling interest and without loss of time he floated in January 1896 a new concern called The Daimler Motor Co Ltd.

When in February 1896 the public were invited to subscribe the prospectus named among others, Gottlieb Daimler and the Hon. Evelyn Ellis to be directors

F. R. Simms' Cannstatt-built Daimler – the car in which King Edward VII had his first motor ride in this country – 14th February 1896

but the right was reserved to Lawson (through the British Motor Syndicate) to install himself as chairman and to nominate one other director. Gottlieb Daimler acted solely in an honorary capacity and never attended any Company meetings, although he along with Simms participated in the famous 'emancipation run'. Daimler died on the 6th March 1900, at the age of nearly sixty-six without having had the satisfaction of seeing in full measure the success of his invention.

With the new Company duly incorporated, the directors left for the Continent in order to visit the factories of Panhard and Levassor, Peugeot and De Dion-Bouton and of course the works of the Daimler Motoren Gesellschaft in order to acquire first hand knowledge. Upon their return they set about looking for suitable premises and after several abortive enquiries and viewings they heard of a disused cotton mill situated on a thirteen-acre site alongside the Coventry canal. The building comprised a double factory which had been largely rebuilt following a fire in 1891. The new company acted with celerity and acquired the premises which more than met their requirements. The acquisition was made in April 1896 and almost at once the Company received an attractive offer for one half

5

of the premises from another new company called The Great Horseless Carriage Company Ltd whose principal promoter was none other than Harry J. Lawson. It is not without interest to note that the proceeds from the sale to the Lawson enterprise more than reimbursed The Daimler Motor Company Ltd for its initial outlay. It has been suggested that Daimler's purchase represented the laying of the British motor industry's largest foundation stone.

The first statutory meeting of The Daimler Motor Company was held in May 1896 when the directors reported on their Continental visit and spoke optimistically about the Company's future but unfortunately subsequent events proved such optimism to be premature, to say the least.

The early directors did not possess much business acumen and even less can be said of their engineering ability and experience. However, a notable exception was J. S. Critchley who was appointed the Company's first Works Manager. He was one of the few men in England at that time with a practical experience of motor engineering and he together with Simms, who had been appointed Consulting Engineer, were responsible for implementing the primary object of the infant Company, namely, the production of motor cars.

Early in 1896, *The Autocar* organized a petition for presentation to Parliament urging it to repeal the subsisting repressive laws and asking that the use of motor vehicles on the public highways be legalized. Furthermore, an exhibition was staged at the Imperial Institute, London between the 9th May and the 8th August 1896. The Daimler Motor Company occupied three stands upon which an assortment of vehicles was displayed but at this date Daimler's own production at Coventry was not far advanced and the exhibits, although powered by Cannstatt Daimler engines, were all of Continental origin.

It was arranged that demonstrations would be given in the grounds adjoining the Institute and invitations were sent to both Houses of Parliament and to distinguished and influential persons with a view to obtaining their support for the new form of transport generally and for the aforesaid petition in particular. Before the exhibition was officially opened, H R H the Prince of Wales (later to become King Edward VII) expressed interest and on the 14th February he was driven by the Hon. Evelyn Ellis through the gallery and out into the grounds in a Cannstatt built Daimler the workings of which were explained to the Prince by its owner F. R. Simms. From this early interest began the close association between the British Royal Family and The Daimler Company which was to endure for many decades.

The unexpected interest manifest by His Royal Highness, and the success of the exhibition itself ensured that the petitioners' prayer would be answered favourably. The long awaited and overdue 'Locomotives on Highways Act 1896' received the Royal assent and came into effect before the end of the year and to celebrate the occasion a drive from London to Brighton was arranged for the 14th November. No effort was spared in making the 'Emancipation' run a success. Several cars were specially brought over from the Continent and every

One of the earliest Coventry-built Daimlers – 1897

The first British-built production Daimler

7

available motorized vehicle was procured. Still no British built Daimler had been made but many of the cars participating were fitted with Daimler engines made at Coventry and elsewhere under licence and furthermore, a number of personnel from The Daimler Motor Company were very much involved.

The first Coventry built Daimlers were constructed during 1897 and although names such as 'Rougemont', the 'Siamese', the 'Wyley', the 'Grafton', the 'Universal' and 'Jaunting car' mentioned in the first catalogue indicated a choice of styles, all were powered by twin-cylinder 4-hp engines with tube ignition. The cars were of course chain driven and the standard production models had driving wheels measuring 3 feet 3 inches in diameter.

On the 28th August 1897 it was reported in the *Hampshire Chronicle* that Major-General Montgomery of Winchester had collected his new Daimler car from the works at Coventry, having submitted what was almost certainly the very first order for a British-made car by anyone unconnected with the motor trade. The report continued – '. . . the riding was simply delightful, the swift, gliding noiseless motion along the level roads being particularly exhilarating.'

Earlier, in July, in a Coventry Daimler with non-standard gear ratios, the Hon. Evelyn Ellis and J. S. Critchley drove to the summit of Malvern Beacon and in so doing caused a mild sensation in the locality and further afield. This achievement was followed during October 1897 by Henry Sturmey (who succeeded H. J. Lawson as Chairman), driving from John o'Groat's to Land's End in a Daimler with bodywork designed by Sturmey and constructed by Mulliners of Northampton. The car had the usual 4-hp engine, solid tyres, chain drive and tiller steering. The journey started on the 2nd October and was concluded on the 19th. Cards were handed out to the many curious spectators en route and these gave the following information:

'WHAT IS IT?'

'It is an autocar.
'Some people call it a motor car.
'It is worked by a petroleum motor.
'The motor is of four horse-power.
'It will run sixty miles with one charge of oil.
'No! It can't explode – there is no boiler.
'It can travel at 14 mph.
'Ten to eleven is its average pace.
'It can be started in two minutes.
'There are eight ways of stopping it so it can't run away.
'It is steered with one hand.
'Speed is mainly controlled by the foot.
'It can be stopped in ten feet when travelling at full speed.
'It carries four gallons of oil and sixteen gallons of water.
'The water is to keep the engine cool.
'It costs less than $\frac{3}{4}$d. a mile to run.
'The car can carry five people.

'It can get up any ordinary hill.
'It was built by the Daimler Motor Company of Coventry and cost £370.
'We have come from John o'Groat's House.
'We are going to Land's End.
'We are not record-breaking but touring for pleasure.'

Although difficulties were encountered none of these proved to be insurmountable, and the trip of 929 miles was accomplished in 93½ hours running time at an average speed of just under 10 mph. If that was not enough, Sturmey then drove back to Coventry making a total of about 1,600 miles for the round trip.

During 1898, the Company introduced 4-cylinder 8 hp engines and the first Daimler car to be so powered was purchased by Prof. Boverton Redwood and it is highly probable that this was the first 4-cylinder engined car produced and sold in this country. Also during the same year wheel steering first became optional and subsequently replaced the tiller used on the earlier cars.

Following the demonstration in 1896 to the Prince of Wales, His Royal Highness had a further opportunity of inspecting more examples of the new form of road transport when on the 27th November 1897 another demonstration was given in the grounds of Buckingham Palace. Among the few vehicles shown was Sturmey's 'End to End' car and another Daimler whose owner was Arthur Mulliner, the coachbuilder. Then in June 1898 while staying at Warwick Castle, the Prince first tried a car on the public highways. Three standard twin-cylinder 4 hp Daimlers with solid tyres and tiller steering were selected: Prof. Boverton Redwood was invited to show his newly acquired 4-cylinder car and the fifth vehicle was again Sturmey's car. It was stated at the time that the Prince was much impressed by the absence of vibration and he obviously enjoyed his experience for shortly afterwards he ordered a Daimler car.

During 1899, about fifty twin-cylinder water-cooled engines of about 4 hp had been received from the German Daimler works at Cannstatt and as it was not envisaged that these units would be used in the Coventry production programme, the Critchley Light car was designed and manufactured for the primary purpose of making use of the surplus engines. Although the Light car differed considerably from models up to that date turned out by the Company, it earned itself a good reputation and sold well. In its way, the Critchley Light car was quite advanced; its engine was mounted transversely so that the flywheel rotated in the direction of travel, it had wheel steering and was equipped with pneumatic tyres and belt transmission. The total weight of the vehicle was only 6¾ cwt.

The *Motor Car Journal*, referring to the Hon. John Scott-Montagu's new 12 hp 4-cylinder Daimler purchased in 1899, said that it was 'the most up to date carriage built in this country.' This was the first petrol engined vehicle ever to enter the near sacred precincts of the Houses of Parliament on the 3rd July 1899 and in September of the same year, the car was taken to France to compete in the celebrated Paris–Ostend event and by all accounts this was 'the first race in

King George VI enjoying a ride on the first Royal Daimler of 1900 (as subsequently modified)

which a British-made carriage has been driven by an Englishman.' The same car was kindly loaned by Lord Montagu of Beaulieu and exhibited on the Daimler stand at the London Motor Show, 1971 on the occasion of the Company's 75th anniversary.

In those early years before the turn of the century, the Company received gold, silver and bronze medals at many notable events for '. . . design, construction and efficiency . . .', 'for the best motor car exhibited' and for innovations and successes in other events. In the famous 'Thousand Miles Trial' held in 1900 (and commemorated by a re-run of the event in 1970), thirteen Daimler cars of the private type started and all finished the course and eleven awards were received. The Trial was the first and perhaps the most famous of its kind ever to be held in Britain.

Shortly after the Trial the car previously ordered by HRH the Prince of Wales, was delivered to him. There has been considerable controversy concerning the date of this vehicle. In *The Autocar* for 3rd February 1939, J. S. Critchley

4-cylinder 12 hp Daimler, 1900

wrote an interesting letter giving details of the car and other data about the first Royal motorist. Critchley was the driver of the car carrying the Prince in June 1898 on the trip from Warwick Castle to Compton Verney and he asserts that it was soon thereafter that the car was ordered. However, in the same article, Critchley concluded that delivery of the car was made late in 1898 or early 1899. This, however, would appear to be incorrect for in another article in *The Motor Car Journal* dated the 16th June 1900 it was stated that the first car owned by Royalty had 'just been delivered'. The car was propelled by a twin-cylinder 6 hp engine fitted with both electric and tube ignition. Originally the paintwork was in chocolate and black with red piping and it almost certainly had pneumatic tyres at both front and rear but it is believed that because of the flints encountered at Sandringham, solid tyres were fitted to the rear at a later date. Over the years a number of modifications have been made to the car which now rests at the Royal Mews, Buckingham Palace and it is one of several Royal Daimlers in the recently started collection there. Twenty-four mph was claimed to be the car's maximum speed but the handbook mentioned a conservative 20 mph! Hooper & Co of St James's Street, London were entrusted with the building of the Phaeton body. Considerable mechanical restoration has recently been carried out to this historic vehicle, and it successfully participated in the 'London to Brighton', 1971.

A Daimler Wagonette of 1900 – note the raked steering

Before the year 1900 closed, His Royal Highness ordered two further Daimlers. One was a 12 hp 4-cylinder car whereas the other was described as a 'Beaters car' designed for use during the shooting season to carry up to fourteen people.

The 'Critchley Light Car' was redesigned and renamed the 'Kimberley' and a new 12 hp 4-cylinder model with raked steering was introduced.

By comparison with the Thousand Miles Trial, the result of the Daimler cars that participated in the Glasgow Motor Trial of 1901 was disappointing but the event is worthy of a brief mention if for no other reason than that two newly designed 6 hp Light Daimlers made their appearance there and they were the first Daimlers to be shaft driven. Also announced during the year was an exciting new 22 hp car fitted with a throttle and both electric and tube ignition.

King Edward VII ordered a new 24 hp Daimler which was delivered to him in time for Ascot 1902 after being exhibited in a partially completed state at The Agricultural Hall, Islington, London, and a fine new seven seater car – nearly 16 feet long and powered by a 22 hp engine – 'making it capable of maintaining level speed over all gradients . . .' was delivered to the Prince of Wales in February 1903.

Seven cars ready for delivery to customers were completely destroyed in a disastrous fire which occurred in April of the same year. Nevertheless, the year

1901 12 hp model

1901 16 hp model

The 22 hp car of 1902 – Oliver Stanton at the wheel

ended with the Accounts revealing a reasonable profit. Sales had nearly doubled over the preceding year and the Company's policy of concentrating on two cars only, namely the 14 hp and 22 hp models was continued. Rendered necessary by the fire was the erection of a new paint and finishing shop and from that time the majority of motor bodies were built and finished in the Daimler works.

The Motor for 11th February 1903 dealing with the Crystal Palace Automobile Show reported:

Greater accessibility of parts is being provided for, the Daimler Company even going so far as to hinge the body of the car so that it can be lifted and held aloft by supports to permit of ready accessibility to the gear box and all other parts of the mechanism.

During 1904, four standard types were offered. The smallest of these was a 7 hp Light car powered by a twin-cylinder engine and was probably the first Daimler to be equipped with battery and coil ignition. *The Motor* commented 'The body is of the familiar Daimler design and this is synonymous with all that is best in carriage work'. From the same source we learn that except where a customer chose differently, the colour most favoured by the makers at the time was 'Daimler green'. Only a few of these Light cars were, however, made. Next in size was the 16/20 having a displacement of 3,309 cc; then there was the 18/22 – (95 × 135 mm – 3,827 cc) followed by the 28/36 – (110 × 150 mm – 5,703 cc).

King Edward VII – c. 1901

Valve seating inclined at an angle to the compression chamber was a new feature on some of the season's models. Some 590 workmen were employed by the Company and output at this period was running at the rate of about one car a day.

King Edward again favoured the Company with his custom and ordered the largest model which was fitted with a limousine body designed and built by Hooper & Co. In the extreme rear of the car there was a fixed seat capable of seating three passengers in comfort and in addition there were two revolving seats in the rear for use by the King and an honoured guest. The central division had an opening centre piece; electric lighting was fitted and the rear compartment was upholstered in blue leather with matching pile carpet. Externally the car was painted in Royal lake picked out with red.

A particular feature of the 1903 cars had been the horizontal fins through the radiator and although the arrangement was retained for some models for 1904, it was in the latter year that the fluted and traditional radiator of the marque emerged. The King's new 28/36 was so fitted and another characteristic of the early Daimlers – the curved scuttle or dash, was also apparent on the Royal car. Much about the same period the Daimler three-piece bonnet came into being and in different forms it remained in use until 1940.

When writing about the Company in *Daimler 1896–1946* (Foulis), St John C. Nixon said: 'Almost from the day of its formation it has been torn by internal

15

HM King Edward VII about to enter his Daimler Car – 1904

His Majesty King George V when Prince of Wales in 1906

16

quarrels and dissent among its sponsors, crippled by lack of working funds and held in check by being controlled by men possessing only just that little knowledge which is so proverbially dangerous.' Now, however, due to the outstanding efforts of the farsighted new Board of business men, The Daimler Company was elevated to the premier position in the British Motor industry. The Company was voluntarily wound up in the autumn of 1904 and a new concern called – 'The Daimler Motor Company (1904) Limited' was formed.

During 1905 King Edward VII ordered yet another Daimler, his seventh, the Prince of Wales (afterwards King George V) ordered a 30 hp model whilst Queen Mary (the Princess of Wales as she then was), ordered a 28 hp landaulette. The Company opened depots in Nottingham and Manchester, appointed agents on the Continent and introduced the Daimler car into America. A Company called the Societa Anonima Officine de Luca Daimler was started in Naples and a number of Daimler cars were constructed there under licence during the years 1906 to 1908.

Daimler cars put up the four best times of the day at the first Shelsley Walsh Hill Climb in 1905. First was a 35 hp car driven by E. M. C. Instone (General Manager of the Daimler Company) and in third position was Percy Martin (Works Manager and later Managing Director).

An outstanding new model – the 45 hp was introduced during the summer of 1906. In place of the earlier practice of using a frame made of flitch plate channel

30/40 hp Daimler – c. 1906/7

steel and wood, a pressed steel frame was used for the new model which had an engine of four cylinders in a block of one casting, with a capacity of no less than 10,604 cc (150 × 150 mm). An unusual feature was the gate change in lieu of the more usual sliding gear lever. Also during 1906 Coventry made Daimlers were for the first time exhibited at the Berlin and Paris Motor shows. A seven-seater Daimler with bodywork of the Roi-des-Belges type was constructed by the Lacre Motor Car Co Ltd, and supplied to the King of Siam.

In twenty-three recorded events during 1907 Daimler cars gained first place in their class. Two further cars were ordered by King Edward and by this date the Company's reputation was such that enquiries and orders were being received from all parts of the world. Development work was being carried on in connection with commercial vehicles and an agreement was negotiated for the manufacture by the Daimler Company of that incredible contraption – the Renard Road-train for most parts of the world. S. C. H. Davis remembers working on the Renard project as an apprentice and has described it as '. . . a horrible affair. . . . The row these joints made when at an angle had to be heard to be believed. Anyway, we swore that you could hear that train going along St Nicholas Street to the London Road while down a pit in the erecting shop.' Perhaps Sammy Davis has vivid recollections of the early experiment as otherwise there would appear to be direct conflict between his testimony and the report in *The Autocar* for August 1910:

On Wednesday last a large company of visitors witnessed a most interesting series of demonstrations, carried out with two road-trains which have been built for the transport of ore by well-known Australian and Canadian mining companies respectively. A great many of us who were present had been acquainted with the old system of traction, as applied on the Renard principle, and therefore were in a position to appreciate the vast improvements which have been effected by the Daimler Company. Perhaps the most astonishing feature of all, when watching these huge motor trains moving on smooth road or rough field, is the wonderful silence of the whole mechanism. This is, of course, primarily due to the Knight engine, and secondly to the efficient transmission system which has been adopted.

Although both trains had been built for freight, on this occasion one of them consisted of the locomotor and several cabs, on which seats were mounted in char-à-banc fashion, so that visitors were able to test the running qualities, especially with regard to comfort. In this respect it should at once be said that these were a revelation as far as smoothness was concerned, even though the ground on which the train travelled had been made as bad as it could possibly be made.

According to particulars given the weight of the locomotor complete in running order, with water and petrol, totals 4 tons 16 cwt. The weight of a passenger follower carrying twenty-five to thirty people works out at 4 tons 18 cwt, and a goods follower loaded with 5 tons of material runs to 8 tons 5 cwt. Taking a long day's work, the cost of running a train of a gross weight of 28 tons 18 cwt comes to £5. 4s. 4d.

The engine, as has already been stated, is of the well-known Daimler Knight type, having six cylinders cast in pairs and listed as 80 hp. There is nothing in this engine that materially differs from the 57 hp pattern except in the cooling system. Here, a very large radiator is provided in front, and above, running the whole length of the bonnet, is a large water tank which would obviously

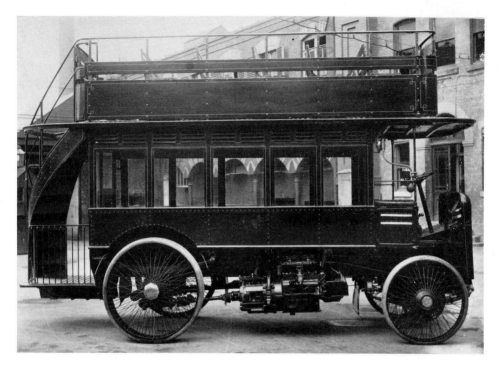

The advanced KPL Bus of 1910

A Daimler Renard Road-train in chassis form

appear to be a necessity, especially in hot climates. From the engine, power is taken through a very large diameter cone clutch and flexible shaft to a gear-box containing four speeds forward and reverse. A direct drive is obtained on third speed, and normally the speeds give two, four, six and eight miles an hour respectively. The top speed is geared up and is used when the train is running light. Each cab or follower has its own differential, and the drive is taken by countershafts and chains in every unit. Instead of employing crown wheels and bevels the overhead worm drive is employed throughout, and a continuing series of driving shafts pass from the locomotor to the last cab.

The Renard 'Automobile Train' was invented by the Renard Freres and was first shown at the Paris Exhibition in December 1903. In its form as developed by Daimler it was supplied to Canada, Australia, USA, South America and several European countries and for military use, Lord Kitchener ordered one for Egypt.

The previously mentioned Italian associate Company entered three Coventry built cars for the 1907 Targa Florio, the cars finishing in thirteenth, twentieth and twenty-sixth place respectively. Also during the same year Daimler engined boats won the Dewar Cup, the May Cup, and a Gold Medal in the Motor Yacht Club's reliability trials, and a little later *Daimler II* won the Motor Boat Challenge Trophy at an average speed of over 26 knots.

The 30 hp and 38 hp cars of 1907 were the first to be equipped with live rear axles. By this time the Company were conscious of the presence in the luxury car market of Lanchester, Rolls-Royce, Napier and one or two other manufacturers. In particular the Rolls-Royce Silver Ghost had emerged triumphant from the RAC observed trial of 1907 and its comparative silence and lively performance were conspicuous attributes. In America, Charles Y. Knight, a young agriculturist of Wisconsin, had demonstrated the practicability and potential of his invention, the sliding or sleeve valve engine. This was brought to the notice of The Daimler Company who invited Knight to visit them accompanied by a car powered by an engine of his design. The idea commended itself to the Coventry engineers and agreements for production were negotiated and after very extensive experimenting and development – much of it under the direction of Dr F. W. Lanchester, the Company decided to adopt the new design. The engine differed from the ordinary type in that the conventional mushroom tappet valves in use at the time were replaced by sleeve valves fitted between the piston and the cylinder wall. The motor was able to run very quietly and, owing to the rapid opening and closing of the valves, higher than normal speeds could be attained. The absence of valve pockets in the combustion chamber was an added advantage and facilitated cooling.

Within the cylinder were two concentric cast-iron sleeves which extended into the crank chamber and were there attached by connecting rods to short cranks on a counter-shaft running at half the speed of the main shaft. On the 22 hp model (1910) the inner sleeve was 4 mm thick and the outer one 3 mm thick and their stroke was one inch. Near to their upper extremities the sleeves had slots which registered with each other and with the inlet and exhaust ports timed to correspond with the motions of the four-stroke engine cycle.

1910 tourer – one of the earliest sleeve-valve models

As soon as the Company's proposed change of policy was made known, 'know-alls' immediately condemned the idea of using sleeves as impracticable. One insuperable problem (among many others) they said, would be satisfactory lubrication. Charles Knight himself gave a number of public lectures and also wrote convincingly a series of articles but these did little to allay the inhibitions. Consequently, with a view to dispelling scepticism, The Daimler Company took a courageous decision and in March 1909 submitted two of their new engines to severe independent testing under close scrutiny by the R A C. The engines selected for the purpose were the 38 hp (124 × 130 mm) and a 22 hp (96 × 130 mm).

Under strict observation the engines were each bench tested at the Daimler works for a total of 132 hours and for the greater part of that time both engines were working under full load. Following this the engines were mounted into standard chassis complete with bodies and the cars were then driven from Coventry to Brooklands track where they were both subjected to further arduous testing, again under strict surveillance. A distance of 1,930·5 miles was recorded at an average speed of 42·4 mph for the larger car and for the smaller vehicle a distance of 1,914·1 miles was recorded at an average speed of 41·88 mph. On their return to Coventry (under their own power) both engines were removed from their chassis and given further bench running tests for more than five hours each. They were then stripped and examined. With the notional mileage calculated from the bench tests and the actual mileage as recorded it was shown that each engine had been tested over an equivalent to appreciably more than 10,000 miles.

The undermentioned remarks by the Judges were appended to the certificates issued in respect of both cars:

The engine was completely dismantled, and no perceptible wear was noticeable on any of the fitted surfaces. The cylinders and pistons were found to be notably clean. The ports of the valves showed no sign of burning or wear.

The certificate relating to the 38 hp engine mentioned that the only visible wear in any part was caused by two joint pins rubbing against adjacent parts. The outcome of the tests had been an undoubted success and the new design was vindicated. One of the motor industry's most coveted awards – the Dewar Trophy was awarded to the Company which promptly challenged any other manufacturer of poppet valve engines to submit to a similar series of tests and in the event of a challenger gaining a more meritorious certificate from the R A C the Company offered to pay £250 which sum was in fact forthwith deposited. That there was no response is a clear indication of the apprehension on the part of all other manufacturers.

In November 1909 a new 15 hp model with a 'Silent Knight' engine (80 × 130 mm) was announced for the following year. Thanks to the careful research and experiments carried out by the design staff, the difficulties encountered with the new power units when put into production were singularly few. For a while both poppet valve and sleeve valve engines were made contemporaneously but for 1910 the new engine dominated the Daimler range.

For a while the Company produced a 'House magazine' under the name of the *Daimler Bulletin*. In the issue for February 1909 it was reported that:

Mr (later Dr) F. W. Lanchester has been appointed Consulting Engineer to The Daimler Motor Company and during the course of the next few months he will commence to actively interest himself with the many engineering matters which the Company has under consideration. In addition to the manufacture of pleasure motor carriages, the Company's field of engineering activity already embraces work in connection with road-trains, commercial vehicles, omnibuses, agricultural motors etc. and as the new Daimler engine opens up possibilities of development in directions in which the internal combustion engine has not fully asserted itself, the scope of this Company's business is certain of still further expansion.

Another new Company – The Societe Francaise de la Daimler Motor Company was established in Paris where premises were fully operational by the end of 1909. At the close of the previous year the Company suffered a severe setback for the accounts had revealed a deficit of nearly £50,000. Due in no small measure to the triumph of the sleeve valve engine tests and the resulting prospects, the position was reversed in 1909 and at the end of the following year's trading the position was even better with a profit of £100,000 being shown. According to St John C. Nixon (*Daimler 1896–1946*) the Daimler Company '. . . had become beyond question the leading motor manufacturing company in this country.'

All Lanchester motor cars from 1897 had used worm gear for the final drive and it is therefore, significant to note that shortly after F. W. Lanchester's appointment, all Daimler cars (from 1910 onwards) were similarly equipped

Daimler hire department – London

Daimler showrooms – Paris

23

and it was not until after the second world war that a change to hypoid axles was made. The new Daimlers equipped with sleeve valve engines, worm drive and beautifully engineered gearboxes were now a match for the Rolls-Royce product in all aspects of silence and quality even if one has reluctantly to concede that the Silver Ghost had a more virile performance.

In the *Financial Times* for the 2nd September 1910, it was disclosed that negotiations were in hand for a possible amalgamation of the Company with the Birmingham Small Arms Company Ltd – manufacturers of machine made arms, bicycles and to a limited extent motor cars and a company held in the highest esteem and whose origins go back at least to 1861. The BSA Company was also in a very sound and prosperous state and in a leading article concerning the anticipated merger, in the *Financial Times* for the 27th September 1910, it was stated that 'The combination is one of the most important ever effected in the motor industry.' The proposal was implemented shortly thereafter and all the previous Daimler activities were continued under the simplified name of 'The Daimler Company'.

Not only were the years 1909–10 significant in the history of Daimler for the reasons already mentioned but it was also in the earlier year that the Company first produced a 6-cylinder engine (124 × 130 mm – 9,421 cc). Then in 1910 another 6-cylinder model, the 33 hp (96 × 130 mm – 5,646 cc) was added but this was dropped for 1911 when three 6-cylinder models appeared, the full range consisting of:

hp	RAC	Cyls.	Bore	Stroke	Wheelbase	Price
12	11.8	4	69	114	8′ 10½″	£375
15	15.9	4	80	130	9′ 8″	£400
23	23.8	6	80	130	10′ 6″	£535
25	25.3	4	101	130	10′ 4½″	£535
38	38.1	4	124	130	10′ 4½″	£625
38	37.9	6	101	130	11′ 6″	£700
57	57.2	6	124	130	11′ 6″	£900

Except in the case of the 12 hp car for which the price was £375 complete, the figures shown indicate the price of the chassis.

Whereas Daimler cars had hitherto almost invariably been fitted with four-speed gearboxes, it became the practice from the end of 1909 and remained so for two to three years to provide only three forward ratios. At about this time, some 600 men at the Works were turning out something like fifty complete bodies each week.

During 1910 another vehicle of advanced thinking and design appeared – the KPL omnibus. The initials indicated that Knight engines were employed, the electric transmission was of the Pieper type and Lanchester worm drive was

SIX-CYLINDER
1911 MODELS.

"As a dream of luxury from the passenger aspect, and as a mechanical achievement surely perfection, from the engineering point of view."

So writes a well-known Motoring Editor in the "Manchester Daily Despatch"—and he is perfectly correct—the 23 h.p. and 38 h.p. six-cylinder models are well on the way to a popularity as great, if not greater than that of their four-cylinder sisters.

It will pay you to investigate the claims of the New Daimler six-cylinders.

The Daimler Company, Ltd.,
Coventry.

1911 25 hp car

Another 1911 model – probably a 38 hp limousine

26

used at the rear axle. Body and chassis were in one all-steel unit, the seats faced forwards (an innovation for the period) and four-wheel brakes were incorporated. Two separate 12 hp Knight–Daimler engines and dynamotors were slung from brackets on either side of the bus, and transmission was taken through two universally-jointed shafts and worm gearing to two short live axles carrying the rear wheels. A magnetic clutch and brake formed part of the power units. In normal running, the two engines drove while the dynamotors were charging the accumulators. When extra effort was required, the accumulators automatically came into action to drive the dynamotors which thus became motors in their own right, to provide an increase in available power. In the event of engine failure, the vehicle could still be driven home on electric power.

Possibly the first British commercial vehicle was the 4 hp parcels van of 1897 which was driven by Critchley in the Emancipation run. The Wagonette of 1898 anticipated the public service vehicles to follow and the connection was unintentionally furthered by the first Royal shooting brake – the fourteen seater 'Beaters car' already mentioned. Sidney Straker, who was the Company's Consulting Engineer at the time designed a true charabanc in 1900. An advanced feature for the period was the drive by propeller shaft from the gearbox to the differential in place of chains which were retained for private cars for another seven or more years. At the Olympia Commercial Vehicle exhibition in 1908 the Company displayed a petrol–electric-driven double decker built for the Gearless Motor Omnibus Company Ltd of London. Following the introduction of the sleeve valve engine, the commercial side of Daimler's business greatly expanded and in 1912 the Company received an order for no less than 350 double deckers. A further look at the commercial side will be taken from time to time.

Meanwhile Royalty had during 1907 and 1909 taken delivery of a number of Daimler cars and in 1910 King George V received two outstanding 57 hp cars with bodies (numbered 4643 and 4665 respectively) by Hooper & Co. One was a landaulette and the other a limousine and both were finished in the Royal colours and their interiors were – 'lined with blue shiny morocco cloth lace and carpet' and polished mahogany was used for the framework of the windows. The wings and valances were in patent leather. HM the Queen also took delivery of a new 38 hp car (Hooper body no. 4694), painted in the colours which were to become traditional for her, – green with black mouldings with a picking-out line of light green. Within, lined dull grain green morocco cloth, lace and pile carpet was used with mother-o'-pearl fittings, polished mahogany glass frames and brass mountings. The Royal crown and cypher in gold appeared on the doors. After disposal, some fourteen years later, one of the King's cars was acquired by Charles Knight who exhibited it in America.

Another 57 hp limousine painted in Royal colours was delivered in June 1912; then in August of the same year a new shooting brake mounted on an 11½ feet long wheelbase chassis was delivered to the King. This was designed to carry five persons on each long side seat and two additional passengers alongside the driver.

27

Testing Daimler chassis before World War I – Sandy Lane, Coventry

A 1910 38 hp (4-cyl. model) – Landaulette body made in Adelaide, Australia by Vivian Lewis Ltd

Hooper Limousine-Landaulette on Daimler chassis for HM Queen Alexandra – 1912

The 57 hp 'Shooting Brake' – 1912. Body no. 4890

Typical Daimler sleeve-valve engine and chassis layout – c. 1911–13

20 hp 'Doctor's Coupe' of 1915

Another 20 hp of slightly earlier date

C

The production of cars shortly before 1914 and, opposite, war department vehicles shortly thereafter

Daimler 'Shooting Brakes' and, by contrast, opposite, an elegant tourer by Hooper & Co – c. 1914

33

HM The Queen watching manoeuvres from her car – first world war

First world war staff car – 20 hp

34

Daimler public service vehicles of the first world war period

The hind seats hinged up to give extra space for luggage when required. The vehicle was beautifully finished in Royal colours and was trimmed in the traditional blue leather. The wings and valances were of steel for added strength and waterproof curtains were fitted to enable the rear compartment to be totally enclosed in inclement weather. The Royal crest encircled by Garter and surmounted by Royal Crown was painted on the body sides, the dash, and rear door. Fitted to the front inside body was a special rack designed to carry eight guns.

Models came and went; some remaining longer than others. For 1912 there were four – the 15, 20, 25 and 38 hp each having 4-cylinder engines and three models with 6-cylinder units, these being the 23, 30 and 38 hp.

Another new limousine (body no. 5706) fitted to a 45 hp chassis was delivered to Queen Mary in December 1913 and this was finished and trimmed in most respects similar to the limousine numbered 4694 supplied three years earlier. In September 1914, the King too had a new 45 hp Daimler with a Brougham body by Hooper, but in June and by way of variation, a Windover bodied Daimler limousine had been delivered to the Queen.

Especially during the years preceding 1914 the Daimler production range was one of fearsome complexity and the situation eased but little during the ensuing vintage years. Within a short period covering part of 1913 and 1914 surviving records indicate that all types of bodies were produced on all available chassis types. For many of the distinctive designs produced by the Company, names were ascribed, the following, but a few of aggregate number, illustrate the diversity: 'Padley, Hollywood, Manchester, Shaftesbury, Granmore, Clacton, Barford, Corston, Barnet, Compton, Calder, Chelsea, Camborne, Dawlish, Dunkeld, Burnley, Bodmin, Sandford, Mitcham, Siston, Monmouth, Forston, Franford, Freethorpe, Midhurst, Selsdon, Morley, Sidcup, Sutherland, Somerset, Avonside, Ainsworth, Maranon, Parana, Ardoe, Lyndhurst, Claremont, Cloncaird, Clovelly, Edgmoor, Charlton, Clarence and Lashborough'. In the same period, there were many other standard and special designs lacking in nomenclature.

The 45 hp Brougham ordered by the King in 1914

Special Daimler car for Indian Prince – 1915

Another splendid example on 'active service'

A magnificent Daimler limousine – probably 1919–20

From 1917 this Joseph Cockshoot & Co bodied Daimler was used by the High Sheriff of the County Palatine of Lancaster

A Light-Thirty tourer (body no. 5460) – November 1921

The Daimler Company was not alone in being unprepared in 1914 for war. Within a week of its declaration, all available vehicles on the Company's premises were comandeered by the War department and the letters 'W.D.' and the broad arrow were plastered on the sides of magnificent 6-cylinder landaulettes, touring cars and lorries alike. The Company had to diversify its activities still further and its factory staff had to be increased from 3,824 men to well over 6,000 in order to produce staff cars, lorries, ambulances and other vehicles.

Most of the ambulances and staff cars were constructed on the 20 hp chassis (90 × 130 mm). Water circulation was by pump and ignition by high tension magneto. The power was transmitted through a leather cone clutch, a four-speed gearbox and a shaft and worm drive to the live rear axle. The staff cars were in effect adapted limousine bodies and provided accommodation for the driver and one other in the front and two in the rear. To the partition were fitted folding tables. In the course of time and experience a number of alternative layouts were contrived.

Tractors which were being built in conjunction with Messrs Fosters of Lincoln, and fitted with the Daimler 105 hp engine and special worm gear, were hurriedly adapted for road transport, especially for pulling 15-inch Howitzers and other gun parts. So successful in cross country conditions were these vehicles that the idea for making the first tank was conceived. This too proved itself to be highly successful. Other important Daimler contributions to the war effort included the manufacture of large-calibre shells, aero engines – commencing with the 'Gnome' rotary engine – complete aircraft, component parts and miscellaneous other items. A contemporary account, attributed to the Prince of Wales, on one of his visits to the battle front, and on seeing a huge fleet of Daimler lorries, the remark: 'It seems to me that the Daimler people are running this war!'

Note the absence of an external radiator cap – distinguishing feature on the Light-Thirty

With the cessation of hostilities, the Society of Motor Manufacturers and Traders announced early in 1919 that its thirteenth Motor Show would be held in the forthcoming November at Olympia, London. As a foretaste of the 1920 programme, the Daimler Company Ltd (the name having again been changed following the BSA amalgamation) exhibited at the show two new models both of which were based on the well tried 6-cylinder 30 and 45 hp cars, the smaller of which had been in steady production since around 1912 and was now offered in two wheelbase lengths which were designated the 'Light-Thirty' and the 'Standard-Thirty'. Both the 'Thirties' were powered by an engine of 4,962 cc (90 × 130 mm); and a novel feature about the 'Light-Thirty' was the absence of an external radiator cap – surely the first British car to have a concealed filler. The other new model was the Special 45 hp with a 6-cylinder engine – sleeve valve of course, 110 × 130 mm – 7,413 cc. Apart from a number of minor improvements made to these post-war engines there was in addition a new and elaborate lubrication system. This relied upon a multiple plunger pump driven from the sleeves eccentric shaft and supplying lubricant to troughs beneath the connecting rods. These troughs were inter-connected with a throttle lever so that the faster the engine ran the deeper the big ends were immersed in oil. Incidentally, the fears uttered by the critics of the sleeve valve engine were ill-founded especially as regards lubricant as this proved to be no problem; indeed, because of the plenitude of oil Daimlers of the period became renowned for the blue oil-smoke haze

40

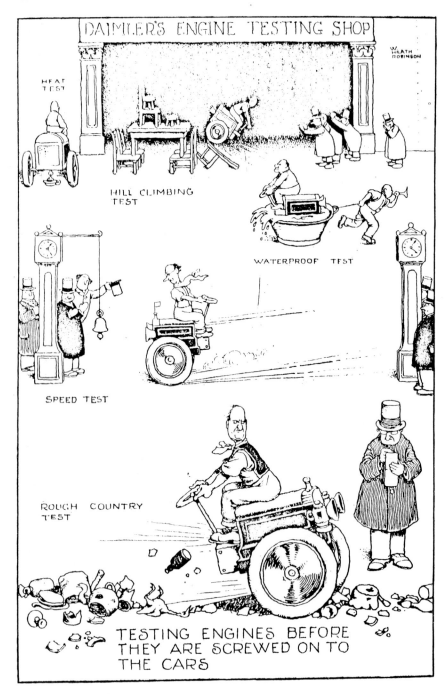

they emitted. A vibration damper was mounted on the front of the crankshaft and this proved itself to be effective.

Very soon after car production was resumed, Daimlers supplied for their larger models a separate steel body frame which of course was matched to the chassis. Before this patented innovation, a coachbuilder had to await delivery of the completed chassis before commencing work on the body but now he could proceed a long way knowing that the coachwork would be an exact fit for the chassis when in due course delivered. In this manner delivery times were substantially reduced to the advantage of all concerned.

An illustrated brochure, entitled 'The Daimler way of ensuring Quality' – (treated seriously by The Daimler Company and humorously by W. Heath Robinson), was issued. The text asserted that:

Only those who have studied the development and manufacture of the motor car can appreciate the stresses and strains which materials must endure if the life of the car is to be lengthy and satisfactory.

At this time the Company possessed one of the most complete metallurgical departments in the world and upon it largely depended the magnificent reputation Daimler cars enjoyed. All materials used had to pass numerous tests and experiments in the research, foundry and chemical laboratories and uniformity of excellence was guaranteed by the standard to which everything had to attain.

Their Majesties King George V and Queen Mary toured Scotland in 1920 in their Daimler cars

43

In the foundry laboratory, qualified chemists were engaged in blending metals, in heat treatment, evolving the best iron and steel for the particular use to which it would be put whilst in the research and chemical departments other chemists tested to the utmost limits the products of their creative work. Tests for hardness, impact tests, and ingenious methods of finding out the fatigue resisting properties of all the metals used were undertaken and in conjunction with the results of chemical analysis, the use of the correct materials for all purposes was scientifically guaranteed.

The Daimler Company had early appreciated the fact that a high standard of machine shop practice was necessary – hence the development and equipment of the Daimler tool room to a standard of efficiency superior to anything existing elsewhere. Tools of such accuracy and precision were used that Daimler craftsmen were able to work to the finest limits of toleration and moreover, many of the master gauges issued during the war through The National Physical Laboratory to the many other factories producing aeroplane engines, were products of the Daimler tool room. From the same source, we learn that a particular branch of tool room activity was the cutting of the Daimler–Lanchester type worm gears. When the ratio of gear had been settled, it was a four months' job to develop a set of tools from the master hob. The intricate tools were hand made and from these a master set of gears were produced and these would be retained for comparison throughout the production run.

During the war special plant had been developed for testing the large number of aeroplane engines built by the Company. Thereafter similar equipment was used for the testing of every vehicle engine, under conditions more rigorous than any normal roads could provide. Nothing was left to chance or imagination. Following the examiners' scrutiny, the engine was run-in on the bench at varying speeds from 400 to 1,500 rpm and not until the required minimum power at each given engine speed was obtained, was the unit passed as satisfactory. Further onerous tests were devised for the transmission. Each gear was subjected to full load for long periods, readings being taken at the axle extremities and again maximum efficiency figures had to be registered before the chassis could be forwarded to the body builders.

Daimler's own coachwork was constructed and finished to a very high standard. It was normal for a total of sixteen coats to be applied in the priming, filling, painting, glazing and varnishing of each body and between the various applications the surface was 'faced down' several times.

William Boddy, Editor of *Motor Sport*, writing in the May 1961 edition of that highly respected journal, noted that:

Daimlers of the vintage era have been dubbed staid, even sluggish, but down the years 'The Autocar'
set out to dispel this notion. Late in 1919, for instance a correspondent took one of the new Light-
Thirty tourers (DU 9475) to the Lake District, the Daimler making light of climbing, even re-
starting, up 1-in-3¼ gradients, carrying six people and much luggage. The steep side of Kirkstone
Pass, for instance, called for second gear over the worst part (although the luckless photographer had

A Daimler Hire Horse Box at Newmarket – 1930

by now been dropped) and took Foolstep's hairpin in first. The ease of changing gear was noted and we were told that the car had 'the usual standard gears and Lanchester worm drive'. The Daimler certainly wasn't spared, for in Little Langdale it nearly became wedged between the stone walls of a bridge, the hub-caps having to be removed to get it through!

As early as November 1907 The Daimler Company operated a chauffeur-driven department from Kensington High Street, London and by 1920 the demand for this facility was such as to warrant the formation of a separate Company to deal with this side of the business. This was called Daimler Hire Limited and some time later it adopted for its slogan the phrase 'Hire by land, sea and air' – for not only did they operate chauffeur-driven and self-drive cars but also from early 1922 an air service between London and Paris (known originally as Daimler Airways – later becoming Imperial Airways) and luxury cruisers – ex-naval MTB's which were powered by the famous Daimler–Ricardo 105 hp tank engines. Throughout the years Daimler Hire had provided transport for count-less official and State functions and as early as 1923 King George V granted the Company the Royal Warrant. Although anticipating the event, it is convenient here to mention that in 1927 and 1928 the Hire Company started a new venture – a Continental coach service called Daimlerways. The Daimler coaches used had sixteen luxury armchair seats, a coffee bar and even toilet facilities and they travelled all over Europe. The Company also operated three-ton lorries and later Daimler horse boxes. BSA sold their controlling interest in Daimler Hire Ltd in 1930 to Thos. Tillings. Reverting to the Daimler Company's own activities . . .

Another use was found for the 105 hp engines, two of which were incorporated in a Daimler petrol electric rail car which was experimented with during 1919. Although it was not produced commercially, it was the forerunner of the now familiar diesel rail cars.

During 1920 the Company settled down to serious production to meet the post-war demand, offering to customers a variety of coachwork which included tourers, saloons, limousines and landaulettes. Probably the most expensive car in the Daimler range at this time was the special 45 hp limousine costing £2,100. The King took delivery of another new car – a model TL 30.

Early in 1921, chassis prices of the Light-Thirty and Standard-Thirty were reduced and in the summer an interesting new model was announced. This was the type TT 4–20; of interest not only because of its own merits, but also because it was the last 4-cylinder car Daimlers produced. The unit, having a bore and stroke of 90 × 130 mm – 3,308 cc, was of course a Knight sleeve valve engine and followed very closely the specification for the 6-cylinder models. The rear brakes were of the expanding type and were adjustable from a turn-screw beneath the bonnet. A novel feature concerned the method of ascertaining the sufficiency of engine lubricant – the owner was provided with a plunger which when depressed, and if all was well, deposited a few drops of oil into a tray 'neatly arranged to conduct it on to the road so that it would not make a mess under the bonnet'!

It was on Daimler cars during 1922 that the experiment was first made with private automobile radio. In conjunction with the Marconiphone Company, wireless apparatus was installed beneath the front seats of Daimler cars and folding aerial frames were mounted on the roof of the vehicles and to eliminate undue interference, the whole of the ignition system was carefully screened. The comparative success of the venture was no doubt aided by the smooth and quiet running of the cars. The experiment was later extended by fitting radio in about a dozen of the Daimler Hire cars but was discontinued owing to lack of demand.

Ernest Instone and Undecimus Stratton both held responsible positions with the Company and from the very early days both had driven Daimler cars in numerous competitions and motoring events and in 1921 they left Daimlers' employ to incorporate a private limited company of their own, under the name of Stratton–Instone Limited, having as its principal object, the supply and distribution of Daimler and BSA cars. The new concern in fact took over control of the Daimler Company's London premises. Subsequently the name was changed to the present title of Stratstone Ltd and for many years the Company has had the honour to supply the Royal family with Daimler and other cars.

Although by all accounts the TT 4–20 was highly thought of, its production was shortlived, for in July 1922 the model was replaced by a 21 hp car which was in most respects similar to the earlier 20 hp car except that the power unit was now of six cylinders with a capacity of 3,021 cc (75 × 114 mm). As a result of improved casting methods it was possible to use on this model a monobloc engine but with detachable cylinder heads.

1922 TT 4-20 in Tasmania (recently destroyed by fire)

The Prince of Wales during his visit to Bath – July 1923

47

Another Royal Daimler, not lacking in ornamentation!

1923 arrived with Daimlers offering their customers a very wide choice. There was a new 12 hp model of 1,542 cc, a 16 hp of 2,167 cc, the above mentioned 21 hp car – one of which was during the year purchased by the R A C of Sweden and presented to the Crown Prince on the occasion of his marriage; the popular Thirty models (4,962 cc) in their two basic forms were continued and finally there was the grand 45 hp model boasting of a capacity of 7,413 cc. An example of the 'giant', fitted with a landaulette body and equipped with Rapson tyres and four-wheel brakes was the following year supplied to H R H the Duke of Connaught. The 12 hp engine was also used to power a B S A model and from the combined efforts of Daimler and B S A no fewer than fifty-six different chassis/body combinations were available. A journalist for *The Autocar*, covering the Six Days Highland Trial wrote concerning a new Light-Thirty tourer that was his transport for the duration of the event and after covering more than a thousand miles:

Its inspiring ideal is an engine which shall suppress its own existence even when it is all-out in bottom gear, and which shall run 25,000 miles with no attention. The engine is more suggestive of steam than of petrol. In its presence one would never mention such words as 'revolution' or 'exhaust' for it does not seem to possess either. Treading on the accelerator pedal does not produce the familiar variations of sound or tremor. The sole effect is that a smooth invisible flow of power, which might well be compressed air, eases off or intensifies its secret pressure.

During the 'twenties, the Company devised an elaborate training scheme for its engineering pupils and apprentices. This involved both categories of trainee being given tuition and experience in all the principal departments of the factory and as a result they became better acquainted with the layout of the Works than anyone except, perhaps, important executives. In consequence, trainees were often called upon to act as guides to visitors.

C. M. Walker, of Cheltenham, who straight from University joined the Company in 1922 as an engineering pupil, recalls two amusing incidents:

All sorts of people came to the Works, the majority of them having only a scant knowledge of the technical processes confronting them. On one occasion, a pupil acting as guide to a group, sought to manifest his knowledge and when asked by one of the party the temperature of the carburising furnaces in the Heat Treatment shop, glibly replied – '720°C'; – he apparently imagined that the question had been posed simply to make conversation and was then shattered when the questioner retorted: 'But my dear sir, it would not even start to carburise at that temperature!' The visitor then disclosed his identity – none other than an engineering professor and the author of the leading text book on the subject with which the pupil was supposedly well versed!

In addition to acting as guides, trainees were also frequently called upon to carry messages. One of the seniors was granted the privilege when acting as emergency messenger of using one of the works runabout cars – a small BSA. This particular character had cultivated the habit of slipping into neutral and coasting with the engine switched off for the last 30 or 40 feet before coming to a halt. Making a visit to the Running Shed, he followed this practice but on the day in question decided to stop beyond the main doors. Just as he inaudibly approached, one of the Royal Daimlers emerged swiftly from the building to start its final test. Overwhelmed by the imminent calamity and without the ability to accelerate, the driver of the BSA could do nothing and ended up impaled on the front of the Royal car!

Coventry must have been a fascinating place in those days, with its numerous motor works in and around the City. There were so many of them – all bursting with activity. The cars were invariably road tested and by convention, each manufacturer kept more or less within a particular region. According to the style of radiator, an informed onlooker could determine his whereabouts. Daimler's sector was the districts of Radford, Keresley and Corley and on two particular hills the testers used to say a given model was performing satisfactorily if it were doing 'x' mph at the bottom of the hill and 'y' mph by the time it reached the first gate or the oak tree at the top.

Towards the end of 1923 a significant new Daimler appeared. This was the 35 hp model having a light chassis and equipped with four-wheel brakes and a much modified engine of 5,764 cc. Up to that time cast iron had been used for the valve sleeves but now all light steel sleeves were substituted. The result was beneficial in several respects: by reducing the weight of the moving parts and by making the sleeves thinner and increasing the size of pistons an increase in horse power was obtained, and in the result performance was much enhanced. Since with sleeve valve engines, capacity is measured by reference to the sleeve bore and not the cylinder bore, there resulted an anomaly exemplified by the 30 hp and the new 35 hp cars. Both were listed as having the same cylinder dimensions but whereas the older model with thicker cast iron sleeves had a cubic capacity of 4,962 cc the new model had a displacement of 5,764 cc.

49

At about this time – Autumn 1923, King George V placed with Stratton–Instone Ltd an order for two new Daimlers to be bodied by Hooper & Co.

A measure of conservatism is to be expected from Monarchs but it is equally true that the service rendered to Royalty must be above reproach, unremitting in its continuity and never failing from the highest standard of efficiency. The fact that the Daimler cars then in use by the King had been in his constant service for upwards of thirteen years in itself constituted all the evidence needed to justify the conservatism of royal patronage. It will be recalled that in 1910 the vehicles delivered to His Majesty were equipped with the large 57 hp engines. The ensuing years were a severe and continuous test of durability and efficiency, but the proof of the good and reliable performance of the early sleeve valve units was clearly demonstrated by the decision of His Majesty to have practically a replica of the original engine built for each of the new cars. He was offered, indeed respectfully advised to have, large contemporary power units, but declined in preference for the earlier type. Apart from the two new limousines, two new shooting brakes were built on a special new chassis having a wheelbase of 13 feet 6 inches and all four were fitted with the specially made sleeve valve engines 124 × 130 mm – 9,420 cc. Standard Daimler practice was embodied throughout the engine design. It was considered prudent to fit cast-iron sleeves and not the new light steel type, but the pistons were of aluminium. For the lubrication system, a multi-plunger pump and variable oil troughs coupled to the throttle were retained but an oil level indicator near the filling orifice was incorporated. Over-filling of the sump was prevented by a cock which opened and and closed simultaneously with the filler lid. Two entirely independent ignition systems, one by magneto and the other by coil and accumulator, were provided. Fuel was fed to the Daimler carburetter from a 22-gallon tank the petrol supply being induced to the carburetter by means of an air pump driven by the engine and supplemented by a hand-operated pump placed on the dashboard, for the purpose of generating air pressure in the petrol tank for starting. An interesting point concerned the carburetter which was so arranged as to draw air through the hollow dashboard with a view to providing a supply of warm air, and also to ventilate the interior of the body. Hartford shock absorbers were fitted all round to ensure steadiness over bad roads, quite a few of which were no doubt encountered in the Highlands of Scotland and elsewhere. Following the introduction of four-wheel brakes on the 35 hp model, the King's new vehicles were so equipped. The top gear ratio was quoted as three-to-one and it was stated that the car could be driven in top at so low a speed as $2\frac{1}{2}$ to 3 miles an hour. The remainder of the small batch of special chassis made with similar specifications was acquired by Stratton–Instone Ltd and sold to privileged customers.

The coachwork was built to the standards associated with the highest class of English carriage builders by, of course, Hooper & Co. All four new vehicles were delivered during August and September 1924.

The limousines (bodies numbered 5985 and 5998) were both finished in Royal

THE DAIMLER BODY MOUNTING.

WITH its rubber buffer support, the Daimler Body Frame gives exceptional comfort to the passengers and increases the durability of the coachwork, both being protected in a very effective manner from the undesirable vibration of rough roads. The Body Frame is an independent steel structure that confers great strength and rigidity on the body and also saves weight. It is the principal technical feature in a perfect system of mounting the body on the chassis.

Body Frame

Rubber Buffer

Chassis Frame

Extracts from 1924 brochures

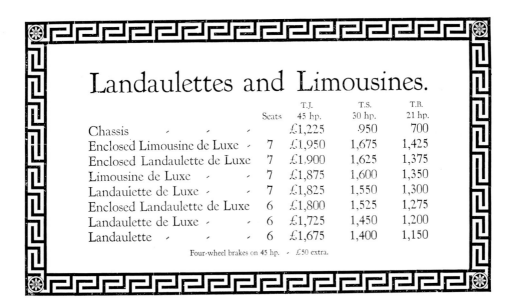

Landaulettes and Limousines.

	Seats	T.J. 45 hp.	T.S. 30 hp.	T.B. 21 hp.
Chassis		£1,225	950	700
Enclosed Limousine de Luxe	7	£1,950	1,675	1,425
Enclosed Landaulette de Luxe	7	£1,900	1,625	1,375
Limousine de Luxe	7	£1,875	1,600	1,350
Landaulette de Luxe	7	£1,825	1,550	1,300
Enclosed Landaulette de Luxe	6	£1,800	1,525	1,275
Landaulette de Luxe	6	£1,725	1,450	1,200
Landaulette	6	£1,675	1,400	1,150

Four-wheel brakes on 45 hp. - £50 extra.

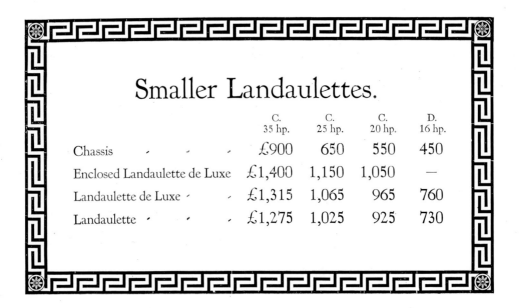

Smaller Landaulettes.

	C. 35 hp.	C. 25 hp.	C. 20 hp.	D. 16 hp.
Chassis	£900	650	550	450
Enclosed Landaulette de Luxe	£1,400	1,150	1,050	—
Landaulette de Luxe	£1,315	1,065	965	760
Landaulette	£1,275	1,025	925	730

Extracts from sales catalogues 1924

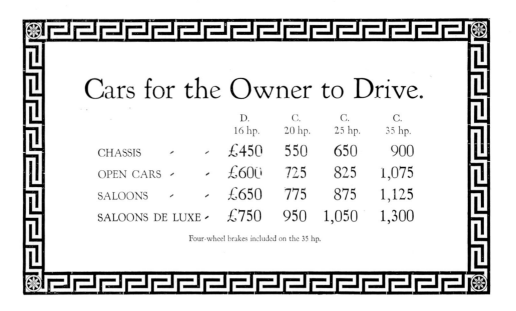

Cars for the Owner to Drive.

	D. 16 hp.	C. 20 hp.	C. 25 hp.	C. 35 hp.
CHASSIS	£450	550	650	900
OPEN CARS	£600	725	825	1,075
SALOONS	£650	775	875	1,125
SALOONS DE LUXE	£750	950	1,050	1,300

Four-wheel brakes included on the 35 hp.

TABLE OF DIMENSIONS.

	C	C	C	D		C	C	C	D
Type	35h.p.	25 h.p.	20 h.p.	16 h.p.	Type	35 h.p.	25 h.p.	20 h.p.	16 h.p.
Engine.					Weight (chassis) ... cwt.	25½	20½	19	17
No. of cylinders	6	6	6	6	Worm ratios, open cars...	9/32	8/33	6/35	6/35
Bore, m/m	97	81.5	73.5	65	,, ,, closed cars	9/32	8/35	6/35	6/37
Stroke, m/m	130	114	104	94	Gear box ratios, Top direct	1	1	1	1
R.A.C. rating	35.0	24.7	20.0	15.7	,, ,, 3rd ...	1.62	1.69	1.69	1.69
Crankshaft bearings ...	7	7	7	7	,, ,, 2nd ...	2.20	2.36	2.36	2.36
Stroke-volume, c.c. ...	5764	3568	2648	1872	,, ,, 1st ...	3.57	4.00	4.00	4.00
Chassis.	ft. in.	ft. in.	ft. in.	ft. in.	,, ,, Reverse...	3.57	4.00	4.00	4.00
Wheel base	11 9½	11 1½	10 9¼	9 9⅜	Tyre sizes (Dunlop) {	880	820	820	765
Wheel track	4 4	4 4	4 4	4 2	{	120	120	120	105
Length (chassis)	15 8½	15 0	14 8	13 5	Eng. revs. at 30 m.p.h. open	1060	1325	1872	1990
Width (wings)	5 5	5 5	5 5	5 0	,, ,, closed	1060	1404	1872	2105
Turning circle (diameter)	44 0	41 0	40 0	38 0	Battery voltage	12	12	12	12
Clearance (engine) ...	10	11½	11½	10¼	Capacity in amp. hours ...	66	66	66	65
,, (axle)	9½	8¼	8¼	8¾	Petrol tank (gallons) ...	15	10	10	9
Height (body floor) ...	26½	24¼	24¼	23¼	Petrol, m.p.g. (as tested)	17	20	24	26

Extracts from sales catalogues 1924

DAIMLER CHASSIS.

Daimler Chassis, Type D   –   –   –   –   –   –   –   –   –   16 h.p., £450.
Daimler Chassis, Type C   –   –   –   –   –   20 h.p., £550 ; 25 h.p., £650 ; 35 h.p., £900.

Four wheel brakes included on 35 h.p.

TABLE OF DIMENSIONS.

	TJ	TS	TB		TJ	TS	TB
Type	45 h.p.	30 h.p.	21 h.p.	Type	45 h.p.	30 h.p.	21 h.p.
Engine.				Weight (chassis) ... cwt.	33	30½	23½
No. of cylinders	6	6	6	Worm ratios, open cars ...	10/33	9/34	7/36
Bore, m/m	110	90	75	,, ,, closed cars ...	10/33	8/33	7/36
Stroke, m/m	130	130	114	Gear box ratios—Top direct	1	1	1
R.A.C. rating	45	30.13	20.9	,, ,, 3rd	1.33	1.55	1.54
Crankshaft bearings ...	7	7	7	,, ,, 2nd ...	2.06	1.99	2.16
Stroke-volume, c.c. ...	7413	4962	3022	,, ,, 1st ...	3.06	3.05	4.01
Chassis.	ft. in.	ft. in.	ft. in.	,, ,, Reverse...	3.96	3.94	3.39
Wheel base	12 2⅛	11 9¾	11 3¾	Tyre sizes (Dunlop) {	895	895	895
Wheel track	4 9¼	4 9¼	4 9¼		150	135	135
Length (chassis)	16 10	16 5⅝	15 8	Eng. revs. at 30m.p.h. open	949	1140	1552
Width (wings)	6 1	6 1	6 1	,, ,, ,, closed	949	1244	1552
Turning circle (diameter)...	45 0	44 0	43 0	Battery voltage	12	12	12
Clearance (engine) ...	14	13⅛	13¾	Capacity in amp. hours ...	80	70	66
,, (axle) ...	9½	8¾	9¼	Petrol tank (gallons) ...	17	17	12
Height (body floor) ...	28¾	28	27¼	Petrol, m.p.g. (as tested) ...	15	17	20

Extracts from sales catalogues 1924

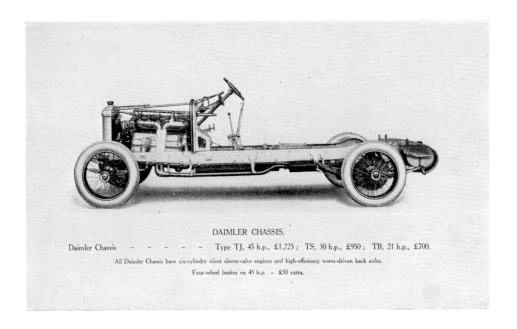

DAIMLER CHASSIS.

Daimler Chassis - - - - - Type TJ, 45 h.p., £1,225 ; TS, 30 h.p., £950 ; TB, 21 h.p., £700.

All Daimler Chassis have six-cylinder silent sleeve-valve engines and high-efficiency worm-driven back axles.

Four-wheel brakes on 45 h.p. - £50 extra.

54

Large Open Cars & Saloons de Luxe.

	T.J. 45 hp.	T.S. 30 hp.	T.B. 21 hp.
CHASSIS	£1,225	950	700
SALOON DE LUXE	£1,725	1,450	1,200
7-SEATED OPEN CAR	£1,540	1,265	1,015
5-SEATED OPEN CAR	£1,525	1,250	1,000

N.B.—Saloons have four doors and open interiors. For Closed Cars with partitions see Enclosed Landaulettes.

1924 price list

claret picked out in vermilion and the external bright parts were of polished brass; blue leather was again used for the upholstery and the interior woodwork was carried out in polished mahogany and interior fitments were in white ivory. Mounted on the division in the rear compartment was a combined speedometer and clock and there was also included an electrically driven fan, silver tray, silver cigarette box and cigar lighter, and two specially sprung rings designed to hold sticks or umbrellas. Exceedingly wide doors were fitted at the rear and the interior headroom was considerable – in the region of 60 inches – necessary in order that His Majesty and distinguished guests might travel in comfort when wearing a Field Marshal's hat and plumes or other tall headdress. The Royal Arms were hand painted – each being an exquisite piece of craftsmanship – on the sides and on the back panel.

One of the shooting brakes (body 6042) was also finished in Royal colours and was trimmed in blue but the other (body 6041) had a wood grain finish with black wings but the chassis side members and springs were painted claret. Both the shooting brakes carried polished ash racks each capable of carrying up to twelve guns.

In addition to the new special models a new 20 hp Daimler was acquired at the Palace. This was a type c 20 with Hooper limousine body (no. 6085) finished in grey with wings and valances in black. Blue leather was, as usual, included with blue cloth headlining and on the roof a luggage rail was fitted.

In all fifty-seven different models (excluding the special 57 hp Royal cars)

1924 Hooper bodied four-door tourer, fitted with four-wheel brakes and a two-door version of around 1925

were catalogued for 1924. W. Boddy, writing in *Motor Sport*, recalls that *The Autocar* – 'also liked to have a Daimler amongst its stud of staff cars and in 1924 ordered a Weymann fabric saloon on a c-type 25 hp chassis costing £250 . . .'.

For a while, on some models, front wheel brakes were an optional extra (costing £50 on the 45 hp car) but soon they were standardized and by the middle of the following year the new light steel sleeves had displaced the cast-iron type and

56

Infinite variety was the theme of the 'twenties – both of the above have Martin Walter coachwork

For HM the King, 1924

LUBRICATION OF ENGINE

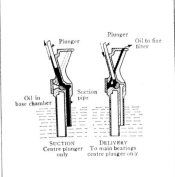

THE CENTRE PLUNGER
(Supplying oil to main bearings)

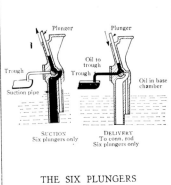

THE SIX PLUNGERS
(Supplying oil to troughs)

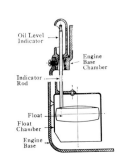

The Oil Level Indicator.
(Not fitted to all engines.)

Diagrams illustrating the Action of the Pump.

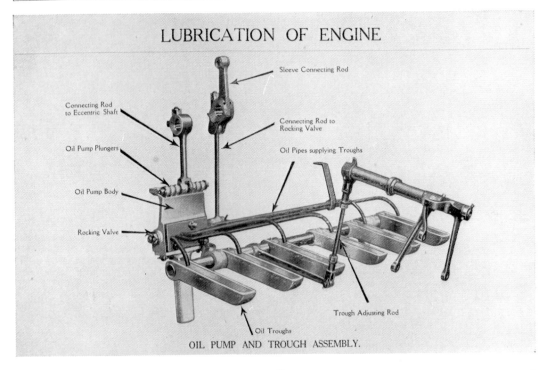

OIL PUMP AND TROUGH ASSEMBLY.

four-wheel brakes were used on all models. A Hooper limousine (no. 6305) on an
N 45 hp chassis was constructed for the Queen and supplied in October 1925.
New long stroke engines having full pressure lubrication and dual ignition were
introduced, these being the 16/55 (1,872 cc), the 20/70 (2,648 cc), the 25/85
(3,568 cc) and the 35/120 (5,764 cc). The trough lubrication was retained only
for the N 30 model. All the new cars had a dropped front axle, four-wheel brakes
and shock absorbers. Moreover, in order to obtain a horizontal bonnet line a new
radiator of deeper appearance was introduced. In all respects the new models
maintained the guarded reputation of the Company and performed and sold
well.

A road test of a 25/85 was prefaced in *The Autocar* by the following remarks:

*Of all cars on the road today there is not one more easily recognized by the average man than a
Daimler. Seen in towns or in the country, at rest or in motion, there is a stateliness, a dignity of
progression, wholly characteristic of the make. The appearance does not belie the actual luxury in
which the passengers travel. To rest reposeful and serene in the embrace of the rear seats, surrounded
by interior carriagework of excellent taste, and idly to watch a countryside of glowing greens roll
past in spring sunshine, to catch with surprising clearness a murmur of the conversation of a chance
pedestrian, by reason of a seating position higher above the ground than normal to see more than
usual of a familiar landscape – these are some of the pleasures of Daimler travel.*

During 1926, the Daimler Company was further honoured by supplying a
25/85 Charlesworth bodied limousine to H M King of Siam, a 35/120 Hooper

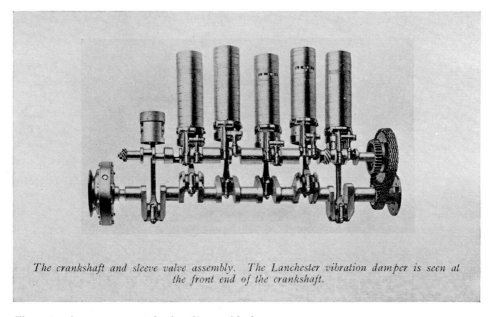

*The crankshaft and sleeve valve assembly. The Lanchester vibration damper is seen at
the front end of the crankshaft.*

Illustration shows arrangement for the 16/20 model of 1931

bodied limousine no 6570 to King George V and a number of other cars to royal and distinguished clients at home and overseas. For the duration of the general strike in 1926 Daimler Hire cars were used for delivering newsprint all over the country and during the coal strike the King made one of his longest road journeys when driven from Balmoral to Buckingham Palace, arriving there the day after departure. That year was, however, more significant in the history of the Company for its introduction of the fabulous 'Double-Six'

At a time when most manufacturers are engaged in the process of producing ever smaller motor cars, it is very gratifying to find a British firm of high reputation with sufficient faith in really big cars to offer an entirely new model of such impressive proportions as the interesting Daimler Double-Six.
(*The Autocar* – 15th October 1926)

In the mid-'twenties, nearly all the European producers of luxury cars favoured 6-cylinder in-line engines and although not first to employ a v-12 layout, Daimlers were certainly alone in doing so in 1926. In the following decade Lagonda, Rolls-Royce, Hispano-Suiza and others introduced or re-introduced 12-cylinder engines of the 'vee' configuration but there could not be another engine quite like the legendary Daimler Double-Six, designed by the late Laurence H. Pomeroy – the Company's Chief Engineer at the time.

The impressive new engine was nothing short of an engineering masterpiece. The first Daimler v-12 engine was made up from two cylinder blocks taken from the existing 25/85 hp engines and these were mounted at an incline on a common crankcase so as to form a 60° vee twelve unit of 7,136 cc. The crankshaft ran in seven plain bearings and the subsidiary crankshafts or eccentric shafts each ran in four bearings and were driven from the rear of the principal shaft by silent chains. Short connecting rods operated the double sleeves (steel of course), in the normal manner. The cylinders were cast in blocks of three, each block having a detachable head. The crankcase was in aluminium and the big ends laid in pairs, the right hand ones being forked so that diagonal pairs of cylinders laid in the same transverse plane.

From the nose of the crankshaft, skew gearing powered two transverse shafts, the lower one being employed to drive the water pumps whilst the magnetos derived their motivation from the other cross-shaft. For each bank of cylinders there was a separate four jet Daimler carburetter which received mixture via a water heated induction system and a separate distributor mounted high up at the front of the cylinder banks. Each distributor was driven by its own vertical shaft.

For lubrication, oil was pressure fed to the main and big end bearings, the sleeve shafts and the sleeves themselves. An ingenious feature of the lubrication system ensured that when starting the engine a supply of oil was directed to the lower ends of the sleeves and the mixture control was so arranged as to provide further lubricant to the other ends of the sleeves as the engine idled. The power was transmitted through a disc clutch to a four speed and reverse conventional

This magnificent R.30 type Daimler was built in 1925 by Hoopers for the Queen of Spain

1926, 25/85 Hooper bodied Landaulette (Body no. 6355)

A typical 35/120 sleeve-valve, Hooper bodied Daimler of 1927

gearbox controlled by a central ball-gate gear lever. The drive was taken through an open propeller shaft to the familiar underslung worm drive back axle.

For 1927 Daimlers introduced Dewandre vacuum servo assistance for their four-wheel, rod operated brakes and the new Double-Six was so equipped. Following earlier Daimler practice, a single hand adjuster was provided. Each bank of cylinders had its own exhaust manifolds which were positioned within the 'v' formation the gases then being led through independent parallel flexible pipes passing through the dash structure to single silencers on the nearside and from thence, by tail pipes acutely angled to pass up and over the rear axle and then down again, beyond the petrol tank to the extremity of the car. Unconventional steering was necessitated by the width of the power unit, the difficulty being overcome by placing a worm and sector reduction box on the bulkhead from which the action was taken by a vertical rod connected to a bell-crank mounted on the offside of the chassis and from that point a horizontal drag link proceeded forward to the front axle.

The chassis was offered in three different wheelbase lengths, and with a choice of high or low radiator and a variety of body styles and coachwork. In the biggest form the chassis was the longest ever built in England for a standard private production car. The independent body frame was still employed.

This superlative new model made its debut at the 1926 Olympia Motor Show where it caused quite a sensation. *The Autocar* for 15th April 1927 carried a report of the car (Registration number RW 9801) following a fairly extensive road test:

Fortunate beings in the immediate future will leisurely survey the moving surface of the earth through the clear windows of their Daimler Double-Sixes as they pass onward in silent dignity. These great cars, with the largest, most powerful, and most expensive of any touring chassis built in the British Isles, are for the lucky few who have the means to purchase them and to keep them in commission. . . .

. . . It is not until one comes close to the car that its great size is realised, for, like a well-proportioned human figure, the bulk is only discovered when some comparative measurement can be made. The Daimler bonnet is nearly level with the chin of the observer. One glance into the coachwork is enough to inspire a desire to enter. Not only is the interior of impressive proportions allowing room and to spare for five people, but the typical Daimler finish of grey upholstery and egg-shell-surfaced ebony woodwork is immensely attractive because of its quiet good taste. There is not display, yet refinement and luxury are both expressed. . . .

. . . According to our own views it seems that the chassis of the Daimler Double-Six was not planned with the idea of providing people with an opportunity to find out what driving behind a powerful twelve cylinder engine feels like but to produce a chassis and engine so excellent and so unobtrusive that no effort of machinery whatever should be noticeable when the duties of carrying the occupants of a luxurious body from one place to another with a minimum loss of time were being performed. In other words, the virtue of the engine lies in its capacity for effacement. There is so much power and so little obvious effort that the speed with which any given journey can be accomplished is not a matter of the capability of the car, but the condition and style of the roads traversed. . . .

. . . So flexible and smooth is the engine that of the four speeds provided by the gear box other than the reverse, not more than two need, in normal circumstances be used. Starting from rest and steep hill climbing are accomplished on third whereas on top gear an absolute crawl through traffic is at

The 'Double-Six-50' – 1927

the command of the driver. It is quite possible for a passenger, whilst the car is travelling dead slow on top gear, to get out of the car, walk round it and get in again. . . .

. . . Summing up this experience of the Daimler Double-Six, we find ourselves impressed with it, so much so that we look forward to the day when smaller cars on the same lines will come within the reach of a wider circle of the motoring public. There is something exceedingly fascinating about the even and effortless flow of power from the twelve cylinders, and once experienced, a strong desire for further runs such as this is aroused.

In addition to the new Double-Six, the existing models – the 16/55, 20/70, 25/85 and the 35/120 were continued for 1927 with the addition of a new light weight version of the 20/70 and as usual, Daimler customers were offered a wide choice of body styles. H M King George V had his 35/120 car modified to receive the new Double-Six power unit but before the end of the year he had delivered to him a complete 12-cylinder car.

In general, bus design retained many pre-war features until the mid-'twenties and during this period it was not uncommon practice for operators to use a vehicle equipped with a charabanc-type body at weekends, and then substitute a truck body for commercial activities of a different nature on weekdays. After a short coalition (1926–29) with A E C, the Daimler Company produced the first of a long line of new type double and single deckers. The first of these was the type CF 6 on which the famous 'fluted top' radiator made its re-appearance, it having been absent from commercial vehicles for many years.

The four basic 6-cylinder cars were continued with only slight modification for the following year. The new 12-cylinder model was re-designated the 'Double-Six-50' and a smaller version of the car utilizing two 16/55 cylinder blocks and giving a capacity of 3,744 cc and called the 'Double-Six-30' was introduced.

SUMMARY OF PRICES

Model	Body Space (ft. in.)	Track (ft. in.)	Chassis Prices: Ratings "50" £	Chassis Prices: Ratings "30" £	Body Prices: Model	Body Prices: £	Car Prices: "50" £	Car Prices: "30" £	Description
P	9 2	5 0	1950	—	PS	850	2800	—	ENCLOSED DRIVE (Driver's leg room 40 in.)
					PT	850	2800	—	PS and OS—Folding head.
O	8 6	5 0	1950	1430	OS	750	2700	2180	PT and OT—Fixed head.
					OT	750	2700	2180	
W	8 6	4 9	1850	—	WS	650	2500	—	ENCLOSED DRIVE (Driver's leg room 40 in.) Folding head.
					WH	650	2500	—	ENCLOSED DRIVE (Driver's leg room 44 in.) Fixed head.
					WB	600	2450	—	SALOON DE LUXE—Fixed head.
V	8 4	4 6	—	1330	VS	640	—	1970	ENCLOSED DRIVE (Driver's leg room 40 in.)
					VT	640	—	1970	VS—Folding head. VT—Fixed head.
					VH	640	—	1970	ENCLOSED DRIVE (Driver's leg room 44 in.) Fixed head.
					VC	565	—	1895	SALOON DE LUXE—Folding head.
M	7 11	4 4	—	1130	MS	540	—	1670	ENCLOSED DRIVE (Driver's leg room 40 in.) Folding head.
					MB	515	—	1645	SALOON DE LUXE—Fixed head.
					MY	320	—	1450	SALOON—Fixed head. Fabric above waist rail.
Q	7 1	4 4	—	1130	QA	440	—	1570	COUPÉ DE LUXE—Fixed head.

TABLE OF CHASSIS DIMENSIONS

Rating ...	"50"			"30"			
Model ...	P	O	W	O	V	M	Q
Bore, m/m ...	81.5	81.5	81.5	65	65	65	65
Stroke, m/m ...	114	114	114	94	94	94	94
R.A.C. rating ...	49.4	49.4	49.4	31.4	31.4	31.4	31.4
Stroke-volume, c.c. ...	7136	7136	7136	3744	3744	3744	3744
	ft. in.	ft. in.	ft. in.	ft. in.	ft in.	ft. in.	ft. in.
Wheelbase ...	13 7	12 11½	12 11½	12 1	11 10	11 9	10 11
Wheel track ...	5 0	5 0	4 9	5 0	4 6	4 4	4 4
Turning circle (diameter) ...	54 0	52 0	52 0	48 0	47 0	42 0	40 0
Height (body floor) ...	25	25½	24½	23½	23	22	22
Length (over tail lamp) ...	18 6	17 10	17 10	17 1	16 5	15 10	15 0
Length (including open luggage grid) ...	19 6½	18 7	18 7	17 8	16 7	16 7	15 9
Width (front wings) ...	6 4	6 4	6 0	6 4	5 9¾	5 5	5 5
Body space (dash to axle) ...	9 2	8 6	8 6	8 6	8 4	7 11	7 1
Clearance (chassis) ...	7	6½	6½	8	7½	8	8½
Clearance (axle) ...	8	7	7	8	7½	6½	6½
Worm ratios—Open cars ...	8/35	8/35	8/35	6/35	7/38	7/36	7/34
„ „ —Closed cars ...	7/34	8/35	8/35	6/35	7/38	7/36	7/34
Tyre sizes ...	7½ for 23	6¾ for 23	33 6.75	33 6.75	33 6	5¼ for 21	31 5.25
Engine revs. at 60 m.p.h.—Open ...	2480	2540	2690	3600	3480	3420	3230
„ „ „ —Closed ...	2765	2540	2690	3600	3480	3420	3230
Gear-box ratio—Top (direct) ...	1	1	1	1	1	1	1
„ „ (3rd) ...	1.56	1.56	1.62	1.6	1.6	1.6	1.6
„ „ (2nd) ...	2.08	2.08	2.2	2.5	2.5	2.5	2.5
„ „ (1st) ...	3.24	3.24	3.57	4.0	4.0	4.0	4.0
„ „ (Reverse) ...	3.24	3.24	3.57	4.0	4.0	4.0	4.0
Weight (chassis) ... cwt.	43½	42¾	41¼	37	30	25	24¾
Battery (12 volts), ampere-hours ...	75	75	75	66	66	66	66
Petrol tank (gallons) ...	24	24	24	19	18½	16	16
Petrol m.p.g. (as tested) ...	10	10	10	12	12	14	14

Extracts from Company sales brochures 1929–30

Summary of Prices

CHASSIS

	Rating	35/120		25/85		20/70		16/55	
Models	High Bonnet	PO	V	PO	V	V	M	Q	
	Low Bonnet	NR	ST	NR	ST	ST			L5
Price		£1200	£1100	£850	£750	£650	£575	£550	£490

Type	Int. Length	High Bonnet Model	Low Bonnet Model	Body £	35/120 PO/NR £1200 Car £	35/120 V/ST £1100 Car £	25/85 PO/NR £850 Car £	25/85 V/ST £750 Car £	20/70 V/ST £650 Car £	20/70 M £575 Car £	16/55 Q £550 Car £	16/55 L5 £490 Car £
LANDAULETTES — Chairs	65 in.	PS1	NS1	800	2000	—	1650	—	—	—	—	—
Chairs	59 in.	OS2	—	700	1900	—	1550	—	—	—	—	—
Chairs	59 in.	OS1	RS1	650	1850	—	1500	—	—	—	—	—
Chairs	59 in.	OR1	—	400	1600	—	1250	—	—	—	—	—
Pillar Seats	56 in.	VS2	—	600	—	1700	—	1350	1250	—	—	—
Pillar Seats	56 in.	VS1	TS1	550	—	1650	—	1300	1200	—	—	—
Pillar Seats	56 in.	VR1	—	375	—	1475	—	1125	1025	—	—	—
Drop Seats	50 in.	MS1	—	500	—	—	—	—	—	1075	—	—
Drop Seats	50 in.	MR2	—	325	—	—	—	—	—	900	—	—
SALOONS de Luxe		VC1	—	525	—	1625	—	1275	1175	—	—	—
SALOONS de Luxe		MB1	—	475	—	—	—	—	—	1050	—	—
SALOONS de Luxe		—	SC1	440	—	1540	—	1190	1090	—	—	—
SALOONS de Luxe		—	LC1	400	—	—	—	—	—	—	—	890
COUPÉ de Luxe		QA1	—	400	—	—	—	—	—	—	950	—
SALOONS "Y"		VY1	—	300	—	1400	—	1050	950	—	—	—
SALOONS "Y"		—	SY1	260	—	1360	—	1010	910	—	—	—
SALOONS "Y"		MY1	—	275	—	—	—	—	—	850	—	—
SALOONS "Y"		QY2	—	250	—	—	—	—	—	—	800	—
SALOONS "Y"		—	LY4	225	—	—	—	—	—	—	—	715
OPEN CARS — Plain		VO1	—	250	—	1350	—	1000	900	—	—	—
OPEN CARS — Plain		—	SO1	225	—	1325	—	975	875	—	—	—
OPEN CARS — Plain		QO1	—	175	—	—	—	—	—	—	725	—
OPEN CARS — Plain		—	LO1	175	—	—	—	—	—	—	—	665
OPEN CARS — De luxe		—	LO4	300	—	—	—	—	—	—	—	790

Notes

LANDAULETTES.—All models in which S is the second letter of the symbol are of the coachbuilt type with enclosed fronts, folding heads and de luxe finish. Similar coachwork with fixed panelled heads can be supplied at the same price.

Type—R is metal panelled below the waist rail and has a fixed fabric-covered head.

Models OS2 and VS2 differ only from models OS1 and VS1 in having the moulding so designed that the upper part of the bonnet and scuttle can be painted in a different colour if required.

SALOONS.—All models in which C is the second letter of the symbol are of the coachbuilt type with folding heads and de luxe finish. Similar coachwork with fixed panelled heads can be supplied at the same price (except SC1 and LC1).

Type MB1 is coachbuilt de luxe with fixed panelled head and is not available in the alternative folding head style.

The Coupé de luxe QA1 also has a fixed panelled head.

All Saloons 'Y' have fixed fabric-covered heads.

OPEN CARS.—These bodies are completely equipped with one-man hood, side screens and rear screen, while the de luxe models are provided with an adjustable front seat and other refinements.

35/120 SALOON

A	= 12 ft.
B	= 27 ft.
C	= 16 ft.
D	= 25 ft.
E	= 18 ft.
F	= 20 ft.
G	= 12 ft.

DAIMLER GARAGE PLAN.

This plan shows the minimum comfortable space for manœuvring the new Daimler 35/120 under conditions that are typical of the approach to many garages. Entering the drive at A the car turns up to the front of a house at B and reverses into a garage at G.

GARAGE

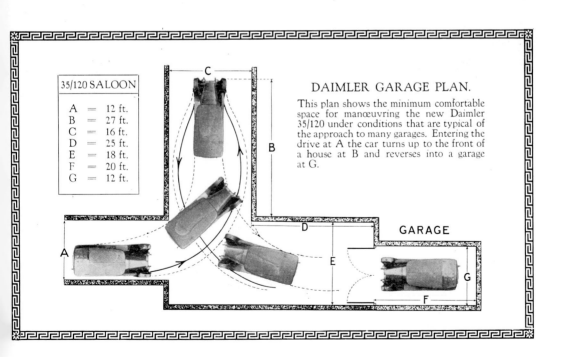

DIAGRAM SHOWING ACTION OF THE DAIMLER SLEEVE-VALVES

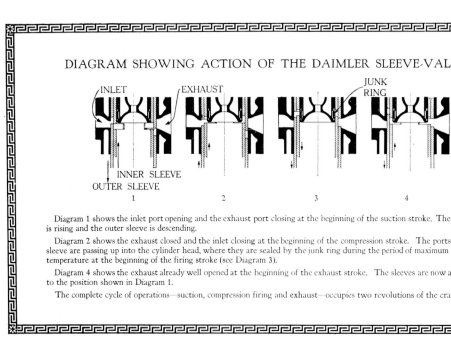

Diagram 1 shows the inlet port opening and the exhaust port closing at the beginning of the suction stroke. The inner sleeve is rising and the outer sleeve is descending.

Diagram 2 shows the exhaust closed and the inlet closing at the beginning of the compression stroke. The ports in the inner sleeve are passing up into the cylinder head, where they are sealed by the junk ring during the period of maximum pressure and temperature at the beginning of the firing stroke (see Diagram 3).

Diagram 4 shows the exhaust already well opened at the beginning of the exhaust stroke. The sleeves are now again moving to the position shown in Diagram 1.

The complete cycle of operations—suction, compression firing and exhaust—occupies two revolutions of the crankshaft.

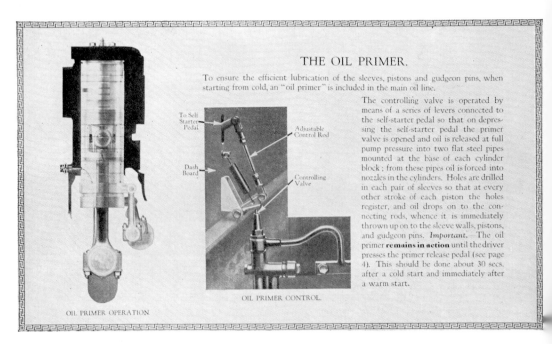

THE OIL PRIMER.

To ensure the efficient lubrication of the sleeves, pistons and gudgeon pins, when starting from cold, an "oil primer" is included in the main oil line.

The controlling valve is operated by means of a series of levers connected to the self-starter pedal so that on depressing the self-starter pedal the primer valve is opened and oil is released at full pump pressure into two flat steel pipes mounted at the base of each cylinder block; from these pipes oil is forced into nozzles in the cylinders. Holes are drilled in each pair of sleeves so that at every other stroke of each piston the holes register, and oil drops on to the connecting rods, whence it is immediately thrown up on to the sleeve walls, pistons, and gudgeon pins. *Important.* The oil primer **remains in action** until the driver presses the primer release pedal (see page 4). This should be done about 30 secs. after a cold start and immediately after a warm start.

OIL PRIMER OPERATION.

OIL PRIMER CONTROL.

Extracts from 35/120 handbooks

DAIMLER CAR MAINTENANCE CHART.

EVERY DAY	**Routine Daily Inspection, plus :—**			
MONDAYS	LUBRICATE CHASSIS.			
TUESDAYS	TEST TYRE PRESSURES.			
Week of the month	*1st*	*2nd*	*3rd*	*4th*
WEDNESDAYS	Change (with Spare) NEAR FRONT WHEEL	Change (with Spare) OFF FRONT WHEEL	Change (with Spare) NEAR BACK WHEEL	Change (with Spare) OFF BACK WHEEL
THURSDAYS	OIL FILTER (Clean)	BATTERY (Fill Distilled Water)	GEAR-BOX (Fill Daimler Gear Oil)	BACK AXLE (Fill Daimler Gear Oil)
FRIDAYS	IGNITION PLUGS (Inspect)		FOOT BRAKE (Oil Power Mechanism)	
JAN. APRIL JULY OCT.	ENGINE BASE (Wash out)	DAMPER (Add Daimler Gear Oil)	MAGNETO (Lubricate)	
FEB. MAY AUG. NOV.	DYNAMO (Inspect)	SPRINGS (Grease Leaves)	STARTER MOTOR (Inspect)	SPEEDOMETER (Oil inside Flex)
MAR. JUNE SEPT. DEC.	PETROL TANK (Clean Filters)	DISTRIBUTOR (Inspect and Lubricate)		
ANNUAL INSPECTION	SILENCER (Clean out) JOINTS (Inspect)	RADIATOR (Drain and Flush) ELECTRICAL (Inspect Cables)	GEAR-BOX (Drain and Flush)	ENGINE (Decarbonize) BACK AXLE (Drain and Flush)

N.B.—*The above table is mainly for the convenience of those who are able and who desire to give their cars systematic attention. It is based on approximately 500 miles per month. So long as the above points are not unduly neglected there is no need to conform strictly to any schedule in order to obtain efficient service from the car.*

ROUTINE DAILY CAR INSPECTION.

Before Starting Out.

PETROL — Refill tank.

RADIATOR — Inspect water level and replenish if necessary.

TYRES — Note appearance and test pressure if any tyre appears flatter than usual.

CLUTCH — Test action.

UNDER BONNET. Inspect for any signs of water leakage at pipe joints as indicated by rusty deposit.

BRAKES — Test (see pages 18 & 22).

HORN — Test action.

SPEEDOMETER. Set trip.

CLOCK — Wind and set.

DOORS — Test action.

WINDOWS — Test action.

NUMBER PLATES. Clean.

LAMPS — Clean and focus before going out at night.

Whilst Driving.

DYNAMO — Note charging (see page 27).

OIL — Note pump action (see page 9).

After Using Car.

OIL — Inspect level in engine base and replenish, if necessary, whilst warm with Daimler engine oil.

TYRES — Note appearance for pressure and inspect for nails and cuts.

WHEELS — Tighten hub caps if necessary.

BODY — Wash. (N.B.—Cover up the petrol tank filler cap.)

SPECIAL POINTS FOR ATTENTION ON A NEW CAR.

WHEELS — Shake road wheels to test tightness on hub every day for the first month.

ENGINE — Drain base-chamber, wash out with paraffin, and refill with Daimler engine oil after a fortnight.

GEAR-BOX — Drain, wash out with paraffin, and refill with Daimler heavy gear oil after one month.

BACK AXLE — Drain, wash out with paraffin, and refill with Daimler heavy gear oil after a fortnight.

A rare Q type 20/70 'Magic Carpet' – one of possibly only three made. The radiator shell, lamps, wheel hubs and deck rail over mahogany deck all gold plated. The vertical dividing line down the radiator was the first to appear on a 6-cylinder model

Daimler 'Double-Six-30' Coupé – 1929

From this year a chromium vertical strip was added to the centre of the radiator of the Double-Six models.

The new '30' version was offered with a choice of four wheelbase lengths and with many body alternatives. The mechanical design and layout, although more compact, was in all essential respects almost identical to that of the larger version – except that on the '50' the fuel supply from the 24-gallon rear mounted petrol tank was by air pressure whereas on the '30' an Autovac was used.

The Autocar, in 1929 tested a Double-Six-30 and recorded a maximum speed of 75 mph and a petrol consumption of 16·5 mpg. Such was the flexibility of the

Further examples of coachwork on the 20 hp chassis

Double-Sixes that either of the models could be started on the level in top gear.

H M the Queen ordered a new '30' limousine (Hooper body no 6861) and this had two additional seats hinged to the division, a domed roof, a patented Hooper signal window for the driver and the vehicle was finished green for the lower part and black for the upper parts, wings and valances. The rear compartment was upholstered with green morocco and cloth to the roof. The interior fittings were in silver and ivory and a tray and cabinet were fitted between the extra seats and the woodwork was described as 'laurel cross veneer'.

The Government commissioned the Daimler Company to make gun turrets

'Vintage selection'

1928 'Double-Six-30' for HM The Queen

Late 'twenties Scottish show stand

for aircraft commencing from 1929. In the same year, the Company, emulating Rolls-Royce, offered three-day training courses for chauffeurs. The tuition was thorough and comprehensive and those who attended were awarded proficiency badges. Among the recipients were chauffeurs from the Royal Mews who received special gold badges. Apart from minor changes, the Daimler range was continued unaltered for 1929. A special two-seater car on a Double-Six-30 chassis was made for Joseph Mackle of Stratton–Instone Ltd which company had on the 1st August 1928 been appointed sole distributors of Daimler cars for the whole of England and Wales.

A new design of aluminium piston radically reducing oil consumption was introduced in May 1929. Hooper & Co supplied the Royal Mews with two additional new cars. The first was in July 1929 and was a limousine (body no. 7208) on a v.3 25/85 chassis and although the coachwork was not dissimilar from that on the 30 hp car supplied to the Queen the previous year, it was unusual in that it was painted grey with black mouldings, wings and valances; silk curtains were fitted to all rear compartment windows. The other car – on a Double-Six-30 chassis was a Brougham (body no. 7209) and was painted in Royal colours but unlike 7208, this one exhibited the Royal Crest encircled by the Collar of the Order of the Garter surmounted by the Royal Crown, on the main doors and back panel and front of the scuttle. It also had a combined speedometer and clock within the rear, similar to the arrangement in the 1924 57 hp limousines.

Laurence H. Pomeroy was appointed Managing Director and for 1930 he announced an entirely new 25 hp car powered by a 6-cylinder engine – 81·5 × 114 mm – 3,568 cc having a monobloc aluminium cylinder block, detachable head and, of course, sleeve valves. The sleeves had changed quite a lot from the early type used when first the Knight engine was marketed. Now, to facilitate lubrication, the inner sleeve had perforations through its lower part, while the outer sleeve was grooved circumferentially throughout its length both inside and out and was also perforated near to its lower end. The outer sleeve was coated inside by a special process with a thin layer of white metal. On the new model, the valve sleeves were balanced to eliminate the minor tremors previously existing at high engine speeds.

Dual pumps within the sump were used in a novel lubrication system. One was employed to circulate oil through a vertical oil cooler incorporated in the nearside of the water radiator and the other pump ensured a constant supply of oil throughout the system at 30 lb psi and the carburation and cross fed hot spot induction system ensured an even distribution of mixture and greatly facilitated starting. The external appearance of the engine was extremely clean and tidy.

The chassis, offered with a standard wheelbase length of 11 feet 10 inches or with a short wheelbase of 11 feet 1 inch, was of conventional Daimler layout but here again use was made wherever possible of alloy. Silentbloc bushes were used throughout and the standard chassis weighed about 22 cwt and the complete car had a maximum speed of 65 mph but with better than average acceleration.

71

E

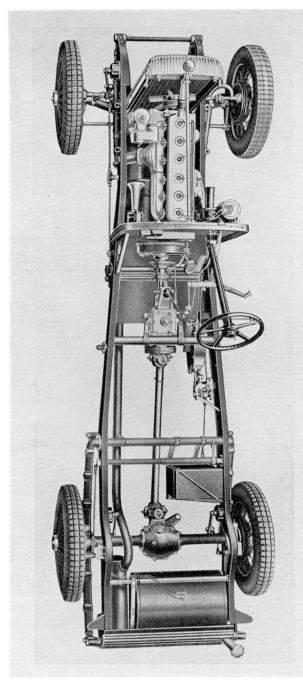

Plan View of the Daimler "Twenty-Five" Chassis

Daimler catalogue, 1930

The petrol tank, showing the accessible filler, which is also designed to prevent splash, and the Daimler slatted shield which gives a neat and finished appearance to the back of the car.

The radiator, with its hand-finished fluted top, characterises the whole car and blends gracefully with the coachwork.

The 'Corsica' drophead coupé on the 'Double-Six' lowered chassis

74

The first specially prepared 'Double-Six' with lowered chassis, by Thompson and Taylor of Brooklands, made for a Captain Wilson

Another low built 'Double-Six' (but not on a lowered chassis) made by Martin Walter – 1932

The Daimler patented brake compensator and single point adjuster were features which were retained. A push-on handbrake operated on the transmission via a drum positioned behind the gearbox. The bonnet was of the three-piece type with the top hinged at the back and the side doors opening outwards and capable of being removed completely when occasion so demanded, and the slatted shield which covered the rear mounted petrol tank and the five-spoke steering wheel – long standing Daimler characteristics – were also in evidence on the new car. The short chassis cost £650 and the long chassis £45 more with prices for completed vehicles commencing at about £875.

At about this time or shortly afterwards, a few special low chassis versions of the Double-Six-50 were produced – the most impressive being evolved at Brook-lands track by Thompson and Taylor Ltd, under the direction of their chief engineer, Reid Railton.

The most notable event of the year was the disclosure of Daimler's revolutionary new transmission system. As first conceived the idea was to use the fluid flywheel in conjunction with an orthodox gearbox but due largely to the initiative of the Company chairman, Percy Martin, the flexible drive was for production purposes, allied to an epicyclic preselective box.

The fluid flywheel was a development of the torque transmitter patented by Dr H. Fottinger in 1906. The simplified form of coupling with constant fluid content, as adopted for motor car transmission was patented by H. Sinclair in 1926 and further patents were registered in 1930 by The Daimler Company and Percy Martin, in respect of the system as devised by them.

The component parts were few and simple. The fluid flywheel had an outer casing which was bolted to the crankshaft. The rear plate of this casing serves as the driving member. On its inner surface are a series of cup-shaped pockets separated by radial webs. Within the outer casing is the driven member mounted on a shaft passing rearwards through a bearing and oil-tight gland in the driving member to the gearbox. The driven member has another set of pockets and webs upon its rear surface facing those of the driving member and the two are separated by a small gap so that they are free to rotate independently. If the reader can at this point imagine two halves of a grapefruit . . .!

The power is transmitted from the driving to the driven member by means of ordinary engine oil of which the fluid flywheel is nearly full. When in motion the oil in the segments on the driving member is flung outward by centrifugal force. This stream of oil strikes the vanes on the driven member at an angle causing it to rotate. After the oil stream gives up its energy in this way, it flows inwards through the pockets to the centre of the flywheel to be caught there for the process to be repeated.

The result was an outstandingly smooth and trouble free system which, in many respects anticipated the fully automatic transmission systems to follow.

J. Dewar McLintock, in that fascinating book *Royal Motoring* (Foulis 1962), mentions that according to his informant, Major E. C. Ball, who had represented the Daimler Company in the south and south-west of England during the late 'twenties and early 'thirties, it was during the summer of 1930 that the Duke of York visited Weymouth and there encountered for the first time a Daimler car equipped with the new fluid transmission. Apparently the Duke was minded to walk through the town following the ceremony but the equerry was asked by Major Ball '. . . tell His Royal Highness that I have a car here which will go as slow as he wants, in top gear.' The author tells how the Duke responded to the invitation and as they drove very slowly through the main street of Weymouth, the Duke was so impressed that he remarked: 'I really must stop looking at this and wave to the public.'

King George V used his Daimlers on every occasion he had to travel long distances by road. An ardent racegoer, he used invariably to motor over from Sandringham or Buckingham Palace to the Newmarket meetings. Whenever he

King Hussein of Jordan's 'Double-Six-40/50'

A replica of King George V's 'Double-Six', with fluid flywheel and self-changing gearbox – 1930

A Special 20/30 with Mrs Joseph Mackle at the wheel, having won first prize in the sporting car class at a Brighton concours d'elegance, 1930

This 1930 car was one of the first to be fitted with Daimler fluid transmission

HM King George V leaving Buckingham Palace in one of the 1931 Daimler 'Double-Six 40/50' State cars

1931 35 hp Daimler supplied to the King of Egypt

elected to stay in his suite at the Jockey Club rooms in Newmarket High Street, a Daimler waited outside.

Likewise the royal procession to Epsom on Derby Day always consisted of Daimler cars. There was a special parking place behind the Grand Stand close to the place where the royal brakes were drawn up which had brought down the royal servants, who wore 'travelling costume' – black coats with the red lanyards that once secured pistols with which to defend the royal personage if attacked by highwaymen or footpads en route.

On those brilliant days when the King drove in open carriages to Ascot, the Daimler was present in the background. Nothing was ever left to chance. In case of rain, the royal fleet was drawn up under the trees behind the race course.

The original Double-Six-30 remained in production until 1932, whereas the Double-Six-50 was dropped during 1930. It is unlikely that either of these models were fitted with the new transmission, except perhaps, for experimental purposes, but the fluid flywheel was employed for the two new 12-cylinder models announced in 1930 and produced between 1931 and 1935. Both had sleeve valve engines and were the Double-Six-30/40 – 73 × 104 mm – 5,296 cc with a taller and more slender radiator and the Double-Six-40/50 – 81·5 × 114 mm – 6,511 cc but the layout of the new units was somewhat modified and some of the features introduced on the new 25 hp 6-cylinder car were incorporated. The combination of the 12-cylinder sleeve valve engine which had now reached its optimum in design, the fluid transmission and the underslung worm drive axle made these powerful Daimlers incredibly quiet and smooth and it is lamentable that so very few of these and other delectable Vintage Daimlers have survived to the present day. If a sleeve valve car was left unused for any considerable period of time, its engine was prone to seizure and not infrequently the application of force in the attempt to restart led to a fracture of the sleeves or the connecting links. Moreover, with the multiplicity of chassis types produced by the Company over the years, spares became a problem exacerbated by the effects of the war and it has been suggested that there were so many valuable materials in Daimler cars that they were much favoured by breakers and scrap metal merchants!

The new transmission system installed in a 20–30 hp car (the former 25 hp model re-named) was thoroughly tested by *The Motor* whose report was published on 6th January 1931. The test extended over five hundred miles varying from heavy traffic conditions in London, over open stretches of the Great North Road and in the Derbyshire Peak District:

No one guards a reputation more jealously than the manufacturer of a high-grade car. However attractive a novel mechanism may appear at first glance, he cannot make use of it until very strenuous tests have revealed every possible source of weakness. Even so, he cannot be absolutely certain that the general motoring public will not bring about (by mishandling) troubles which the works testers were unable to discover.

All honour is therefore, due to the Daimler Company for having pioneered a very novel 'fluid flywheel' or hydraulic clutch, for having ingeniously combined this with the well-known self-changing gearbox, and for having engineered the whole system so thoroughly that from its initiation onwards no troubles have been experienced.

This new system of power transmission has been accepted with avidity by the Daimler clientele and by many motorists who had not previously owned Daimler cars. It has also created a world-wide interest amongst car manufacturers. . . .

A driver strange to this transmission very soon becomes accustomed to it because he has really nothing new to learn. He is spared the fatigue of elaborate gear changing operations with a delicate control of engine speed, such as are ordinarily required. He is also relieved of responsibility for skilful and cautious clutch engagement. Consequently both in traffic and in hill country the advantages of the system are particularly noticeable. . . . The gear lever works in a quadrant handily placed below the steering wheel and moves with a slight click from position to position, so that it can easily be worked in the dark without looking down. . . . A great feature of this gearbox is that the lever is of the pre-selective type; by using it the driver settles which gear will next be brought into operation but does not actually cause a change to take place. . . .

The next point is that the fluid flywheel automatically disconnects the engine from the gearbox when the revolution speed of the former drops to a sufficient extent. Consequently, when bringing the car to a standstill there is no need to trouble about clutch or engine – the former will disconnect and the latter will idle. Similarly, when starting from rest it is only necessary to depress the accelerator. The engine speed then rises to about 600 rpm, the clutch picks up the load smoothly and progressively and the car moves forwards. The clutch consists of rotating members, one driven by the engine and the other driving the transmission shaft, which can turn independently when running slowly. As the speed increases, the fluid which fills the clutch casing is forced to flow through a tortuous path and drags the driven member around after the driving member. . . .

It is also possible to stand beside the car with top gear engaged and the engine idling, and then to cause it to move very, very slowly forwards by opening the hand throttle two notches, while walking alongside. It is practically impossible to fix a lower limit for the top gear speed, but a steady ¼ mph is certainly feasible. This is a great advantage for traffic crawling and similar performances; in short the fluid flywheel confers upon the petrol vehicle a flexibility almost equal to that of a steam car. . . .

As an aside to their principal objective, the writers of the above report commented on the car generally, mentioning that

the engine, which represents a development of the original aluminium cylindered 25 hp unit is extremely smooth, silent and flexible. Furthermore, it gives excellent torque and power, so that the acceleration is good all the way up the scale. . . . Furthermore, the road holding can be classed as very good indeed.

Other cars in the 1930 range were the 20 hp (formerly the 20/70) and the 35 hp (formerly the 35/120) – the 16/55 being discontinued. For 1931 the range continued basically unchanged except that when equipped with the fluid transmission the 20 was re-designated the 16–20 with a wheelbase of 10 feet 1 inch from March 1931 and from May 1932 with a wheelbase length of 10 feet 4 inches and chassis and body modifications and a new radiator with 'shoulder ledges' and a centre radiator strip similar to that first exhibited on the Double-Six-50. For a while some models were offered with the option of sliding gear or the new Daimler transmission.

Five new Royal Daimlers were delivered in April 1931. Three of these, for

H M the King, were enclosed limousines – two being Double-Six-40/50s – (chassis OP 32349 with Hooper body 7505 and chassis OP 32348 with Hooper body 7506) and the other was a v-type Double-Six-30/40 (chassis 32336 – body 7508). All three were painted in royal colours and had mahogany woodwork with silver and white ivory fittings. The remaining two new cars – limousines of similar design to those made for the King were on a Double-Six-40/50 chassis (number OP 32347 – body no 7504) and on a Double-Six-30/40 chassis (number 32335 – body 7507). The larger car was supplied to Her Majesty and was painted in royal colours but the v 30 was finished traditionally in the Queen's own distinctive colours of green and black.

In 1931, the assets of The Lanchester Motor Company Ltd were acquired by The Daimler Company. It would be an unwarranted digression to seek to chronicle the progress of the first mentioned Company but the reader is warmly commended to read *Lanchester Motor Cars* by Anthony Bird and Francis Hutton-Stott (Cassell 1965). It must, however, be mentioned that the Lanchester brothers were the first in this country to produce a petrol-driven four wheeled car. Referring to the amalgamation in *Daimler 1896–1946* St John C. Nixon said:

Although designed originally on opposite lines, there has always been a certain affinity between the Daimler and Lanchester cars. Both were the pioneers of British motor construction; both played important roles in giving birth to the industry in this country and making it what it is today. There has, too, been a liaison in other directions; no Daimler or Lanchester car has ever been designed to accomplish the sensational; no effort has ever been made by the sponsors of either to achieve anything of a spectacular order.

As soon as practicable after the take over, a new Lanchester 15/18 was shown to the public and this like all succeeding Lanchesters (with a few exceptions – the 14 hp Roadrider de luxe of 1938–9 offered with the alternative of a synchromesh gearbox and the Sprite equipped with Hobbs automatic transmission) were fitted with Daimler fluid transmission and poppet valve engines.

For 1932 the Daimler range comprised the 16–20; the 20–25, the 35, the Double-Six-30, the Double-Six-30/40 and the Double-Six-40/50. Opportunity was shortly to be taken to supersede the sleeve valve units which had proved themselves so faithful. Lanchester had never departed from the poppet valve and moreover such progress had been made in metallurgy and design technique since 1908 that no longer was there such a disparity in degrees of silence and efficiency between sleeve and poppet valves.

The public in general, were demanding a return to smaller cars and Daimlers responded by offering a completely new model of modest proportions. The Daimler 'Fifteen' was announced in October 1932 and was made available for the following season. For it an entirely new 6-cylinder overhead valve engine, $63 \cdot 5 \times 95$ mm – 1,805 cc, was developed and with the new fluid transmission and worm drive rear axle, it was silky smooth in operation and quickly found favour with all who sampled the car.

Daimler 'Twenties' of the early 'thirties – both with coachwork by E. D. Abbott of Farnham

Our first reactions to the behaviour of the Daimler 15 hp, saloon may be summarized by saying we felt that the car possessed all the refinements for which the products of the Daimler Company have long been noted. It is, in fact, a small luxury car built of the finest materials to a design which to say the least, is thoroughly up to date. One might go a step further and say that it is a little in advance of the times, for there are certain special features concerning the engine and transmission which place it almost in a class by itself. . . .

Finally, a word may be said concerning the general construction of both the chassis and body-work. Everything seems to be taut; rattles and squeaks do not exist and there is a notable absence of drumming. It might be added that the Daimler Company has gone to a great deal of trouble to produce this state of affairs, every component used in the make-up of the chassis and bodywork having been carefully scrutinized to see if it could possibly be the cause of trouble in this direction, and the object has been achieved. . . . (The Motor – 6th February 1934)

The London Motor Show (probably 1933)

It was in 1932 that the stylized 'D' was first used on the hub caps – first on the 16/20 which incidentally, in sleeve valve form was continued for 1933 but then known simply as the '20' (chassis type LQ) – 2,648 cc and then on the Fifteen. Similarly the former 20/25 reverted to the simple title of '25' and this too was continued with sleeves and fluid transmission as were the two Double-Sixes, the 30/40 and the 40/50. These latter three in the same form were also retained for 1934 but from September of the year previous the '20' was given a new engine with poppet valves (72 × 110 mm – 2,687 cc – chassis symbol LQ 2.20) which in limousine form had a wheelbase extended by 3 inches to 10 feet 4 inches and then from March 1934 the LQ 3.20 was the chassis designation for the longer version and in this form the '20' continued in production until April 1936.

Confronting most automobile manufacturers in the early 'thirties, were problems of considerable magnitude and for many these problems proved to be insuperable and directly or indirectly brought about their collapse. In addition to the economic and other difficulties common to most concerns, the Daimler Company had a particular problem. As previously noted, the sleeve valve power units had been developed to a peak of efficiency, the Double-Sixes had added further merit to the Company's prestige; patronage from Royalty and the nobility

84

both at home and overseas had not merely been retained but had expanded; the new Daimler transmission had been heralded as revolutionary and the Daimler Fifteen was proving itself to be very popular. There was a need for something entirely new to replace the highly esteemed 12-cylinder cars and the renowned '35'. Gaining a good reputation is one thing; keeping it is quite another! What next?

The Company's answer was the Straight-Eight. Daimlers were not, of course, alone in adopting eight cylinders in line. Both before and afterwards, in England, on the Continent and particularly in the United States, other manufacturers too aimed in this way to attain the ultimate in internal combustion engine design. The majority who chose to explore the idea did not find success easy to come by. Lord Montagu, in his book – *Lost Causes of Motoring* (Cassell), generously asserts that: 'of the firms who toyed with this impressively lengthy power unit in Britain, only Daimler emerged scatheless . . .'.

It will be recalled that at the time of the absorption of The Lanchester Motor Company, that concern were still producing their famous overhead camshaft

Hooper bodied 'V 26 Straight-Eights' of 1934/5. The Sedanca above was built to private order and the touring saloon below was made for Stratstone Ltd

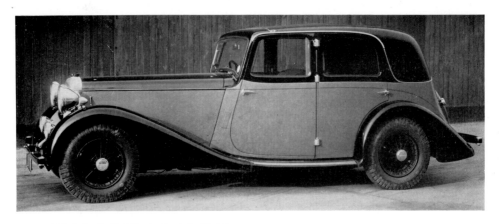

1935–6 Daimler bodied 'Light Straight-Eight'

This Symbol
of Daimler Fluid Flywheel Transmission means for you
'Motoring smooth as flight' which will not tire you.
Perfectly easy, silent gear-changing. Smooth pick-up in
any gear from rest without clutch work.
Traffic-strain eliminated.

straight-eight, and there is little doubt that the knowledge and experience acquired by Daimlers from this source, was not dissipated but, at least to some degree, appropriated to the design of the new Daimler engine. Moreover, several 8-cylinder cars of other makes were acquired and very carefully examined and their merits and demerits assessed.

James Young award-winning design on 'V 26 Straight-Eight' chassis – 1935

An early example of a 'Straight-Eight limousine'

Rare indeed is the occasion when fault can be found with the erudite writings of St John C. Nixon but in his aforementioned book *Daimler 1896–1946* he erred when introducing the Straight-Eight which emerged in 1934. Others too have repeated his erroneous assertion that the original power unit had a displacement of 3·42 litres (although in the appendix, Nixon correctly stated the dimensions

F

as 72×115 mm and the capacity as 3,746 cc) but of greater importance he suggested that the Straight-Eight was conceived and first built as a sleeve valve unit. Such was not the case. Daimlers were anxious to find a convenient way to depart from the now outmoded Knight design and the amalgamation with Lanchesters provided just this opportunity.

Various considerations prompted Laurence Pomeroy to select the eight-in-line arrangement for the new engine which was designed to give a high power output and yet to remain wholly unobtrusive up to a maximum speed of around 4,000 rpm. Advantages which were cited by the designer were that individual cylinder dimensions were kept to an efficient minimum, the mechanical balance was excellent, the relatively small size of the pistons, valves and other such moving parts assisted in maintaining silence and the carburation problem was solved by treating the unit as a combination of two 4-cylinder components.

The carburetter was a dual Stromberg down-draught instrument each part of which was entirely independent and fed its own inlet pipe, one of which served the end pairs of cylinders numbers 1, 2, 7 and 8 while the other pipe conveyed the mixture to cylinders 3, 4, 5 and 6. The crankshaft was fully counter-balanced, was fitted with a vibration damper and ran in nine main bearings. The overhead valves had exceptionally wide clearances (as did the Fifteen, Twenty and later models – in some instances in excess of 60 thou.) and of course these were push-rod operated from the camshaft driven by chain from the rear end of the crank. 95 bhp was, according to the report in *The Motor* (1st May 1934) recorded on the bench but 90 bhp on a compression of 5·5 was the power claimed in the sales literature.

A very sturdy chassis utilised tubular cross-members and the front of the frame was stiffened by box-sectioned side members. The dash was also used as part of the structure and was built from Elektron castings to provide additional rigidity without undue weight and at the front, the bumper was of the harmonic stabilizer type. On the early cars the front axle was a forging of light alloy and the rear axle casing was built from a central aluminium casting and two tapered steel tubes. The separate body frame was no longer part of the Daimler specification, but the brake compensator and single point adjustment were still used in conjunction with a mechanical braking system incorporating a Clayton Dewandre servo motor.

Semi-elliptic springs were used all round and on the offside an anti-kick shackle was included to obviate steering wheel shocks from rough road surfaces. The Luvax hydraulic shock absorbers were of exceptional size – in fact those at the rear were of the type actually used on Daimler motor coaches of the period!

The new model was announced as the 'Twenty-five' but at the works the chassis, having a wheelbase of 11 feet 10½ inches was known as the 'v 26'. With standard coachwork the maximum speed of the car was around 75 mph. The first batch of Straight-Eights were mainly of the formal limousine variety but thereafter more interesting versions appeared. In August 1934, Stratstone Ltd announced that they would shortly be able to supply owner–driver models and in their London showrooms they had for inspection several saloons and an all-weather foursome costing £1,515, with coachwork by Hooper & Co and other examples by Arthur Mulliner.

. . . we were able to verify the exceptional degree of silence and smoothness which has been attained in the design of this engine. Every detail of the construction has been considered from this important viewpoint. . . .

The car handles very nicely both on main roads and in country lanes. The brakes are excellent, the steering light and springing extremely comfortable. . . .

. . . Summing up, the new Daimler '25' represents a very important addition to the list of high-grade British cars. In every detail it bears the stamp of long experience both in design and workmanship.
(The Motor – 1st May 1934)

In the autumn of 1934, the 'Fifteen' was revised in several respects for the forthcoming year. The bore was kept at 63·5 but the stroke was increased to 105 mm giving a capacity of 2,003 cc and providing approximately 46 bhp. The radiator, headlamps, wing valances and other design aspects were improved and so also was the chassis and steering. Girling mechanical brakes, without servo assistance, were installed with a pull-up handbrake, the engine was mounted on rubber (as was the radiator from August 1935) and a thermostat cooling control was added. The basic chassis price remained unchanged at £350 and the car was available with as wide a choice of coachwork as ever. The Company built several types and variations on the theme were available from independent coach-builders.

During the three years it has been in the hands of the motoring public, the car has built up for itself a considerable reputation by reason of its good all round balance.

Restraint of a kind to appeal to people who can appreciate a proper reserve has marked the outward appearance of a car which has a particularly quiet and smooth running overhead-valve engine, superlative ease of handling given by the fluid flywheel transmission with its preselective self changing gearbox, effective insulation from vibration, secured by the flexible mounting of the power unit, and two points which are gained by the use of an underslung frame, namely, a low floor level to give free space in the body and the low centre of gravity necessary for stability on the road; these are the major points of the car.
(The Autocar – August 1935)

The 1935 Fifteen had a maximum speed of 70 mph and returned a fuel consumption of 24–25 mpg.

His Majesty King George V commanded the Daimler Co to produce a new State car, similar to the 1931 Double-Sixes but with extra width in the rear. Stratstone Ltd (shortly to come under the control of Thos. Tillings) delivered the completed vehicle in April 1935. It was the thirtieth Daimler to be supplied to the then King and Queen and the thirty-seventh Daimler car to be ordered by a British Sovereign!

The wheelbase was 13 feet 1 inch and the track 5 feet 4 inches, the latter dimension being 4 inches greater than that in the earlier Royal Double-Sixes; the overall length was 17 feet 10 inches.

For this very special car a significant change to the engine was made with the concurrence of His Majesty. In place of the sleeve valve Double-Six design used previously, a vee-twelve poppet valve engine was specially evolved. Approximately 140 bhp was developed by the new engine, the dimensions of which were $81 \cdot 5 \times 104$ mm – 6,511 cc (49·4 hp). The crankshaft was carried in seven main bearings, the two monobloc banks of cylinders were of cast-iron mounted on an aluminium crankcase, and the detachable cylinder heads were also of cast-iron and the pistons were of special aluminium alloy. The overhead valves were operated by rockers and push-rods from camshafts positioned in the crankcase and driven from the rear end of the crankshaft.

Located in the vee of the blocks were the exhaust and inlet manifolds. Duplicate distributors and coils provided sparks for the plugs accessibly placed on the outsides of the banks, but a single dual carburetter fitted with an automatic choke control fed the twin inlet manifolds. Special care was taken to secure silence at the air intake and the system of exhaust silencing was the result of considerable experiment, the silencers being of a new type, of large size and arranged in tandem. Twin submerged gear pumps were employed for the pressure fed engine lubrication system.

Daimler transmission was of course incorporated with gear ratios: first 18·9, second 10·7, third 6·6 and top 4·38 to 1.

Another special feature was the chassis frame which was exceptionally strong. Long and wide semi-elliptic springs were used at both ends and all had self-lubricating graphite bronze tips to maintain constant flexibility and to avoid squeaking. Moreover, hydraulic shock absorbers were fitted to both front and rear and by the turn of a knob on the floor, the driver could adjust the ride whilst the car was in motion.

The limousine body (no 8258 on chassis 39701) was again the work of Hooper & Co and was in most respects similar to the earlier Royal cars. The traditional floor to roof internal measurement of 60 inches was retained but the rear seat width between the wheel arches was increased to 50 inches. The radiator surround was finished in dull black and all the exterior metal fittings were of burnished brass.

In December of the same year, Queen Mary took delivery of an almost identical car (body 8430 on chassis 39700). Both the King and Queen's cars were painted in Royal colours and both gave outstanding service. After the second world war, a DE 27 4-litre 6-cylinder engine was substituted for the original unit in the Queen's car which Lord Montagu has in his collection at Beaulieu.

Some of the earliest experiments with Daimler fluid transmission were carried out on public service vehicles and before long this reliable and foolproof system was standardized on all Daimler buses. When sleeve valves became obsolete new poppet-valve bus engines were developed but within a short period, Gardner Diesel engines were offered (from about 1933). Two years later other power units could be specified, for example, some of Coventry's buses were fitted with AEC

The two 1935 poppet-valve 'Double-Sixes' supplied respectively to the King (above) and Queen

diesel engines whilst the power units in Newcastle's Daimler buses (type COS 4) were Armstrong Saurer diesels. In 1936 the Company formed its own bus division under the name of Transport Vehicles (Daimler) Ltd and shortly before the war it had developed its own diesel power unit with a capacity of 8·6 litres, but more of this later.

On the private side, one of the new '25' Straight-Eights was introduced to the Royal Mews in October 1935 and was used by the Royal Household. This was chassis 38438 mounted with Hooper enclosed limousine coachwork (body 8440).

The new 8-cylinder car had proved itself to be satisfactory to the Company and of more importance, to the customer and so two new Straight-Eights followed, the first in December 1935.

The 'V 4½' – (80 × 115 mm – 4,624 cc) had a treasury rating of 31·74 hp and in most respects this was simply a bored out version of the V 26 which it replaced, but with the compression ratio increased to 6 to 1. The track and wheel-base dimensions remained unchanged. An extra long chassis, the 'VF' version

1933 Martin Walter bodied Daimler '15' coupé – (1,805 cc)

Another 1933 Daimler '15' with Martin Walter 'Denton' coachwork

1933 Daimler '15' with drophead coupé body by Abbotts of Farnham

Ranelagh coachwork on 1937 Daimler '15' (2,166 cc) chassis

Young coachwork on Straight-Eight 3½-litre chassis no. 43672. A 'one-off' built for Joseph Mackle, Esq

Light Straight-Eight – Melbourne, Australia, 1939

R. S. (Bob) Crouch with the 1937 Charlesworth bodied 3½-litre Light Straight-Eight Monte Carlo Rally car

This 4½-litre Straight-Eight with Rippon coachwork (registration no. DWT 100) was a car of many parts. Seen above, it was being driven by Col. Rippon in the Scottish Rally; overleaf it is shown as it featured in the British film version of Esther McCracken's play – 'A Quiet Weekend' (1945) and then in 'The Motor' for 27th March 1946 it was reported that the car had been presented to HH The Aga Khan by his followers on the occasion of his Diamond Jubilee. Elaborate cabinet work was a feature of the rear compartment in which there was also included radio and a foot warmer

The 4½-litre 'Straight-Eight' DWT 100 (see previous page)

The Lanchester Straight-Eight landaulette – registration no. JJ 4

and another similar Lanchester ordered by HRH The Duke of York before his accession

The 1939 Royal Lanchester with Hooper landaulette coachwork on the Daimler 4½-litre 32 hp Straight-Eight chassis

being 9 inches greater in wheelbase length was available from February 1937. The 4½-litre cars were designed principally for formal coachwork and they found their place with Royalty at home, in government service throughout the Commonwealth and Empire and with the well-to-do the world over. In normal limousine form the complete vehicle weighed between 47 and 48 cwt and had a maximum speed of about 70 mph and consumed fuel at the rate of 1 gallon every 13–14 miles. The Straight-Eights, especially the 4½-litre version, were worthy successors to the Double-Sixes and their design was a personal triumph for Laurence Pomeroy. Prices varied for standard coachwork from £1,575 to £1,825.

After their amalgamation in 1931, Lanchesters confined their models to the small to medium size and price range. In the main Lanchester cars during the 'thirties, were slightly smaller and cheaper versions of their Daimler counterparts. In order to satisfy the Lanchester clientele, a number of 8-cylinder cars were made to special order from 1936. In reality these were 4½-litre Daimler Straight-Eights but displaying Lanchester radiators. Early in 1936 HRH the Duke of York (later King George VI) ordered two such cars – chassis 41289 and 41290 with Hooper bodies numbered respectively 8524 and 8523. The first mentioned was an attractive and distinctive enclosed landaulette whilst the other car was a typical enclosed limousine. Another 'Lanchester', endowed with a truly magnificent Vanden Plas drop-head coupé body was made for HH the Maharajah Jam Sahib of Nawanagar. During the 'sixties this car was still receiving envious glances and it won the premier award in the all India concours d'elegance. At that time the total mileage of the vehicle was claimed to be only 4,000. This Maharajah had more than forty Lanchesters!

Referring to the 32 hp Straight-Eight on road test, *The Motor* in 1938 said:

. . . it is a paradox that the more expensive a car may be, the more difficult it is to render praise; one's standards are raised so that a point that would be below notice on a car costing £500 becomes a major thorn in the flesh in one of £1,500. It is therefore, the more remarkable that we are able to give this large Daimler full marks from practically every point of view.

From around April 1936, the 'Twenty' was uprated to 24 hp – (80 × 110 mm – 3,317 cc) and for a short while the chassis symbol LQ 3/24 was employed but by the late summer EL 24 was applied to the model, opportunity being taken to effect a considerable number of improvements – particularly as regards the chassis which was strengthened and given greater rigidity. A deeper radiator was mounted a little further forward and anonymity was again restored by the removal of the 'D' from the nave plates – the 'Twenty-four' having splined hubs as did the Straight-Eights. The new 6-cylinder car proved itself to be immensely popular and reliable and remained in production until the outbreak of war. When testing one with light limousine coachwork, the following comments were made by *The Motor* (6th April 1937):

. . . We took the Daimler from the Midlands to Brooklands, where acceleration, maximum speed and braking tests were carried out. Despite the handicap of large, well-built coachwork, the car performed extraordinarily well, being capable of accelerating quickly throughout its speed range.

The engine and the whole transmission showed the refinement which is to be found in all Daimler products. This limousine struck us as being one of the quietest and smoothest-running cars produced. Hardly any vibration can be detected when running on top or in any of the indirect gears at any reasonable speed. . . .

We actually completed a lap of Brooklands at a speed slightly in excess of 70 mph, which considering that the maximum speed of which the car is capable on level going is 73 mph speaks well for the engine.

Altogether this Daimler is a fine car, designed and built to afford comfortable travel at a cost which is not unduly high.

The final stage in the production of every Straight-Eight power unit is an exhaustive eight-hour bench test in which the engines are run from slow speed right through to maximum. During this process they are tested for oil and water leaks after which they are washed down and finally inspected and adjusted. When the Straight-Eight takes the road, maximum speed can be obtained without fear of damage to the engine.

[Extract from Catalogue]

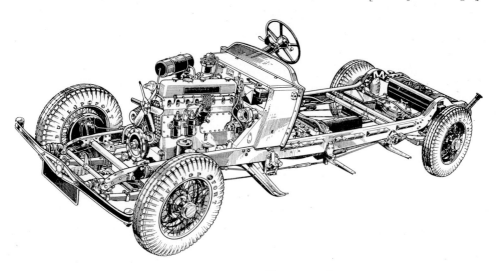

The 1936–39 Daimler 4½-litre Straight-Eight chassis. Chassis price £975

4½-litre Landaulette – body no. 8864, built by Hooper & Co. for J. M. Ryrie, Esq, 1936

1938 4½-litre Straight-Eight Continental Sports Saloon by Arthur Mulliner

For 1936, a smaller version of the Straight-Eight was designed specifically for the owner-driver and having similar general qualities to the 4½ litre but with a more lively performance. To distinguish it, the new model was given the title 'Light Straight-Eight'. It had an entirely new engine (72 × 105 mm – 3,421 cc) with a five bearing fully counter-balanced crankshaft and a non-detachable cylinder head. The wheelbase measured 10 feet 3 inches and the track, the same as on the bigger 8-cylinder car, 4 feet 9 inches. The chassis type was 'E 3½'.

1938 Daimler Straight-Eight Limousine Model 954 (coachwork by Windover)

This Daimler is in a sense representative of the progressiveness shown by a firm which in experience and traditions goes back to the commencement of the British Motor industry. . . .

so began *The Autocar* road test in March 1938. It continued:

. . . rather special effort has been made to provide high performance and yet retain the quiet and comfortable running always associated with this make. The 3½-litre engine . . . is efficient, stands up admirably to hard driving, and not least, is extremely well finished, so that it is a pleasure to open the bonnet. The car as a whole is of handsome appearance; it 'looks fast' and it is, but no sacrifice has been made of comfort and interior room.

The car tested was a Charlesworth four-door, four-light sports saloon weighing 39 cwt unladen and provided an average fuel consumption of 15–16 mpg and at its best would travel 85 miles an hour. The cost of that particular model was £1,050. During the first year of its introduction, a Light Straight-Eight open car with thin oil in the hubs, achieved a maximum timed speed at Brooklands of slightly in excess of 90 mph.

As a companion to the Light Straight-Eight, the Company also brought out during 1936 a new 'Light Twenty' with a displacement of 2,565 cc (72 × 105 mm). The 6-cylinder engine followed very closely the design of the 8-cylinder version; in particular the head was of the non-detachable variety which form of construction eliminated distortion of the cylinder barrels, improved valve cooling and avoided gasket trouble. For a fairly sober looking motor car, the 'Light Twenty' had a very commendable performance of up to about 75 mph.

With the coming of the Fifteen, Light Twenty and the Straight-Eights, coachwork design both at Daimlers and with the Specialists reached a very high standard and many of the examples depicted exhibit an almost unsurpassable quality of style and elegance.

Freestone & Webb Special Touring Limousine on 4½-litre Straight-Eight chassis

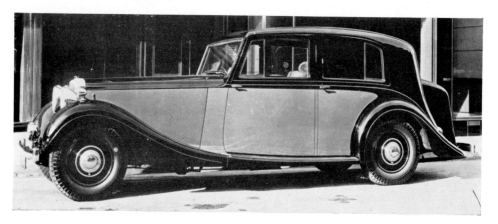

Another example by the same coachbuilders

4½-litre Straight-Eight with James Young Special Touring Limousine body. Price £1,660

Hooper seven seater Landaulette on 4½ Straight-Eight chassis. Price £1,710

4½-litre Straight-Eight with Hooper Touring Limousine body. Price £1,725

4½-litre Straight-Eight with 'Rippon' special design 6/7 seater Enclosed Limousine body. Price £1,800

*4½-litre Straight-Eight with 'Rippon' special four-door close-coupled Touring Limousine body
Price of car illustrated £2,012.15.0*

*This fine car, built for Colonel Rippon by his Company, won the premier award on its first appearance
at the R A C rally coachwork competition at Blackpool in the spring of 1938. Externally the car was
painted ivory white whilst the leatherwork within was tastefully carried out in Air Force blue which
blended well with the grey sycamore woodwork.*

*The rear compartment had a sliding roof and glass division, both controlled electrically from switches
on the armrests and on the dash. In the beautifully panelled centre division were concealed a lady's and
a gentleman's dressing-case. The lady's case was elegantly equipped in gold and blue enamel with
clothes and hair brushes, comb, compact, powder bowl, mirror and cigarette and match containers. In the
other case there was provided for the gentleman's use hair and clothes brushes, comb, flask, cigarette and
cigar boxes and all these were set in ivory and silver. Between the two was a cocktail cabinet and
beneath that a grille for the electric heater outlet. The absence of a pillar between the rear door and
quarter light afforded excellent visibility. Moreover, the quarter lights could be opened and could also be
partially covered by sliding panels with mirror insets. In addition to the usual roof lights, special reading
lights were fitted and these were suitably screened from the driver; a door pillar switch enabled the
rear interior to be lit automatically when a door was opened and an electrically operated rear blind was
under the control of the driver from the dash.*

*The front compartment was equally well equipped. In addition to all normal controls and equipment,
there were the following items: under the dash, first aid kits, fire extinguisher, reserve petrol tap, radio
and inspection light, and on the passenger's side a glass covered sliding map case which was illuminated
when in use. Above the compartment there was an unusual sliding roof capable of being fully opened
or optionally a masking panel could be slid back revealing a water-tight Perspex panel still in position.
On account of the large number of electrically operated gadgets the car was fitted with two 48 amp
batteries and the system was interposed by master switches mounted on the front floor.*

*In the boot were supplied fitted suitcases and a trunk and a hinged bulkhead concealed them so that
further light luggage could be carried on the inside of the lid. Above the luggage compartment was a tool
chest which was automatically illuminated when the lid was raised.*

*Detail equipment, such as lighters and ashtrays, was lavishly carried out. There were no fewer than
four driving mirrors. On the roof there was an identification lamp and a socket for rally pennants. On
each rear armrest were placed switches to raise and lower the division and operate the rear sunshine roof
and above the offside armrest was another concealed companion containing shopping list, visiting card
case and mirror.*

'Light Twenty' of 1938

HM King Edward VIII, in June 1936, had delivered to him a new Hooper enclosed limousine (body 8599 on 32-hp Straight-Eight chassis 41326) and then early in the new year an EL 24 (chassis 43728) was used as the basis for a new motor carriage for Queen Mary.

The accession of HM King George VI makes 1937 another important year in the chronicle: of this ruler, St John Nixon wrote (*Daimler 1896–1946*):

When King George VI came to the throne, he owned three Lanchester cars, one being a 'sports' model which he always drove himself. It was in this car that he used to take Queen Elizabeth and the two Princesses from 145 Piccadilly to his country house at Royal Lodge, Windsor Forest, every weekend.

King George has worthily carried on the tradition of his illustrious father; as soon as he became King he ordered at once certain additions to the existing fleet of Daimler cars. His first new car was delivered at the end of April 1937; it was specially designed to be both a means of transport and a travelling office. It contained elaborate reading lamps, and fitted into the centre arm of the back seat was a small writing desk, which could be used for writing when travelling from place to place.

A vast number of Daimler cars were in service during the Coronation celebrations of 1937. It was estimated at the time that a thousand figured in one way or another, and the photograph of Whitehall shows a long procession of Daimler cars which took part. There were 150 Daimlers – of the 'straight eight' type – specially chartered for the use of Empire Prime Ministers and other distinguished guests. Many were sent to the coastal ports to bring visitors from overseas direct to London by road. It was an impressive sight and one of which there is good cause for the Daimler Company to be proud when, on Coronation Day, a long procession of Daimler cars swept out of

'This Model No. 724 by Salmons and Sons is an example of the finest type of "all weather" body available on any Daimler chassis. On the "Twenty" an extremely attractive appearance is obtained. Price £835.' (1938 catalogue)

Daimler bodied Light Twenty (Model 722). Priced at £615

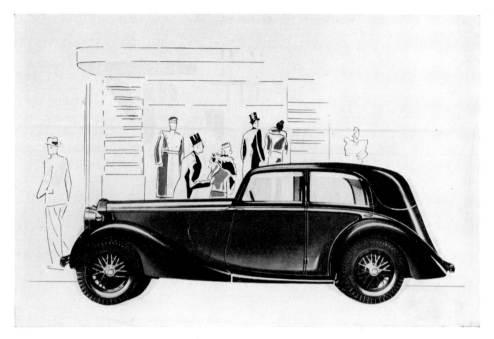

'Here illustrated is Model 723 built by Charlesworth Bodies (1931) Ltd. This alternative bodywork is of sturdy construction with an excellent practical specification. Price £755.' (1938 catalogue)

The Daimler bodied Six-Light Twenty Saloon (Model 721). Price £595

Buckingham Palace to the Abbey in a line containing Princes and Princesses, Ambassadors, Ministers, Admirals and Generals.

It is a wonderful record, this long connection between the Royal Family and the Daimler Company; although the British motor industry is but fifty years old, three generations of Kings have honoured the Company with their patronage.

The new car delivered in the April was an enclosed limousine (Hooper 8840) and this was followed two months later by an enclosed landaulette (8857) and then in July a 'Shooting Omnibus' (8869) was made. All three were 4½-litre Straight-Eights with chassis numbered respectively, 44209, 43584 and 44235 and

Special Light Straight-Eight much used by Royalty – 1937. Painted grey with turquoise upholstery

Another impressive and elegant 4½-litre Straight-Eight

before the end of the year another enclosed limousine – chassis 44254 with Hooper limousine coachwork (8925) was made for Queen Mary.

Reverting to the smallest model in the Daimler range – the 'Fifteen' – this was further revised for 1937. The most important innovation was independent front suspension and the system selected was an adaptation of the design patented by Andre Girling employing large coil springs. From August the year previous, the engine had been enlarged to 2,166 cc (66 × 105·4 mm) and now the track and wheelbase dimensions were modified to 4 feet 4 inches and 9 feet 6 inches. The overall gear ratios remained unchanged and notwithstanding the increase in weight of the new model the maximum speed of around 70 mph was sustained. At about this time the post-war 'DB 18' characteristics became clearly discernible. In 1938 the power unit was further enlarged to 2,522 cc (69·6 × 110·49 mm) and this gave 64 bhp. The various chassis in the series were designated in 1937, first DB/17–1 and then DB/17–2 followed in 1938 by DB/18, which, strangely enough, remained the symbol for the 2½-litre cars produced until 1953 notwithstanding the many further improvements and alterations yet to be announced.

Of this car *The Motor* said (20th September 1938):

Thus the engine is certainly one of the smoothest which we have experienced and is also remarkable for its quietness not only at low speeds but also when cruising at between 60 and 70 mph. . . . Moreover, and in our judgment, just as important, is an unusual degree of high speed stability. This is doubtless aided by the general build of the car which gives a low centre of gravity.

We regard this car in fact, as being one of the best examples of what independent suspension can be if it is applied in a really intelligent way to suit British conditions.

Such a basically sound chassis, possessing so many fine attributes was quickly seen to be worthy of further experiment and development. Several variants of the 2½ litre appeared.

This special bodied Sports saloon on the 4-litre Straight-Eight chassis was built in November 1938 by Gurney Nutting for Mr Ashley MacLean

The Daimler 'Ritz' was built on the standard chassis but capable of about 78 mph maximum speed. The model possessed numerous special features. To ensure the 'exclusiveness of The Daimler Ritz sports saloon' output was strictly limited. The vehicle was meticulously hand constructed and the whole appearance of the car was most commendable and attractive. The bodywork was finished in silver grey with raised chromium moulding, alternatively in black or irridescent blue. The upholstery was of light-grey leather with contrasting piping and the interior woodwork was of beautifully figured grey sycamore finish, toned to match the upholstery – the cappings and mouldings being specially hand

4-litre Straight-Eight with Vanden Plas Pillarless Saloon body. Price £1,330.
This was a strikingly handsome car and viewed from any angle it had aesthetic appeal. Best quality materials were used throughout

Martin Walter 'Wingham' cabriolet on the 4-litre chassis (£1,215)

4½-litre Straight-Eight with Windover Sedanca de Ville body (£1,675)

4-litre Straight-Eight Freestone & Webb 'Round' type saloon (£1,325)

4-litre Straight-Eight Freestone & Webb touring saloon (£1,345)

2½-litre coupé 1938

Pre-war 2½-litre DB 18 with Tickford cabriolet coachwork

One of only four such cars made during 1938–9 – 2,522 cc DB 18 chassis, with drophead coupé bodywork by E. D. Abbott, Ltd, Farnham, £565 ex works

Daimler 'Ritz' – awarded 2nd prize for coachwork in the 1939 RAC Brighton Rally

Bob Crouch and George Fabel in the 1939 'Dolphin'

"The Motor" Data Panel (2½-litre Daimler Dolphin)

Price, £700; 19 m.p.g.; tax, £13 10s.; weight (unladen), 28½ cwt.; turning circle, 38 ft. (2½ turns of steering wheel).

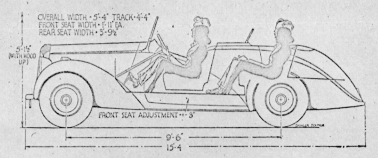

OVERALL WIDTH · 5'-4" TRACK · 4'-4"
FRONT SEAT WIDTH · 1'-11" EA.
REAR SEAT WIDTH · 3'-9½"
5'-1½" (WITH HOOD UP)
FRONT SEAT ADJUSTMENT · 1 - 3"
9'-6"
15'-4"

ENGINE

No. of cyls.	..	6
Bore and stroke	..	69.6 x 110.4 mm.
Capacity	..	2,522 c.c.
Valves	..	O.h.v., push-rod operated
Rating	..	18.02 h.p.
B.H.P.	..	90 at 4,200 r.p.m.

CHASSIS

Frame	..	Underslung cruciform
Springs	..	Ind. coil spring, front; half-elliptic, rear
Brakes	..	Girling mechanical
Tyres	..	Dunlop Std., 6.00 x 16 ins.
Tank	..	13 galls.
Glass	..	Triplex

PERFORMANCE

m.p.h	O.D. secs.	Top secs.
10-30	12.9	8.0
20-40	13.1	9.0
30-50	15.0	9.5
40-60	15.4	11.2
Max.	82	83

0-30 m.p.h.	..	.. 5.3 secs.
0-50 m.p.h.	..	.. 11.8 secs.
0-60 m.p.h.	..	.. 17.0 secs.
0-70 m.p.h.	..	.. 25.7 secs.
Standing ¼-mile	..	.. 21.1 secs.

GEARS   HILLS

O.D. Top	3.54	Max. grdnt. 1 in 12.9
Top	.. 4.87	Max. grdnt. 1 in 8.0
2nd	.. 8.0	Max. grdnt. 1 in 4.8
1st	.. 14.6	Max. grdnt. 1 in 2.6

Engine speed, 2,210 r.p.m. at 50 m.p.h., O.D.; 3,030 r.p.m. at 50 m.p.h., Top. PULL, Tapley Q figure, 280 on First and Top.

BRAKES

30 m.p.h. to stop		lb. on pedal
120 ft.	..	41
60 ft.	..	65
Best 33.5 ft. (89%)	..	120

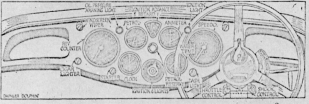

OIL PRESSURE WARNING LIGHT · IGNITION ADVANCE & RETARD · IGNITION LIGHT · WINDSCREEN WIPER · PETROL · AMMETER · SPEEDO · REV COUNTER · WATER TEMP · CIGAR LIGHTER · STARTER · CLOCK · PETROL · DASH LIGHT · IGNITION & LIGHTS · THROTTLE CONTROL · SHOCK CONTROL · DAIMLER DOLPHIN

SEATING.—Black figure portrays woman 5 ft. 5 ins. high, 26 ins. from hips. White figure shows 6-ft. man, 30 ins. from hips. Scale of drawing ¹⁄₂₀ actual size.

HILL-CLIMBING.—Maximum gradients for each gear are shown. Where 1 in 6.5' is recorded the car will climb Edge, South Harting, Kirkstone, and Rest and Be Thankful Hills.

BRAKES.—Scale gives distance in feet from 30 m.p.h. as determined by a Ferodo-Tapley meter. Pressures needed to stop in shortest distance, in 60 ft. (normal short stop) and in 120 ft. or "slow up" are also shown. Average figures are 50 lb. for 60 ft., and about double for shortest; 100 lb. is the maximum pressure for average woman. If the 60-ft. and shortest-stop pressures are close together (e.g., 60 ft., 50 lb.—shortest, 72 lb.), the brake tends to fierceness.

May 16, 1939.

finished. A 'Philco' car radio was included as standard equipment and the fascia and glove box were illuminated. The rear seats were specially sprung and smokers were well catered for by the provision in the rear centre arm rest of a divided box for cigars and cigarettes, with a lighter which was incorporated in the fascia. In the rear side armrests were concealed Thermos flasks. Picnic tables and footrests were included and the sales brochure made reference to the fact that provision was made for the installation of an air conditioning unit – 'In winter this unit heats the car and demists the windscreen, even when the windows are tightly closed. In summer it keeps the air within the car cool and fresh.' Consistent with the high class finish of the coachwork, the engine was smart in appearance. Many parts – the rocker box cover in particular – were chromium plated and an inspection lamp was fitted to the bulkhead where a comprehensive tool kit was also to be found. The 'Ritz' sold for £575 complete as against £485 for the standard saloon.

In the Monte Carlo rally 1939 a sports saloon not only earned an award for its coachwork but the car also performed exceptionally well. On its return to the works, the closed body was removed and in April it reappeared with a most attractive foursome open body. The car, registration number DVC 681 was successfully driven in the English, Scottish and Welsh rallies by Bob Crouch (today Sales Manager – Daimler Transport Vehicles Ltd) and George Fabel (today Chief Development Engineer within the same division).

Better than average performance was achieved for the new car – christened the 'Dolphin', by inclining at an angle the overhead valves and positioning the sparking plugs to fire in the region of greatest volume across into a steadily diminishing space in the combustion chamber. The valves themselves were made of an austenitic steel and seated on screwed-in inserts of Monel metal – two thirds nickel and one third copper alloy and by research were shown to be resistant to burning and corrosion. An increase from 5·5 to 1 to 7 to 1 in the compression ratio was achieved and the resultant power output was improved by over 36 per cent – from 64 bhp to approximately 90 bhp. Separate inlet and exhaust ports to each cylinder were provided and separate exhaust down pipes were used for the front three and rear three cylinders. A departure from normal, exclusive at the time to the 'Dolphin' was the rearrangement of the gear ratios to provide an overdrive on top and this proved so satisfactory that the car formed the basis for the post-war Special Sports series. With twin carburetters acceleration was quite impressive and the top speed of the car was up to around 83 mph. The whole of the road test report contained in *The Motor* for 16th May 1939 is worthy of reproduction verbatim, but restricted by space, a concluding paragraph must suffice:

At a time when motorists may be seeking the attributes of a thoroughbred high-performance car and, at the same time, wishing to combine these with medium-rated horse-power, the Daimler Co have produced a car which ranks as one of the best available in any country today.

For those who imagine that all Daimlers are 'hearse-like' with corresponding performances, take note!

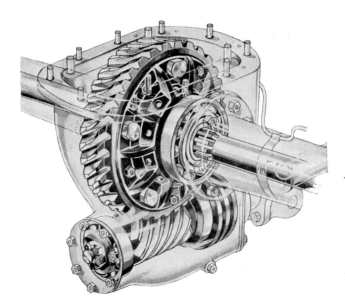

The Daimler rear axle worm drive is acknowledged to be the finest type for maximum transmission efficiency combined with smoothness and silence. The special teeth design gives low working stresses which permits thorough and constant lubrication. It also makes possible a low flush floor without wells or tunnels

Illustrations from 1938 EL 24 Sales brochure showing worm drive axle and diagram of fluid flywheel

FIGURE 1

Frame is of the rigidly built cross braced box girder type. With engine floating on rubber mountings and with a rubber cushioned rear axle all road noises are isolated. Radiator, wings and lamps are mounted in a special independent assembly so that front end movement, even on the worst of roads, is practically eliminated.

DIMENSIONS
Overall length (luggage grid folded)   16′ 0″
  (Limousine)
Overall length (luggage grid open)   16′ 11″
  (Limousine)
Overall length (Saloon)   16′ 3″
Overall width   5′ 9″
Wheel base   10′ 4″
Wheel track   4′ 9″

CHASSIS PRICE
£595

CHASSIS OF THE DAIMLER TWENTY FOUR

117

EL 24 hp chassis with Charlesworth de Luxe limousine body. Model No. 854A. List Price £870

Daimler EL 24 hp Saloon by Charlesworth. Model No. 858. List Price £795

EL 24 chassis with seven-seater enclosed limousine, by Daimler. Model No. 851. List Price £795

The ES 24 of 1939 – the first Daimler to have a slightly raked and curved radiator

Early in 1938, the Company was consulted by the Army authorities concerning the design and possible production of a high speed versatile vehicle for most exacting war service. Clearly the contemplated vehicle would have to be capable of traversing rough terrain, negotiating bomb and shell craters, ditches, hedges and almost every other conceivable natural obstacle as well as being capable of travelling at high speed over semi-normal highways.

Daimler engineers deserve full credit for the resultant 'Scout' which satisfied all demands and surpassed expectations. This incredible vehicle had independent suspension all round, Daimler fluid transmission (specially modified to reduce slip by about 50 per cent) a five speed epicyclic gearbox and a 2½-litre engine of 2,522 cc – in fact the standard DB 18 unit incorporating some of the modifications sampled on the 'Dolphin'. The ignition system was screened to eliminate interference with radio transmission and reception and because of the sort of terrain over which the 'Scout' had to travel, a dry sump type lubrication system was employed.

A 'Twenty-four' specially built for the Maharajah of Nawanagar, adopted son of Ranjitsinhji, the great cricketer was delivered in the closing month of 1938. The car had lavish equipment and externally there were fitted a sun shield and chromium plated 'slats' along the bonnet sides – similar to those first used (but not exclusively) on the Light Straight-Eights.

Continued almost without change for 1938 were the EL 24, Light Straight-

119

Eight, and 4½-litre Straight-Eight but in August the programme for the year following was announced. This included an improved Light Straight-Eight with a larger engine (77·47 × 105 mm – 3,960 cc – the E 4-litre) first seen at the 1937 London show and some exceptionally fine bodies were constructed on this new chassis. The track and wheelbase dimensions remained unaltered, but the new power unit offered 95 bhp and a top speed of just below 90 mph, and much improved acceleration. The body styles included saloons, sports saloons, cabriolets and coupés and prices varied according to design and coachbuilder from £1,070 to £1,345. On some few late 3½-litre cars and all the 4-litre examples, vertical chromium plated radiator grilles replaced the honeycomb and provided a mark of distinction.

All the pre-war Straight-Eights were run in and bench tested before being installed in the chassis. Each of them had that 'undefinable something' which placed the car in a category all of its own. The characteristic is epitomised in the following extracted from a contemporary Daimler brochure:

Daimler ideals demand the production of a car with an outstanding performance achieved at all times and under all conditions with complete silence and unobtrusiveness. In short, car control that is by every standard the easiest and most pleasurable.

These standards can only be maintained by unsparing attention to detail in design and craftsmanship and a continued striving to give Daimler owners a car of unquestioned supremacy in the motoring world.

Road safety receives one of the greatest encouragements from the spread of Daimler ownership. Unfailing dependability and pleasantness of operation are qualities which are taken for granted in a marque of Daimler's eminence. But it is the almost indefinable manner of its performance that is the special quality which distinguishes the Daimler from all other cars. It is a car which will be the deserving object of great admiration.

By putting a 24 hp 6-cylinder engine into a v-type Straight-Eight chassis extra length was obtained either for limousine or luxurious saloon coachwork. Quite a few of such vehicles were produced during 1938 and early 1939 and to distinguish the type they were known as 'ELS 24'. Windovers built a good many of the bodies. A new standard design of body was evolved by Daimlers and was

Within the Royal Mews early in the reign of HM King George VI

A procession of Daimler cars conveying the Lord Mayor of London and his retinue when they visited Buckingham Palace in March 1937

The new limousine delivered to the Royal Mews, February 1939

mounted on the long chassis to become the ES 24 type. The car was beautifully fitted out and was the first of the marque to possess a rounded and slightly sloping radiator grille.

HM King George VI ordered another Straight-Eight – (chassis 43615) and this was received in February 1939. It was the first State car (Hooper landaulette 9045) to have a glass roof over the rear compartment and then in July, the King took delivery of another of the rare Lanchester Straight-Eights, this one having a Hooper landaulette body (9114). King George V detested ostentation. To him nickel or chromium plating was taboo and it will be seen from the photographs of most of the State Daimlers that the famous flutes of the radiator were enamelled black and even after his death, the convention was followed almost up to the war. For private use King George VI had a DB 18 coupé (chassis 46123) painted black with the registration number FGJ 865 and a 24 hp limousine (chassis 47997) also painted black with the registration number FLN I was kept for use by members of the Royal Household.

The Daimler Company acquired several other interests shortly before the war, including the famous coachbuilding concerns of Barker & Co (Coachbuilders) Ltd, and Hooper & Co (Coachbuilders) Ltd. Thereafter Hoopers made under the name of Barker about nine bodies on various chassis and after the war the name of Barker was used for prestige purposes by the Daimler Company on their own 'coachbuilt' bodies constructed at Coventry. Hoopers carried on more or less as before, but like so many other firms they were obliged to concentrate on other 'things' – mainly aircraft components, until 1946 when they resumed building motor bodies mainly on Daimler, Rolls-Royce and Bentley chassis

To commemorate his fortieth year as secretary of the Royal Scottish Automobile Club and in recognition of his services to the automobile movement, Mr Robert J. Smith was presented in December 1939 with a new 24 hp Daimler. Scottish motorists subscribed to the gift and the car had the registration number 'G I' – the first issued in Glasgow and which Mr Smith had always held.

A further 32 hp Straight-Eight Lanchester (43616) with Hooper limousine body no. 9164 was delivered to the King in May 1940 and then in 1941 His Majesty reluctantly inclined to the view that it would be prudent, having regard to the hostilities, for him to have additional protection whilst travelling and accordingly two further Straight-Eight Daimler limousines (chassis 48314 and 48327 with Hooper bodies 9103 and 9105) were supplied with bullet proof glass and concealed armoured plating.

Extensive work was carried out at the Daimler Works during 1937 and 1938 to enable production to be speeded up. New plant and equipment were installed and the body-building section was completely reorganized. It was anticipated that production would be almost doubled but before much benefit could be gained the war intervened. How the Company suffered!

The diverse activities and sufferings of the Daimler Company throughout the period 1939–45 are a stimulating history in themselves.

Daimler Hire cars 5am Coronation Day, 1937

Daimler cars in the Coronation procession — 1937

King George VI visits Aldershot – April 1938

A 4½-litre Straight-Eight under military control during the war

The Daimler Armoured Car

New 'Shadow Factories' were erected and in the shortest possible time the Company was engaged in the production of aircraft engines and components, gun turrets, rocket projectors, Bren and Browning gun parts, shell fuses, spare parts running into millions and in addition repairs and overhauls on a large scale were undertaken. Of special importance were the 'Scout' cars already referred to of which 6,665 were produced, and armoured cars of which 2,764 were constructed.

For the latter, an entirely new 6-cylinder unit having bore and stroke measurements of $85 \cdot 09 \times 120 \cdot 015$ mm $-4,095$ cc was developed and by working frequently from dawn to midnight, seven days a week, the Company produced a successful working vehicle within six months from the time the 'go-ahead' was given by the Government. The engine with twin Solex carburetters of the non-spillable type, produced 100 bhp and to cope with a total weight of about seven tons, an emergency low ratio of 80 to 1 was incorporated in the epicyclic gearbox. The Armoured car was equipped with wading equipment and disc brakes! The Armoured car and the Scout were both held in the highest esteem in military and civilian circles and both gave outstanding service in all theatres of the war. The 'Scout' was succeeded by the post-war 'Ferret' which is still being built by the Company for the Army.

That Coventry was very severely bombed is common knowledge but it may not be known that the Daimler factories were made special targets for the German

A 'convertible' coach of the early 'thirties

In 1965 London Transport bought eight Park Royal bodied Daimler Fleetline double-deckers for assessment under all operating conditions. Several hundreds of similar buses were subsequently ordered

onslaught. Approximately 70 per cent of the Radford factory area was demolished by no less than 170 HE bombs and mines, but notwithstanding the ordeal, war production actually increased.

Following the Coventry raids of 1940 and 1941, bus production was transferred to Wolverhampton and during the war 1,083 bus chassis were made under not ideal conditions! From 1936 the Company had been making trolley-buses and output was expanded during the 'fifties to meet demand both at home and abroad. In 1949 a larger Daimler diesel engined bus (type CD 650 – 10·6 litres) was a notable success and it featured hydraulic power-assistance for steering, gearchange and brakes. The same power unit was utilized for the 'Freeline' under-floor engine single-deck bus which appeared in 1951 although optionally a Gardner diesel engine could be had. After a long period of production, it was superseded in 1964 by the even more advanced 'Roadliner'. Reference is later made to the advances made with the Daimler transmission as adapted for public service vehicles from 1957. The rear engined double-deck 'Fleetline', introduced in 1960 is one of the most modern and comfortable double-decker buses in the world, and its popularity is borne out by its high rate of sales. Today, Daimler Transport Vehicles Ltd leads the way in public service vehicle design, meeting the stringent demands of operators in all parts of the world.

Towards the end of the war, the Company received an order for the supply of Daimler cars (mainly of the Straight-Eight and Twenty-four types) for use by high ranking military and civilian officials. In December 1945 a new 24 hp limousine was delivered to Dr Benes, President of Czechoslovakia. About that time, ill-founded rumours were heard, that the Daimler Company would not again produce private cars but this was officially denied, opportunity being taken to make it known that at the earliest possible date, production of cars would be resumed. Part II of this work describes in detail the cars which in fact appeared in furtherance of 'The Daimler Tradition'.

H

PART II

The Living Tradition

Contents

Strenuous efforts have been made to ensure, so far as may be practicable, that the chassis numbers quoted at the beginning of each section refer to vehicles actually produced. Nevertheless, Jaguar Cars Ltd, did not inherit from Daimler complete and reliable records and although they have to the best of their ability verified the author's data, regrettably no assertion as to accuracy can be made in every instance.

CHAPTER I

The DB 18's and Consort

2½-litre saloons and foursome coupés chassis numbers 50013–50031; 50040–51039; 51800–52799; 53000–53749; 54500–54949; 56000–56135
Consort chassis numbers 55000–55999; 56200–56699; 57010–59009; 59240–59989
Special Sports series chassis numbers 53750–53999; 56136–56188; 56700–56774; 59010–59239

IN September 1945, the Company officially announced that in order to have a car available at the earliest moment, it had been decided to continue with the very successful Daimler 15 with 'its now famous 2½-litre engine.' The basic price for the post-war saloon version was £1,020 basic – £1,340.1.8 including purchase tax (July 1946). For a detailed description of the car:

The chassis, in many respects unchanged from the pre-war model, was straightforward and robust in design with U-section side members and cruciform cross bracing. Front independent suspension incorporated heavy duty coil springs, while semi-elliptics were retained for the rear. Luvax shock absorbers of the piston type were employed at both front and rear and to ensure a smooth ride and stability, an anti-roll bar was used at the front.

Completely mechanical Girling braking was fitted with 11-inch drums to all wheels. The compensating mechanism had self-lubricating bushes and maintenance in this respect was thereby obviated.

Many of the improvements first introduced pre-war on the 'Dolphin' and further proved in the most practical way, on the military 'Scout', were incorporated in the 1945 power unit. The re-designed cylinder head (in cast iron) was employed in which the push-rod operated valves were set at an angle of approximately fifteen degrees. The combustion chambers and ports were re-shaped and the resulting improvement in gas-flow and turbulence enabled the compression ratio to be raised to 7 to 1 and from 64 bhp on the pre-war standard unit, the output was raised to 70 bhp at 4,200 rpm. As is usually the case, the more efficient the motor, the better the fuel consumption. In this instance the later car returned 22 mpg as against 18 mpg for the pre-war equivalent.

Another feature having a direct bearing both on power and petrol consumption was the redesigned induction system. An integral cast water manifold jacket was provided and this was connected to the main cooling system by a by-pass from the thermostat. When starting from cold, the thermostat remained closed and the warmed water from the adjacent cylinder head facilitated carburation and quick warm-up. A single 1½-inch SU horizontal carburetter was fitted, the supply being fed by an AC mechanical pump from the 14 gallon fuel tank.

The water pump had also been redesigned and this was driven by belt from the crankshaft pulley which belt also served to drive the dynamo. Incidentally, the pulley angles were revised to eliminate the possibility of squeak from the belt.

Special attention was also paid to the cooling of the valves, the water jacketing being so arranged that water passing from the block to the cylinder head was deflected through jets into close proximity of the exhaust-valve seats, which were inserts of hard iron alloy.

Engine lubrication was provided by gear pump from the sump holding 11 pints. An external filter was fitted through which all oil passed at 40 psi and on the outside of the filter a pressure relief valve was to be found. On the fascia a pressure warning light was fitted but in the Daimler custom no calibrated gauge.

Ignition was by battery and coil with automatic advance and retard mechanism and there was an over-riding manual control that could be used to compensate for varying grades of fuel. The lessons learned from the 'Scout' influenced the designers in their decision to omit the annular ring on the rotating members in the flywheel thus permitting greater torque – particularly at low revs and consequently improving acceleration. The pre-selector box (with top gear ratio of 4·375 to 1 overall) remained virtually unchanged and an open propeller shaft with Hardy Spicer needle bearing joints at both ends transmitted power to the three-quarter floating underslung worm drive axle.

To all but six points, chassis lubrication was automatic. The fixing of the radiator and front wings was so designed as to facilitate comparatively easy removal. As standard equipment, a built-in DWS jacking system was included.

Adjustable steering of the Marles worm and double roller type was fitted with an 18-inch steering wheel. The turning circle was 41 feet.

Mulliners of Birmingham produced the standard Six-Light saloon body which incidentally was the last Daimler production car to possess a sunshine roof. By employing steel body members and laminated timber it was possible to reduce the thickness of the actual body sides and thereby obtain a quite substantial increase in accommodation. Thinner pillars were also possible without weakening the structure and this of course improved the all round visibility. Additional legroom was afforded to the rear passengers by recessing the backs of the front seats. Running boards were totally eliminated (although retained for the larger and more luxurious 27 and 36 hp models). At the front, the body was secured to a stout bulkhead of laminated wood faced with aluminium which in turn was secured to the chassis by really massive brackets – thus achieving a completely rigid scuttle.

The interior was upholstered in leather and polished wood was used for the door fillets and the fascia.

The 1947 2½-litre Drop-head Coupé by Tickford

The following extracts are taken from *The Autocar*, 9th April 1947:

... the Daimler 2½-litre displays an unusual blend of qualities. On the one hand, it offers the comfort and refinement which is expected of a car carrying the fluted Daimler radiator. On the other hand, however, it provides the lively performance and responsive controls which are more often associated with the best products of continental factories. It is a car which should appeal strongly to motoring enthusiasts of matured tastes.

For passengers, the 2½-litre Daimler must be judged as a delightful car in which to ride. Progress is smooth and peaceful, the scenery is in full view and the car reaches its destination in quick time without feeling to hurry. It would somehow seem a waste to buy this model and hand it over to a chauffeur, however, for it is difficult to name any car which is more pleasant to drive.

The springing is soft and the car can readily be rocked by hand when stationary. Our test included city streets and country lanes which had suffered severely from frost and floods, and the car always rode comfortably, although perhaps with not quite the exaggerated softness which is favoured on transatlantic models. An unplanned test for the suspension system was provided when a large lorry dropped its spare wheel flat in the roadway – the result being quite a mild bump as the car rode over an obstacle which was actually too high for mudguard damage to be avoided. In open country, high speed actually seems to improve the riding comfort, and road irregularities of horrifying aspect can be completely ignored.

In sum, we feel that, by present-day standards, the car represents very excellent value at the price of £1,304. Offering attractions to any motorist who can afford a medium-sized quality car, its strongest appeal is undoubtedly to the driver who can appreciate genuine mechanical excellence.

Some standard post-war DB 18 saloons carried a coachbuilder's name plate, but from this it should not be deduced that the entire body was constructed by the specialist. At most, the painting, trimming and general finishing was the responsibility of the coachbuilder in question.

An attractive and practical version of the model was offered in foursome two-door drop-head coupé form. The standard chassis and power unit (70 bhp) was employed.

The Barker bodied DB 18 foursome drop head coupé (1946–50)

2½-litre (DB 18) saloon supplied to Mr Douglas Fairbanks, January 1950

134

The more common of the two variants produced was the Barker bodied version but for a while an alternative body, very similar in appearance, was offered by Tickford of Newport Pagnell, the latter car costing an additional £85 in the basic price. The Barker cost (in 1946) a total of £1,425.9.5 (chassis £815; body £300 and purchase tax £310.9.5).

Hoods on both cars were spring assisted and folded into a recess behind the rear seat and with hinged cant rails folding across the body an intermediate 'De ville' position was possible.

The standard saloon and foursome drop-head models were for a short while made contemporaneously with the Special Sports and Consort models mentioned next. The standard saloons and coupés were discontinued in 1950.

With the successful re-introduction of the saloon after the war it was natural that the Company should wish to offer as soon as possible an alternative and somewhat more specialized version of the DB 18.

The $2\frac{1}{2}$-litre Special Sports introduced in the autumn of 1948 enhanced the Daimler tradition in a most appealing manner. Twenty and more years later, good examples of the model were much sought after and commanded a relatively high price. The new car was warmly received by the motoring public and press alike. The 'Special Sports' fell into that rare and exclusive category of car in which luxury is blended with performance. Designed for effortless high speed cruising, rather than for sheer maximum speed, the car owed much to its predecessor, the 'Dolphin'. In external appearance and mechanical layout the two power units differed but little. Hard wearing cylinder liners were fitted with a four bearing crankshaft. In noting that the power output for the 'Special Sports' was 85 bhp as against a claimed 90 bhp for the pre-war 'Dolphin' it should be mentioned that the latter was designed primarily for and initially used in rallying, whereas the former was from the outset conceived as a production model. In describing the car submitted for road test, *The Motor* report reads in the following terms:

. . . proudly carrying a fluted Daimler radiator devoid of name or mock-heraldry, the Barker drop-head body is outstandingly handsome, exploiting to the full the opportunity provided by a chassis of unusually graceful proportions. Inconspicuously as it may travel, the car nevertheless attracts unceasing favourable comment which mechanical silence renders almost embarrassingly audible to driver and passengers. If the quality of finish occasionally falls just short of the best standards of traditional craftsmanship, interior and exterior detail work is nevertheless far above the standard of today.

The fluted radiator on the standard DB 18 saloon retained its vertical appearance of the 'thirties, but for the 'Special Sports' subtle but distinct alterations were made without in any way detracting from the worthy emblem of Daimler. As is apparent from the photograph the famous edifice was now given a slightly rounded and sloping profile with chromium plated vertical grilles to convey an indication of sportiness and blending well with the delightful frontal design of the car. Even this was not entirely new for the ES 24 car driven by C. M. Simpson

The Motor Road Test No. 4/47

Make: Daimler   **Type:** 2½-litre Saloon

Makers: The Daimler Co. Ltd., Coventry

Dimensions and Seating

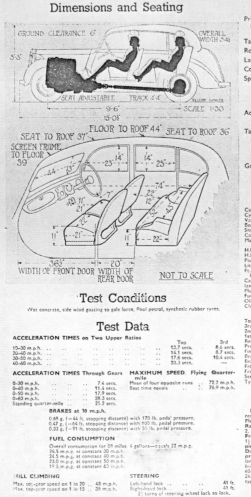

GROUND CLEARANCE 6"
OVERALL WIDTH 5'4"
5'3"
SEAT ADJUSTABLE   TRACK 4'4"
9'6"
15'0½"
SEAT TO ROOF 37"   FLOOR TO ROOF 44"   SEAT TO ROOF 36"
SCREEN FRAME TO FLOOR 39"
SCALE 1:30
36½" WIDTH OF FRONT DOOR   20" WIDTH OF REAR DOOR   NOT TO SCALE

In Brief

Price £1,020
plus Purchase Tax £284 1s. 8d. =
£1,304 1s. 8d.

Tax	..	£26
Road weight unladen..		31 cwt.
Laden weight as tested	..	34 cwt.
Consumption	.. ..	22 m.p.g.
Speed	.. ..	72.2 m.p.h.

(mean both ways)
57 m.p.h. 3rd
38 m.p.h. 2nd

Acceleration .. 10-30 on top, 13.7 secs.
0-50 through gears, 17.9 secs.

Tapley lb. per ton and
gradients : 175 lb. max. on top=1 in 13
275 lb. max. on 3rd=1 in 8
370 lb. max. on 2nd=1 in 6

Gearing .. 18.3 m.p.h. in top at 1,000
r.p.m. 63 m.p.h. at 2,500 ft.
per min. piston speed

Specification

Cubic capacity	.. ..	2,522 c.c.
Cylinders	.. ..	6
Valve gear	.. ..	Pushrod o.h.v.
Bore	.. ..	69.6 mm.
Stroke	.. ..	110.5 mm.
Compression ratio	..	7.0
Max. power	.. ..	70 b.h.p.
at		4,200 r.p.m.
H.P. per sq. in. piston area ..		1.98
H.P. per ton, unladen		45.0
Piston area per ton, unladen		23.0
Litres per laden ton-mile	..	2,440
Ft./min. piston speed at max.		
h.p.		3,050
Carburetter	.. ..	S.U. horizontal
Ignition	.. ..	Lucas coil
Plugs : make and type	..	Lodge CB14
Fuel pump	.. ..	A.C. mechanical
Oil filter	.. ..	Tecalemit, full-flow
Clutch	.. ..	Fluid flywheel,

with preselective gearbox

Top gear	.. ..	4.375
3rd gear	.. ..	6.84
2nd gear	.. ..	10.17
1st gear	.. ..	17.85
Reverse	.. ..	23.6
Propeller shaft	.. ..	Hardy Spicer
Final drive	.. ..	Underslung worm
Brakes	.. ..	Girling mechanical
Brake drum diameter		11 ins.
Friction lining area	..	127 sq. ins.
Friction area per ton, unladen		82 sq. ins.
Steering gear	.. ..	Marles
Tyre size	.. ..	6.00 × 16

Maintenance

Fuel tank : 14 gallons (including 1½ gallons reserve). **Sump :** 11 pints. **Gearbox :** 5 pints. **Fluid flywheel :** 8½ pints. **Rear axle :** 6 pints. **Radiator :** 3½ gallons. **Firing order :** 1, 5, 3, 6, 2, 4. **Chassis lubrication :** Luvax automatic. **Front wheel toe-in :** ⅛ in. to ¾₆ in. **Castor angle :** 1½ degrees. **Camber angle :** 1½ degrees. **King-pin angle :** 5 degrees. **Wheel offset :** 1.2 ins. **Damper fluid :** Luvax piston type. **Tyre pressure :** 28 lb. front, 30 lb. rear. **Lights :** Head-lamp bulbs, 12-volt, 36-watt ; side and tail lamp bulbs, 12-volt, 6-watt ; pass. lamp bulb, 12-volt, 60-watt ; stop and reverse lamp bulb, 12-volt, 24-watt. **Battery :** Lucas 12-volt 69-amp./hr., type SLTW13A.

Ref. No. D/26/47

Test Conditions

Wet concrete, side wind gusting to gale force, Pool petrol, synthetic rubber tyres.

Test Data

ACCELERATION TIMES on Two Upper Ratios

		Top	3rd
10-30 m.p.h.	.. .. ..	13.7 secs.	8.6 secs.
20-40 m.p.h.	.. .. ..	14.1 secs.	8.7 secs.
30-50 m.p.h.	.. .. ..	17.6 secs.	10.4 secs.
40-60 m.p.h.	.. ..	23.3 secs.	—

ACCELERATION TIMES Through Gears

0-30 m.p.h.	.. .. ..	7.4 secs.
0-40 m.p.h.	.. ..	11.4 secs.
0-50 m.p.h.	.. ..	17.9 secs.
0-60 m.p.h.	.. ..	28.3 secs.
Standing quarter-mile	.. ..	25.2 secs.

MAXIMUM SPEED Flying Quarter-mile

Mean of four opposite runs .. 72.2 m.p.h.
Best time equals .. 76.9 m.p.h.

BRAKES at 10 m.p.h.

0.68 g. (=44 ft. stopping distance) with 170 lb. pedal pressure.
0.47 g. (=64 ft. stopping distance) with 100 lb. pedal pressure.
0.33 g. (=91 ft. stopping distance) with 50 lb. pedal pressure.

FUEL CONSUMPTION

Overall consumption for 88 miles 4 gallons—equals 22 m.p.g.
26.5 m.p.g. at constant 30 m.p.h.
24.5 m.p.g. at constant 40 m.p.h.
23.0 m.p.g. at constant 50 m.p.h.
19.5 m.p.g. at constant 60 m.p.h.

HILL CLIMBING

Max. top-gear speed on 1 in 20 .. 48 m.p.h.
Max. top-gear speed on 1 in 15 .. 38 m.p.h.

STEERING

Left-hand lock	.. ..	41 ft.
Right-hand lock	.. ..	41 ft.

2½ turns of steering wheel lock to lock.

for the Company in the 1939 RAC Rally was the first Daimler to possess this innovation.

In the construction of the body for the 'Special Sports' care was taken to avoid excessive weight, although normal coachbuilding methods and principles were observed. A light but strong seasoned ash frame was used with aluminium panelling except for the front wings which were of steel to provide rigidity and strength.

Special attention was given to the ease of operation of the head by the provision of spring assistance. External landau irons were omitted and although the head when lowered did not completely disappear, it laid less prominently than was the case with many folding hoods of a similar type. The covering was of mohair and in keeping with the general quality of the car, the interior of the hood was suitably lined.

Occasional seating for three was possible on the bench-type front seat and in the rear a single seat was transversely positioned and could be removed to accommodate large suitcases or other luggage – it could also be positioned to face either left or right. This seating arrangement was not, however, new. In 1926 (and more than likely the practice appeared earlier), a third seat positioned sideways but mounted on a revolving support, was included in a Daimler 'three-quarter coupé cabriolet', available on several different chassis. In that instance, however, two more passengers could be carried in the 'dickey'. In the 'Special Sports' the front seat squabs separately tilted forward to facilitate entry to and egress from the rear. All the seats were made of high grade leather. Polished walnut was used for the fascia board, the same natural material being used for the surmounting roll into which was set a pair of ashtrays.

Instruments were centrally grouped with a lockable glove box on the near side and an open cubby hole on the driver's side. The instrumentation was dominated by a large speedometer to the right of the group and a rev counter to the left with smaller dials between the two. These comprised a water thermometer, ammeter, petrol gauge and clock. In addition 'pulls' were provided for mixture, hand throttle and petrol reserve. Ignition and oil pressure lights were included together with a cigar lighter. Provision was made for the fitting of a radio and a heater/demister unit was incorporated.

Incorporating Daimler transmission with, like the pre-war 'Dolphin', an overdrive epicyclic gearbox, the 'Special Sports' was not outstanding for acceleration but was eminently suited for and well capable of sustaining high cruising speeds over long distances.

Appleyard of Leeds Ltd, announced in June 1952 that they could undertake the conversion of the Special Sports drophead coupé into an attractive fixed-head version. The standard body was not altered in any way, all that was necessary being the removal of the complete fabric and roof framework, and the fitting of a new ash framework panelled in aluminium. This was welded to the existing body at the back, and lap-jointed at the base of the steel windscreen pillars in the front. The rear window and quarter lights were designed specially for the conversion which was approved by The Daimler Company.

137

Reprinted from "The Motor," June 14, 1950.

The Motor Continental Road Test No. 6C/50

Make: Daimler **Type:** 2½-litre Special Sports Coupe

Makers: The Daimler Co., Ltd., Coventry

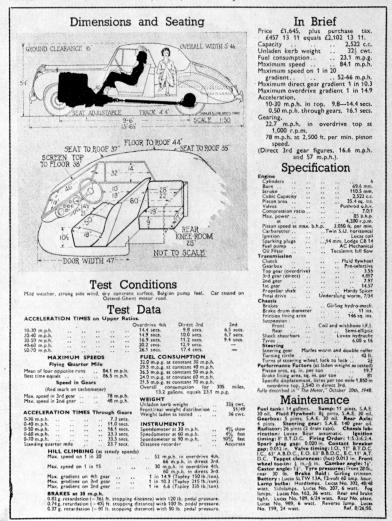

Dimensions and Seating

GROUND CLEARANCE 6"
OVERALL WIDTH 5' 4½"
SEAT ADJUSTABLE TRACK 4' 4"
9'-6"
15'-6½"
SCALE 1:50

SEAT TO ROOF 37" FLOOR TO ROOF 44" SEAT TO ROOF 35"
SCREEN TOP TO FLOOR 38"
32" 14"
10" 28"
19" 22"
60"
19"
9"
10½"
18"
REAR KNEE-ROOM 25"
DOOR WIDTH 47"
NOT TO SCALE

In Brief

Price £1,645, plus purchase tax, £457 13 11 equals £2,102 13 11.
Capacity .. .. .. 2,522 c.c.
Unladen kerb weight .. 32½ cwt.
Fuel consumption.. .. 23.1 m.p.g.
Maximum speed .. .. 84.1 m.p.h.
Maximum speed on 1 in 20 gradient.. .. .. 52-66 m.p.h.
Maximum direct gear gradient 1 in 10.3
Maximum overdrive gradient 1 in 14.9
Acceleration,
10-30 m.p.h. in top. 9.8—14.4 secs.
0-50 m.p.h. through gears. 16.1 secs.
Gearing,
22.7 m.p.h. in overdrive top at 1,000 r.p.m.
78 m.p.h. at 2,500 ft. per min. piston speed.
(Direct 3rd gear figures, 16.6 m.p.h. and 57 m.p.h.).

Specification

Engine
Cylinders 6
Bore .. .. 69.6 mm.
Stroke .. .. 110.5 mm.
Cubic Capacity .. .. 2,522 c.c.
Piston area .. .. 35.4 sq. ins.
Valves .. .. .. Pushrod o.h.v.
Compression ratio 7.0/1
Max. power .. .. .. 85 b.h.p.
at .. .. 4,200 r.p.m.
Piston speed at max. b.h.p. 3,050 ft. per min.
Carburetter .. .. Twin S.U. horizontal
Ignition .. .. .. Lucas coil
Sparking plugs .. 14 mm. Lodge C.B 14
Fuel pump .. .. .. AC Mechanical
Oil Filter .. .. Tecalemit full flow
Transmission
Clutch .. .. .. Fluid flywheel
Gearbox .. .. .. Pre-selective
Top gear (overdrive) 3.55
3rd gear (direct) 4.857
2nd gear 7.97
1st gear 14.57
Propeller shaft .. .. Hardy Spicer
Final drive .. .. Underslung worm, 7/34
Chassis
Brakes .. .. Girling hydro-mech.
Brake drum diameter .. 11 ins.
Friction lining area .. 146 sq. ins.
Suspension:
Front .. .. Coil and wishbone I.F.S.
Rear .. .. .. Semi-elliptic
Shock absorbers .. Luvax hydraulic
Tyres .. .. .. 6.00 x 16
Steering
Steering gear Marles worm and double roller
Turning circle .. .. 42 ft.
Turns of steering wheel, lock to lock .. 2⅜
Performance Factors (at laden weight as tested)
Piston area, sq. in. per ton .. 19.7
Brake lining area, sq. in. per ton .. 81
Specific displacement, litres per ton mile 1,850 in overdrive top, 2,540 in direct 3rd.
Fully described in "The Motor," October 20th, 1948.

Maintenance

Fuel tank: 14 gallons. Sump: 11 pints, S.A.E. 30 oil. Fluid Flywheel: 8½ pints, S.A.E. 30 oil. Gearbox: 5 pints, S.A.E. 30 oil. Rear Axle: 4 pints. Steering gear: S.A.E. 140 gear oil. Radiator: 26 pints (2 drain taps). Chassis lubrication: Luvax Bijur automatic. Ignition timing: 8° B.T.D.C. Firing Order: 1.5.3.6.2.4. Spark plug gap: 0.020 in. Contact breaker gap: 0.012 in. Valve timing: I.O., 11° B.T.D.C., I.C., 63° A.B.D.C., E.O. 63° B.B.D.C., E.C.41° A.T.D.C. Tappet clearances: (hot) 0.013 in. Front wheel toe-in: ⅛ in.-¼ in. Camber angle: 1½°. Castor angle: 1½°. Tyre pressures: Front 28 lb., rear 30 lb. Brake fluid: Girling crimson. Battery: Lucas SLTW 13A, 12-volt 60 amp. hour. Lamp bulbs: Headlamps, Lucas No. 302, 48/48 watt. Sidelamps, Lucas No. 207, 6 watt. Fog lamps, Lucas No. 162, 36 watt. Rear and brake light, Lucas No. 189, 6/24 watt. Rear No. plate, Lucas No. 989, 6 watt. Reverse lamp, Lucas No. 199, 24 watt. Ref. 8/26/50.

Test Conditions

Mild weather, strong side wind, dry concrete surface, Belgian pump fuel. Car tested on Ostend-Ghent motor road.

Test Data

ACCELERATION TIMES on Upper Ratios

	Overdrive 4th	Direct 3rd	2nd
10-30 m.p.h.	14.4 secs.	9.8 secs.	6.5 secs.
20-40 m.p.h.	14.9 secs.	10.0 secs.	6.7 secs.
30-50 m.p.h.	16.9 secs.	11.2 secs.	9.4 secs.
40-60 m.p.h.	20.2 secs.	12.9 secs.	—
50-70 m.p.h.	26.1 secs.	17.4 secs.	—

MAXIMUM SPEEDS
Flying Quarter Mile
Mean of four opposite runs .. 84.1 m.p.h.
Best time equals .. .. 86.5 m.p.h.
Speed in Gears
(Red mark on tachometer)
Max. speed in 3rd gear .. 78 m.p.h.
Max. speed in 2nd gear .. 48 m.p.h.

ACCELERATION TIMES Through Gears
0-30 m.p.h. .. .. .. 7.3 secs.
0-40 m.p.h. .. .. .. 11.0 secs.
0-50 m.p.h. .. .. .. 16.1 secs.
0-60 m.p.h. .. .. .. 23.3 secs.
0-70 m.p.h. .. .. .. 33.5 secs.
Standing quarter mile .. 23.7 secs.

HILL CLIMBING (at steady speeds)
Max. speed on 1 in 20 .. 52 m.p.h. in overdrive 4th, 66 m.p.h. in direct 3rd.
Max. speed on 1 in 15 .. 30 m.p.h. in overdrive 4th, 60 m.p.h in direct 3rd.
Max. gradient on 4th gear .. 1 in 14.9 (Tapley 150 lb./ton).
Max. gradient on 3rd gear .. 1 in 10.3 (Tapley 215 lb./ton).
Max. gradient on 2nd gear .. 1 in 6.6 (Tapley 335 lb./ton).

BRAKES at 30 m.p.h.
0.82 g. retardation (=36¾ ft. stopping distance) with 120 lb. pedal pressure.
0.74 g. retardation (=40¾ ft. stopping distance) with 100 lb. pedal pressure.
0.37 g. retardation (=81 ft. stopping distance) with 50 lb. pedal pressure.

FUEL CONSUMPTION
32.0 m.p.g. at constant 30 m.p.h.
29.5 m.p.g. at constant 40 m.p.h.
26.5 m.p.g. at constant 50 m.p.h.
24.0 m.p.g. at constant 60 m.p.h.
21.5 m.p.g. at constant 70 m.p.h.
Overall consumption for 305 miles, 13.2 gallons, equals 23.1 m.p.g.

WEIGHT
Unladen kerb weight .. 32¼ cwt.
Front/rear weight distribution .. 51/49
Weight laden as tested .. .. 36 cwt.

INSTRUMENTS
Speedometer at 30 m.p.h. .. 4% slow
Speedometer at 60 m.p.h. .. 4% fast
Speedometer at 90 m.p.h. .. 10% fast
Distance recorder .. Accurate

The last 85 bhp chassis (no. 59239) was built in 1953. About 500 Barker 'Special Sports' were produced – most of them after 1950. Some 108 of the chassis type were mounted with Hooper coachwork and of these 97 were of the 'Empress' style.

Without doubt the 'Special Sports' was a classic design and worthy of its fine reputation. 1953 marked the close of another chapter of Daimler history. From 1910 all Daimler cars had Dr Lanchester's worm final drive and although hypoid axles were fitted on the Twenty-Sevens and Straight-Eights from 1946 and the Consort from 1950, worm drive was retained until 1953 for all the 'Special Sports' chassis.

The distinguished 'Consort' was another successful model. It has sometimes been described as a 'revamped' DB 18. This is the truth but not the whole truth.

Announced in September 1949, the 'Consort' was first destined for export and was made for a while concurrently with the standard 2½-litre saloon, the foursome coupés and 'Special Sports'. The all steel body was the responsibility of Mulliners and was mounted with the bowed radiator used on the 'Special Sports' except that for the new saloon the vertical grilles were not normally chromed but painted to match the particular car. The radiator was flanked by headlamps faired distinctively into the detachable wings. The body itself was very similar to the standard DB 18 saloon but had a more pronounced rear end. Further external differences were to be seen in the use of disc wheels and larger

1950–53 DB 18 'Consort'

hub caps, new style rounded bumpers, an unenclosed rear number plate and the omission of a sunshine roof and opening windscreen, but to a limited extent the last mentioned omission was compensated for by the provision of hinged quarter lights on the front doors.

The separate seats were so aligned as to carry three abreast – albeit, in such an event without much room to spare! Armrests were provided and a standard provision was telescopic adjustable steering. Curved glass in thin-framed windows was fitted and by following the curvature of the panel the windows were capable of being lowered into doors of minimum width thereby increasing the effective internal width of the car. Slight alterations were also apparent on the fascia.

The power output remained unchanged at 70 bhp but the pistons were now fitted with three compression rings – (two plain and one tapered – and a slotted scraper). Other fairly minor detail changes were also made to the engine.

Girling hydro-mechanical brakes replaced the wholly mechanical type previously used and wider base wheel rims (5 inch instead of 4 inch) were fitted. As already noted a bevel final drive was employed in place of the revered worm drive. The overall length of the 'Consort' was $1\frac{1}{2}$ inches greater than the $2\frac{1}{2}$-litre saloon and the turning circle was increased to 42 feet.

Autocar's road test report was in the following terms:

For the sterling qualities it exhibits, most of them well known to connoisseurs as inherent in the Daimler character, this latest $2\frac{1}{2}$-litre Consort saloon is quickly liked. . . . Quality without ostentation is strongly suggested by this car and it has all the performance ordinary motorists require, plus the ability to carry a full load up to six people, without apparently making any difference to the handling or performance. . . . Total weight is lower than might be expected with a body generous in all dimensions and acceleration is useful, the car quickly getting up to a cruising gait of between 50 and 60 mph on the open road, and proving lively if the driver wants to handle it briskly. That it is in no sense a dull car is the point that is being stressed; but conversely, through the special properties with which it is endowed by the hydraulic transmission it is specially suitable to quiet, peacable driving and pottering round the by-ways. Its suspension shows up well over poor surfaces. . . .

No car is easier to drive, since starting from rest is only a matter of engaging first or second gear by moving the lever mounted on the steering column to the appropriate position on its visual quadrant, depressing the gear changing pedal, which takes the place of a normal clutch pedal, and then depressing the throttle pedal to move away. Subsequent gear changing is carried out similarly, without risk of making a noise, and top and third gears serve for almost all normal driving. Second gear remains in reserve – as practically an emergency ratio on which, fully laden, the car will climb a hill of 1 in 6 calibre. . . .

On a journey this car swings along very satisfactorily at 60 mph plus, and up to a full 70 mph which is not by any means the maximum, the running is free from suggestion that the engine is being forced. It is found that good times are achieved on a journey without the driver making a special effort to hurry, and that it is a restful car psychologically as well as physically, to the driver and passengers. The handling qualities are good and there is a very strong impression of safety about the behaviour at all times.

Suspension characteristics are firm rather than soft. Shocks from road surface deteriorations are absorbed well though at times there is some vertical movement, strictly limited in its degree. Laterally

SPECIFICATION

DESIRABLY balanced in comfort, appearance, and performance, the "Consort" Saloon is equally at home in city or country, providing effortless motoring under all conditions of speed. Its ability to carry a full complement of 5 or 6 passengers in no way detracts from its exceptional handling and performance qualities. A genuine cruising speed of 70 m.p.h. can be quickly reached, with a very lively performance well above that when required. The distinguished body style incorporates a modern bowed Daimler radiator, wide doors affording easy entry, with pivoting ventilators in the forward door windows and excellent all round driver and passenger visibility. Seating at the front is of the bench-type divided into two, each half of the seat being separately adjustable, with ample leg room for the tallest of passengers. The roomy rear compartment has a deep seat with centre armrest. Upholstery is of soft leather throughout and the interior is furnished with the finest fittings and materials, with polished figured walnut for the instrument panel and woodwork. An interior heater and demister is fitted and provision is made for fitted radio. Luggage accommodation is provided in the spacious boot at the rear.

The chassis is engineered and built with customary Daimler skill and care, providing those running qualities which can only emanate from the highest degree of mechanical refinement. Performance of the six-cylinder power unit is unusually flexible for all-round performance, crisply willing in acceleration and economical in fuel consumption. In combination with Daimler fluid transmission and four-speed pre-selective gearbox it provides quiet, untroubled power at all road speeds and long term reliability.

An exceptionally comfortable driving position is afforded in the "Consort" by provision of adjustable arm rests on the front doors, ample support from the seat, and an adjustable steering wheel.

ENGINE: Six cylinder, o.h.v., bore 69.6 mm., stroke 110.49 mm., capacity 2,522 c.c., compression ratio 7 to 1, b.h.p. 70 at 4,500 r.p.m. Four bearing crankshaft, statically and dynamically balanced; four bearing camshaft; pistons fitted with three compression and one scraper rings; full pressure lubrication to all bearings at 40 lb. sq. in. full flow oil filter; vibration damper ensures smoothness at all speeds. Horizontal S.U. carburetter, oil bath air cleaner and silencer; mechanical fuel pump; 14 gallon fuel tank, including a 1½ gallon reserve controlled from instrument panel. Thermo-static temperature control; full-length water jacket cooling.

ELECTRICAL SYSTEM: 12 volt system; dynamo voltage controlled, battery capacity 69 ampere hours, distributor with automatic advance mechanism, starter motor with solenoid control switch; long-range headlamps; tail, stop, and automatic reversing lights; self-cancelling trafficators.

TRANSMISSION: Fluid flywheel with four-speed pre-selector epicyclic gearbox; ratios 4.08 to 1, 2.32 to 1, 1.56 to 1, 1 to 1, with 3.16 to 1 reverse. Pre-selector change lever on steering column.

SUSPENSION: Independent front suspension by coil springs; semi-elliptic rear, hydraulic piston-type shock absorbers.

FRAME: Underslung box section, cruciform braced.

DRIVE: Hardy Spicer open propeller shaft, hypoid bevel final drive, three-quarter floating rear axle ratio 4.30 to 1.

STEERING: Worm and double roller type steering box with centre arm steering, 18" diameter spring steering wheel mounted on a telescopic column adjustable for length, turning circle diameter 41 feet left and right.

BRAKES: Daimler-Girling hydro-mechanical; independent mechanical handbrake with pistol grip type handle mounted under dash.

WHEELS AND TYRES: Disc type bolt-on wheels with 6.00 by 16 tyres with one spare wheel and tyre in special compartment under luggage boot.

CHASSIS LUBRICATION: Thermal automatic chassis lubrication system.

JACKING SYSTEM: D.W.S. mechanical built-in jacking system.

AIR CONDITIONING: Interior heater mounted under dash with control on instrument panel delivers warm or cool air as desired; demister ducts deliver on to windscreen.

PRINCIPAL DIMENSIONS: Wheelbase 114"; track—front and rear 52"; overall length of Saloon 182"; overall height 65", overall width 64½"; ground clearance 6".

the car is extremely steady with the result that, although the owner may never wish to indulge in such methods, it can be taken round bends fast without swaying or any feeling of insecurity. This has the valuable and perhaps more practical corollary by average standards, that a quick swerve necessitated by an emergency can be safely performed, for in addition the steering is fairly high geared and therefore quick. It is reasonably light steering, however, at low speeds and for manoeuvring, and at speed feels safe and definite, not calling for any special concentration to keep the car on a normal course. There is nice castor action, the steering wheel coming back positively after taking a 90 degree turn, without the return movement being aggressive. No road shocks worthy of note are transmitted from the road wheels. . . .

. . . Effective and tasteful use is made of polished hardwood in the body which in conjunction with the fine quality grained leather upholstery gives an unimstakable touch of quality, superimposed on the very real quality which is built in beneath the surface of a Daimler. Extended experience of this car, as gained during the present test, produces a strong impression of dependability.

The maximum speed of the Consort was around the 77–78 mph mark and between 17 to 20 mpg could be expected. The car in 1951 cost £1,623.10.7 (including tax) but at one period the total rose to over £2,000.

A few 'Consort' chassis were sold separately and some were mounted with Barker special four-seater two door touring bodies similar in most respects to the DB 18 foursome previously depicted but incorporating the head and side lamps in the wings.

At Earls Court in 1948 a Barker Special Sports (chassis 53750), painted in red and cream was awarded The Institute of British Carriage Builders and Automobile Manufacturers' silver medal for standard convertible coachwork for cars listed up to £3,000 (exclusive of purchase tax).

The Hooper bodied Daimler Empress was first built on the DB 18 Special Sports chassis and very popular it proved itself to be, so much so that in various forms and on 2½-, 3-, 3½- and 4½-litre chassis production was continued until 1958.

The 1950 London show 'Empress' (chassis 53811) was finished in two shades

2½-litre DB 18 Barker Special Sports drop-head coupé

142

The distinguished Hooper bodied 2½-litre Daimler Empress

2½-litre (DB 18) Empress interior

of green and trimmed in pale green leather piped with beige. The car was fitted with separate adjustable front seats, beautifully made and shaped, into the rear of which occasional tables were fitted. Special features included: low overall height of car, curved windscreen glazed with laminated glass, double sealing round all doors for dust and draught exclusion, fixed roof specially insulated against heat, large carpeted boot to accommodate luggage and spare wheel, headlamps built into the front wings, detachable covers partially covering rear wheels, radio, demister, screen wash equipment and heating and ventilating equipment. Some examples of the model (like the one illustrated) had built-in fog and spot lights and a one-piece bonnet hinged at the rear. Others had air intakes at the front and centre hinged bonnets. There were other differences in the fascia layout.

The car was constructed to the highest standards according to traditional coachbuilding principles and the example exhibited justifiably received first prize in Section VII (enclosed cars, the retail list price of the complete vehicle being over £1,000 but not exceeding £3,000) of The Institute's Coachwork competition.

Again the following year, another 'Empress' on chassis 56183 was exhibited by Hooper & Co and it too in the same category as before was awarded The Institute's silver gilt medal (first prize). This car was identical to the 1950 model except that for 1951 the exterior was painted maroon and cream and internally was trimmed throughout in cream leather.

One of the few specially bodied post-war DB 18's was the very delightful two-door fixed head coupé constructed by Hoopers for Lady Docker. Mechanically it was identical to the 'Special Sports', that is to say, it was built on the 2½-litre 'special series' twin carburettor chassis producing 85 bhp and although the body

The special Hooper bodied 2½-litre Sports saloon (chassis 53790) – Lady Docker

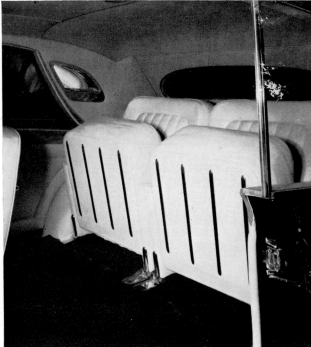

Rear interior of the Lady Docker Sports saloon – (1950)   *Another view of the Lady Docker car with rear seats up-turned*

design could be described as a two-door version of the Empress, which is partially true, there was more to the car than that.

The most conspicuous alteration was made to the frontal aspect. The head, side and fog lamps were all encompassed within a Perspex shield blending in well with the wing contours. The Perspex moulding had a chrome surround, the upper part of which was 'fluted' in typical Daimler fashion.

The car, being specially designed, was intended to be used primarily for touring purposes. The rear compartment contained two exceptionally comfortable individual seats upholstered in the best hide. Centrally and either side were padded armrests. Both the rear seats folded back so as to leave the floor space clear for additional luggage.

Six special drop-head coupé versions of the DB 18 were made by Hoopers. The chassis in each case was again the 'Special Sports' version and the cars offered exceptional comfort for four or occasionally five passengers. The hood was power operated and when lowered a lid covering a recess behind the rear seat opened electrically and after the entire hood was enveloped, the lid closed completely concealing the hood. To make these processes operate reliably and in sequence was no mean achievement.

The first of such cars (chassis no 53806) was delivered in July 1950 to His Majesty King George VI. Another (on chassis no 53898) was in March the following year delivered to ex-Queen Marie of Roumania. The other four (chassis nos 53890, 53903, 59113 and 59114) were made to private order and were built between March 1951 and August 1952.

2½-litre four seater drop-head coupé by Hooper & Co – one of six made

One of the six special Hooper power operated hood coupés built on the Special Series chassis

CHAPTER 2

The 'Twenty-Sevens'

Type DE chassis numbers D 50000–D 50005; D 51040–D 51133;
D 51250–D 51354

I T was the established practice of the Company to produce a wide range of cars
headed by the State carriages used by Royalty and the Nobility and at the other
end of the scale, a model of approximately 20 hp rating offering comfortable
travel with moderate power. Between the two extremes, were cars of medium
engine capacity but capable of carrying coachwork suitable for social purposes
in town or long distance country travel. It will be recalled that at the time the
second world war was declared, this middle category was occupied by the
'Twenty-fours'.

When the Company could again direct its attention to the provision of private
transport, it decided to utilize the well-proven 4-litre engine (4,095 cc) which
had powered the Armoured cars, and install it in a new chassis and endow it
with a coachbuilt body. The new model was the post-war exposition of the
'middle type' of Daimler above referred to but to think of the new car as being
of medium size would indeed be inept, for at the time of its announcement it was
one of the largest production cars in the world.

During the years 1938 and 1939, the average wheelbase for all British cars
exceeding 25 hp and tested by *The Motor* was 10 feet 6 inches. The wheelbase of
the 'Twenty-Seven' was 11 feet 6 inches! Similarly the average leg room on the
pre-war examples was 60 inches measured from the pedals to the front of the rear
seat. On the Daimler the corresponding figure was 78 inches. Some 70 per cent
of the area within the wheelbase was available for passenger accommodation.

Careful overall design eliminated the possibility of disproportionate appearance and in fact the whole car was an example of what a Daimler should be and
due credit was acclaimed for its designer, C. M. Simpson.

The massive frame depth was 7 inches but notwithstanding this, the upper
side of the chassis member was only $1\frac{1}{2}$ inches above the hub centre. Moreover,
even on full bump of the rear wheels, the propeller shaft remained below the
floor level. To achieve this desirable arrangement both the rear axle and the
engine were inclined downwards – the engine by some five degrees from the
vertical. Further the line of the pinion shaft was tipped downwards so that in
conjunction with an initial $1\frac{1}{2}$ inches offset obtained by using a hypoid gear, the

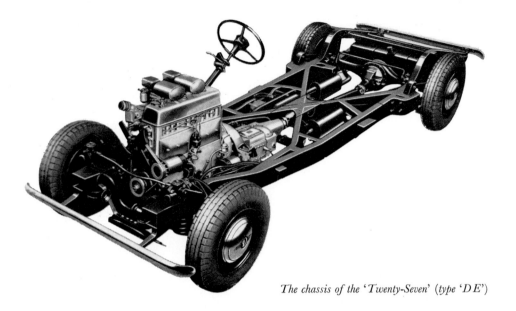

The chassis of the 'Twenty-Seven' (type 'DE')

rear end of the propeller shaft was brought $3\frac{1}{2}$ inches below the hub centre. *The Motor* pointed out that as a consequence of this feature, the universals were running at a slight angle even when the car was fully laden, but that it was actually advantageous as it would prevent the bearings being loaded constantly on one spot as they would have been if they had run exactly in line for the greater part of their life.

The inclination of the rear axle combining with the softness of the rear springs which had a total deflection of 9 inches, made it necessary to control the angular movement of the rear axle casing. This control took the form of arms attached to the rear axle at one end and running forward to the chassis frame to a point immediately above the true pivot of the semi-elliptic spring. By this means the arms did not distort the normal spring motion and the arms were given sufficient freedom in two planes so as not to restrict the accurate travel of the axle should one wheel only encounter a bump.

The rear springs were damped by Luvax–Girling shock absorbers with an inter-connecting torsion anti-roll bar.

As will be seen from the drawing, the frame itself was x-braced from the scuttle to the rear wheel arch, the outer members being of box section both ahead and behind the braced portion. The front of the frame was inswept to provide ample lock and upswept to accommodate the motion of the connection linkages and the front wheels were independently suspended, a coil spring each side which gave a total deflection of some 8·6 inches. The linkage was of the wide-base bottom wishbone type and one arm of the bottom triangle was so disposed as to resist torque from braking.

The chassis bearing points were rubber insulated throughout, the bushes being Silent-bloc and needing no lubrication. The Luvax–Girling dampers at the front were operated by a separate arm and the front anti-roll bar was connected from one damper across to the other.

The track rods were so disposed that they swung about the same radius as the suspension links and as the radius of the top arm was less than that of the lower one, the front independent suspension provided a roll-centre above the ground with a slight departure from vertical wheel motion.

Another somewhat unorthodox arrangement was in relation to the steering geometry. The steering itself was by a Marles roller gear but in place of the normal king pin inclination to provide castor angle, the hub centre was positioned slightly to the rear of the king pin centres. Such an arrangement had previously been used on other cars having outstanding controllability and *The Motor* suggested that it was significant that Daimler should adopt this – an indication of 'the designers' belief that good handling is of first-class importance on all types of motorcars.'

The power unit – slightly modified from the original as developed and proved in the Armoured car, gave an output of 110 bhp. The combined cylinder block and crankcase was carried well down and gave ample support for the four bearing counter-balanced crankshaft which ran in Glacier strip-type bearings. The bearings in the big ends were flanged over thus locating the rod sideways against the webs of the shaft and preventing a minor source of noise and rattle. A full flow Tecalemit oil filter was provided.

The cylinder head followed the design features adopted for the post-war DB 18 and provided a compression ratio of 6·3 to 1. The manifold and induction arrangement also followed the layout on the 2½-litre. Two downdraught SU carburettors were used together with twin Blundell air cleaner-silencers.

As with the smaller versions of the power unit, Brivadium dry liners were used and for the exhaust valve seatings, Brimo-chrome pressings were utilized. (Brimo-chrome contained 3 per cent chrome and 4½ per cent molybdenum.)

The whole engine gearbox unit was mounted forward by a rubber block just underneath the water pump, with two stabilizing points at an angle just above the crankshaft centre line. The gearbox was also supported on rubber and, in order to eliminate engine vibrations being transmitted to the chassis, there were no centre bearings on the Hardy Spicer propeller shaft. To keep the length of shaft in proportion, there was fitted to the rear axle a 15 inch extension.

For the first time on a British production car braking was provided by the Girling Hydro-mechanical arrangement with servo assistance. The braking on the front was actuated hydraulically whilst rods and levers were employed for the rear and the servo operating on the rearward system was of the Clayton–Dewandre vacuum type.

Consistent with the prevailing practice before the war, the DE 27 chassis could be purchased separately so that coachwork of the customers' choice could be mounted. When first announced the chassis price was listed at £1,200, but was increased to £1,400 by the time production got into its stride and in 1949 the price rose to £1,700.

Hooper & Co built thirty-three limousine bodies of differing styles on the DE 27 chassis. In the standard Four-Light and Six-Light designs the front compartment was generally fitted with a bench seat in leather quite capable of accommodating the driver and two passengers seated side by side, and in the rear – where the overall width was 61 inches – a further three passengers were seated in extreme comfort. The seat measured 48 inches between armrests; even with the two occasional seats in use for two additional occupants, there was

Hooper Six-Light limousine made for the King of Siam – 1950

The well proportioned features of the 'Twenty-Seven' as exemplified by Freestone and Webb

Princess Elizabeth's DE 27 entering Buckingham Palace

The 4-litre Daimler presented to HRH Princess Elizabeth

I

virtually no restriction of leg room or interference with general comfort. When, as was usual, a division was fitted this was electrically raised or lowered and separate electric motors were used to operate the rear window blind and the driver's door window. Push buttons were installed in both front and rear compartments and to order separate front and rear heaters could be built in and a radio and speaker could be installed in the rear of the division between the occasional seats. In some cars, spring-rolled silk blinds could be lowered behind the division glass to afford maximum privacy. In addition to the normal high quality carpeting, the rear floor was covered with a luxurious wool carpet. In the Six-Light Hooper body (as illustrated p. 150), there was no pillar between the rear door window and the quarter light and visibility was quite exceptional. From the driving seat the view was exceedingly good and three wipers were provided for the wide screen.

As noted in the 'DB 18' chapter, the first production models to have sloping and rounded radiators were the post-war 'Twenty-Seven' and 'Straight-Eight'. Combined with the Lucas P.100 headlights the frontal appearance was not only pleasing but exceedingly dignified.

For its size and weight of 52 cwt, the car had surprising acceleration and a creditable maximum speed of around 80 mph. The whole performance of the car, whether travelling at a mile a minute on main roads or jostling through heavy town traffic, could only be described as impeccable. The fine chassis and coachwork combined to give a feeling of solidarity and security whilst the ride was firmly smooth.

As with most Daimlers, drivers were pleasantly surprised to discover the cornering abilities of the car. *The Autocar* road tested the Hooper version – in January 1948 – and found the fuel consumption to be in the region of 12 to 14 mpg. At that date the basic price of the car was £3,795 and with the addition of purchase tax, the total cost was brought up to £5,904.16.8 – no small sum for the early post-war years! The report commented –

Probably even today, after the Daimler firm have been making for many years overhead valve-engined cars of high performance characteristics, there are people who are not aware that they have departed as far as this model indicates from the days of long ago when smoothness and silence were the chief aims of the sleeve-valve-engined Daimlers and performance as such was not achieved. The latest designs, of which the 'Twenty-Seven' is an excellent post-war representative, combine the traditional Daimler silkiness and silence with performance to satisfy most requirements.

Much of the 'silkiness' was, of course, attributable to the fluid flywheel.

In June 1947, Queen Mary took delivery of a special bodied limousine (Hooper no. 9424 on chassis 51101) and at 57 inches the interior headroom was 3 inches greater than normal for the post-war cars.

It will be recalled that Barker & Co had been integrated into the Daimler Company, but for a number of years after the end of the war, the highly esteemed coachbuilding name of Barker was used for models with bodies built by the Daimler Company to traditional high standards. Although Hooper & Co had

The Barker bodied DE 27 limousine

similarly been part of the Daimler organization within the BSA group, they retained to a far greater degree, their individuality. Under a mutual arrangement between the parent company and the two coachbuilders, for a while after 1938, Hoopers made a few – in fact, about nine – bodies under the name of 'Barker'. Post-war 'Barkers' were made at Radford Works, Coventry by both craftsmen from the old coachbuilders and from Daimlers.

In 1949, there was specially designed for private hire work, a new Barker limousine on the 'Twenty-Seven' chassis. Normally upholstered in leather throughout, the limousine was able to accommodate nine passengers including the driver – three rows of three! In September 1949, the car sold for £4,341.10.0 (basic £2,790).

Reverting to the pre-war 'Twenty-four', it is interesting to recall that a considerable number of the model were endowed with coachwork by Windovers of London – whose beginnings dated from 1796 in Huntingdon.

During the second world war, Windovers, like many of the other coachbuilders, including Hoopers, turned their attention to the manufacture and service of aircraft components.

On account of the established association with Daimlers, it was not unnatural in 1946 for Windovers to be given further orders. Initially the coachbuilders were asked for fifty limousine bodies (design no 116) suitable for mounting on either DE 27 or DE 36 chassis. Of this number, thirty and one prototype were in fact made. Five were fitted to the Straight-Eight chassis and the remaining number were mounted on to 'Twenty-Sevens' (see next page). Design 116 is illustrated on p. 154 (albeit mounted on the DE 36 chassis) and the specification for these limousines required them to be 'constructed of best quality well seasoned ash framing, strengthened by steel body plates where necessary, built as light as possible consistent with the required strength; the whole of the exterior panelled throughout in hand beaten sheet aluminium.' A spring blind

Body no.	Chassis no.	Chassis rec'd	Body no.	Chassis no.	Chassis rec'd
6646	51042	Feb 1946	6693	51102	1947
6679	51061	1946	6694	51103	July 1947
6680	51065	1946	6695	51105	1947
6681	51067	1946	6696	51129	Mar 1948
6682	51068	1946	6697	51256	1948
6683	51066	1946	6698	51257	July 1948
6684	51076	1946	6700	51258	1948
6685	51069	1946	6701	51254	1948
6687	51077	1946	6702	51289	Sep 1948
6688	51078	Dec 1946	6703	51296	1948
6689	51070	Jan 1947	6704	51299	Oct 1948
6690	51071	1947	6705	51300	Jan 1949
6691	51072	1947	6706	51304	1949

The Windover limousine – design 116

The Windover 'Twenty-Seven' saloon (design no. 136)

over the rear window operated by the driver was provided and the division windows were operated manually by sliding from side to side.

In common with the designs by Hooper and Freestone and Webb, on the same chassis the specification provided that the Windover cars should have concealed running boards.

The limousine provided similar accommodation to that of Hoopers – that is, three including chauffeur on the front bench seat, three on the rear seat and two on the face-forward occasionals. All interior woodwork was of walnut. For each complete body, the contract provided that Windovers should be paid £688!

The only owner driver saloon on the DE 27 chassis in standardized form was offered by Windovers. In September 1946 the Daimler Co ordered twenty-five bodies (design 136) and again they were to be suitable for mounting on either of the two chassis types.

In all salient points the same specification was applied to this alternative design. In normal form a division was not contemplated but a 'sunshine-roof' was incorporated. The saloon was built as a six-seater but where a division was added to special order, then two occasional seats were generally included. As is apparent, the rear part was 'pillarless'; the upholstery and woodwork was according to customers' choice. The division, when fitted, was normally electrically operated as on the Hooper examples and at extra cost an alternative seating arrangement in the front could be had. This consisted of a separate adjustable seat for the driver and a fixed bench seat alongside to accommodate two passengers.

For each completed and fitted body the agreed price to be paid to the body-builders was £753.10.0 and an extra £70 where a division was included. Of the twenty-five bodies (design 136) contemplated, twenty were completed and all but five of these were mounted on 'Twenty-Sevens':

Body no.	Chassis no.	Chassis rec'd	Body no.	Chassis no.	Chassis rec'd
6729	51091	8.5.1947	6738	51131	19.3.1948
6730	51107	23.7.1947	*6741	51261	1.7.1948
6732	51123	3.2.1948	6742	51262	3.9.1948
6733	51127	16.2.1948	6744	51306	7.2.1949
6734	51276	16.8.1948	6745	51305	11.2.1949
6736	51125	6.2.1948	6746	51307	15.2.1949
6737	51265	17.8.1948	6747	51312	1.3.1949
			6748	51319	23.3.1949

The car marked with an asterisk was exhibited at Earls Court in the autumn of 1948. It had no division, but possessed the optional front seating as above described. The exterior was finished in black and maroon and the interior was upholstered in best quality maroon leather. As shown, the total price for the complete car including purchase tax was £3,267.

One of the DE 27 Lanchesters by Vanden Plas

The Hooper built Daimler ambulance on the DC 27 chassis

Charlesworth did make a few bodies in the post-war years. Certainly several 'Twenty-Sevens' had Charlesworth coachwork as did one or two DB 18's and possibly a few bodies found their way on to DE 36 chassis. Unfortunately it seems that their records were destroyed when they went out of business more than twenty years ago.

Where non-standard coachwork was contemplated the customer would normally select the DE 36 chassis in preference to the DE 27. Having regard to the comparative overall costs of such a special vehicle, the reason for such a choice can perhaps be appreciated. Nevertheless a few 'specials' were made. Although displaying Lanchester radiators, two cars on the DE 27 chassis were built by Vanden Plas for the Royal House of Nawanagar, for the use of 'Ranji', the famous cricketer (bodies 4031 and 4032 on chassis 51049 and 51050). These two were the only Daimler/Lanchester bodies constructed after the war by Vanden Plas until the arrival of the DS 420 limousine. This distinguished customer also had two DE 27's with Hooper Six-Light bodies (nos 9187 and 9188).

Freestone and Webb designed and built an attractive body for the DE models. Typical of this coachbuilder's work, was the body of the razor or semi-razor edge style and the result was a combination of dignity and elegance. One or two bodies were built for the owner–driver without partition, but by far the majority were constructed as limousines. Between 1946 and 1949 the following were made as 'Twenty-Sevens':

Body no.	Chassis no.		Body no.	Chassis no.
1359	51064		1369	51290
1363	51113		1371	51302
1364	51104		1372	51310
1365	51128		1373	51308
1367	51273		1374	51320
1368	51282		1375	51328

Type DC (Ambulance) chassis numbers 54000–54499

Similar in many respects to the DE 27 chassis was the DC 27 chassis which was designed and developed for use as an ambulance. The power unit was the Twenty-Seven engine as already described but in place of the twin SU downdraught carburettors on the limousine, the ambulance version was fitted with a single Solex downdraught and a modified distributor. The effect was to slightly reduce to 105 bhp, the power output at 3,600 rpm.

The chassis for the DC 27 although in most respects similar to the DE 27, differed in a number of ways. The most significant variation concerned the transmission layout.

Two propeller shafts were mounted in series – the forward one being supported by a rubber mounted centre bearing. The shafts were fitted with needle

157

The chassis of the DC 27 (ambulance)

roller bearings and transmitted the drive from the gearbox to the rear axle, which was of the hypoid bevel type but incorporated the differential in a housing offset to the nearside. The engine was not only inclined backwards but also positioned slightly diagonal to facilitate the transmission arrangements. Ambulances in several different forms were produced by Barker & Co, Hooper & Co, and a few other specialists. Rarely has there been an ambulance to equal the smoothness and comparative silence of the Daimler Twenty-Seven.

Type DH chassis numbers D 52900–D 52949

The virtues of the 'DC' chassis were well appreciated and without significant modification, it was adopted for a new limousine made by Hooper to the order of Daimler Hire Ltd. In this form the chassis was appropriately designated the 'DH 27' and some fifty limousines were made.

The principal dimensions of the hire limousine were: wheelbase 12 feet 6 inches; track 5 feet at the front and 5 feet 3 inches at the rear; overall length 18 feet 9 inches; width 6 feet 6 inches; height (unladen) 6 feet 11 inches; unladen weight 2 tons 16 cwt 1 qr. The gearbox ratios were identical on all three versions (DE, DC and DH 27).

It is believed that these DH Twenty-Sevens were the largest hire cars ever to be built in quantity. Up to seven passengers (in addition to chauffeur), could be carried. The cars were designed for comfortable touring being provided with air conditioning, efficient heaters and special 'sight-seeing' windows and electrically operated partitions.

158

A Daimler Hire limousine in service

The 'DH 27' – fifty of which were built by Hooper & Co for Daimler Hire Ltd

CHAPTER 3

The Daimler Straight-Eight

Type DE 36 chassis numbers D 50006–D 50011; D 51150–D 51243;
D 51700–D 51749; D 51750–51759 (L.H. drive); D 52800–D 52855*

The post-war Straight-Eight Daimler is an entirely new design and is a car of such striking performance and qualities that one searches almost in vain, for the appropriate adjective. Possibly 'fabulous' is the most embracing term for a car that is considerably the most expensive in the world, has the largest wheelbase and biggest body space of any European car, has all the qualities of silence and dignity of which Daimler is a synonym with speed acceleration and road holding which would evoke praise in a sports model. (*The Motor* – December 1947)

THE chassis of the DE 36 was virtually identical with that of the DE 27 – 4 litre, except that the wheelbase was 12 feet 3 inches in length and overall the car was more than 18 feet long. The 8-cylinder engine had the same cylinder dimensions as the 'Twenty-Seven' but with a one-third increase in capacity the power output was raised to 150 bhp at 3,600 rpm. The handling and general running qualities of the car clearly impressed the motor journal testers for their commendations excelled the complimentary comments made about the 'Twenty-Seven'.

It was immediately appreciated that the chassis offered almost unlimited scope for the coachbuilder and during the seven years – 1946 to 1953 – the car was in production, some of the finest and most elegant bodies ever constructed were mounted on the DE 36 chassis. The outstanding examples are illustrated.

Most of the standard body designs from Hooper & Co, Windovers, and Freestone & Webb were so made as to be suitable for mounting on either the 'Twenty-Seven' or the 'Straight-Eight' chassis.

Five Windover saloons (design no. 136 – as illustrated on p. 154) were made:

Body no.	Chassis no.	Date chassis received
6731	51214	13th September 1947
6735	51218	10th February 1947
6739	51231	11th May 1948
6740	51715	3rd September 1948
6743	51731	16th December 1948

*Chassis nos 54950–54999 were also allocated for DE 36 left-hand drive cars, but it is improbable that any chassis bearing numbers within this sanction were built.

Reprinted from "The Motor," December 17, 1947.

The Motor Road Test No. 15/47

Make: Daimler. **Type:** Straight-Eight Hooper 4-Light Limousine.

Makers: The Daimler Co. Ltd., Coventry.

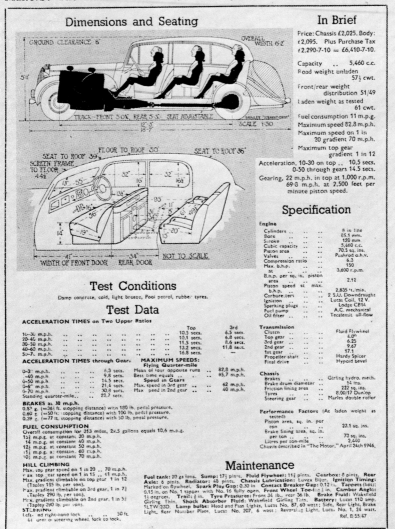

Dimensions and Seating

GROUND CLEARANCE 8"
OVERALL WIDTH 6'2"
5'11"
TRACK—FRONT 5'0¾", REAR 5'3"
SEAT ADJUSTABLE
12'3"
18'7"
SCALE 1:50

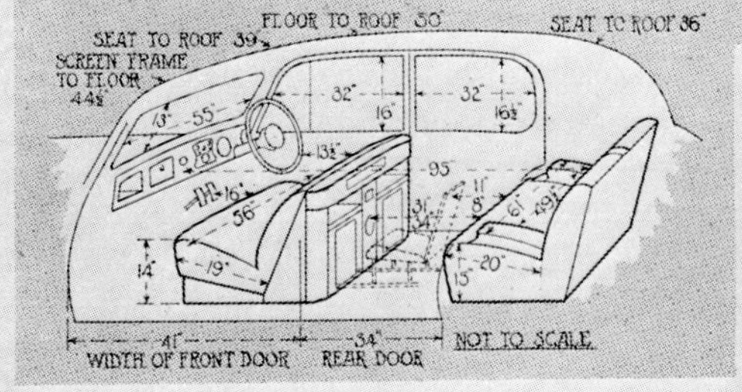
SEAT TO ROOF 39"
FLOOR TO ROOF 50"
SEAT TO ROOF 36"
SCREEN FRAME TO FLOOR 44½"
WIDTH OF FRONT DOOR
REAR DOOR
NOT TO SCALE

In Brief

Price: Chassis £2,025. Body: £2,095. Plus Purchase Tax £2,290-7-10 = £6,410-7-10.

Capacity ..	5,460 c.c.
Road weight unladen	57¼ cwt.
Front/rear weight distribution	51/49
Laden weight as tested	61 cwt.
Fuel consumption	11 m.p.g.
Maximum speed	82.8 m.p.h.
Maximum speed on 1 in 20 gradient	70 m.p.h.
Maximum top gear gradient	1 in 12

Acceleration, 10-30 on top .. 10.5 secs. 0-50 through gears 14.5 secs.

Gearing, 22 m.p.h. in top at 1,000 r.p.m. 69·8 m.p.h. at 2,500 feet per minute piston speed.

Specification

Engine

Cylinders ..	8 in line
Bore ..	85.1 mm.
Stroke ..	120 mm.
Cubic capacity ..	5,460 c.c.
Piston area ..	70.5 sq. ins.
Valves ..	Pushrod o.h.v.
Compression ratio ..	6.3
Max. b.h.p. ..	150
at ..	3,600 r.p.m.
B.h.p. per sq. in. piston area ..	2.12
Piston speed at max. b.h.p. ..	2,835 ft./min.
Carburetters ..	2 S.U. Downdraught
Ignition ..	Lucas Coil, 12 V.
Sparking plugs ..	Lodge CB14
Fuel pump ..	A.C. mechanical
Oil filter ..	Tecalemit full-flow

Transmission

Clutch ..	Fluid Flywheel
Top gear ..	4.09
3rd gear ..	6.25
2nd gear ..	9.67
1st gear ..	17.1
Propeller shaft ..	Hardy Spicer
Final drive ..	Hypoid bevel

Chassis

Brakes ..	Girling hydro. mech.
Brake drum diameter ..	14 ins.
Friction lining area ..	222 sq. ins.
Tyres ..	8.00/17 Dunlop
Steering gear ..	Marles double roller

Performance Factors (At laden weight as tested)

Piston area, sq. in. per ton ..	23.1 sq. ins.
Brake lining area, sq. in. per ton ..	73 sq. ins.
Litres per ton-mile ..	2,440

Chassis described in "The Motor," April 24th 1946.

Test Conditions

Damp concrete, cold, light breeze, Pool petrol, rubber tyres.

Test Data

ACCELERATION TIMES on Two Upper Ratios

	Top	3rd
10–30 m.p.h. ..	10.5 secs.	6.5 secs.
20–40 m.p.h. ..	10.1 secs.	6.8 secs.
30–50 m.p.h. ..	11.5 secs.	8.6 secs.
40–60 m.p.h. ..	13.2 secs.	11.8 secs.
50–70 m.p.h. ..	16.8 secs.	—

ACCELERATION TIMES through Gears

0–30 m.p.h. ..	6.3 secs.
0–40 m.p.h. ..	9.8 secs.
0–50 m.p.h. ..	14.5 secs.
0–60 m.p.h. ..	21.4 secs.
0–70 m.p.h. ..	30.8 secs.
Standing quarter-mile ..	22.7 secs.

MAXIMUM SPEEDS:

Flying Quarter-mile

Mean of four opposite runs ..	82.8 m.p.h.
Best time equals ..	85.7 m.p.h.

Speed in Gears

Max. speed in 3rd gear ..	62 m.p.h.
Max. speed in 2nd gear ..	40 m.p.h.

BRAKES at 30 m.p.h.

0.83 g. (=36½ ft. stopping distance) with 180 lb. pedal pressure.
0.60 g. (=50 ft. stopping distance) with 100 lb. pedal pressure.
0.39 g. (=77 ft. stopping distance) with 50 lb. pedal pressure.

FUEL CONSUMPTION

Overall consumption for 313 miles, 29.5 gallons equals 10.6 m.p.g.
15½ m.p.g. at constant 30 m.p.h.
14 m.p.g. at constant 40 m.p.h.
12½ m.p.g. at constant 50 m.p.h.
11½ m.p.g. at constant 60 m.p.h.
10½ m.p.g. at constant 70 m.p.h.

HILL CLIMBING

Max. top gear speed on 1 in 20 .. 70 m.p.h.
Max. top gear speed on 1 in 15 .. 61 m.p.h.
Max. gradient climbable on top gear 1 in 12 (Tapley 185 lb. per ton).
Max. gradient climbable on 3rd gear, 1 in 7¾ (Tapley 290 lb. per ton).
Max. gradient climbable on 2nd gear, 1 in 5¼ (Tapley 390 lb. per ton).

STEERING

Left- and right-hand lock .. .. 50 ft.
4½ turns of steering wheel, lock to lock.

Maintenance

Fuel tank: 20 gallons. **Sump:** 17½ pints. **Fluid Flywheel:** 11½ pints. **Gearbox:** 8 pints. **Rear Axle:** 6 pints. **Radiator:** 48 pints. **Chassis Lubrication:** Luvax Bijur. **Ignition Timing:** Marked on flywheel. **Spark Plug Gap:** 0.30 in. **Contact Breaker Gap:** 0.12 in. **Tappets (hot):** 0.15 in. on No. 1 tappet with No. 16 fully open. **Front Wheel Toe-in:** ⅛ in. **Camber Angle:** 1½ degrees. **Trail:** ⅜ in. **Tyre Pressures:** Front 34 lb., rear 36 lb. **Brake Fluid:** Wakefield Girling Thin. **Shock Absorber Fluid:** Wakefield Girling Thin. **Battery:** Lucas 110 amp. SLTW/23D. **Lamp bulbs:** Head and Pass Lights, Lucas No. 87, 60 watt; Side, Rear Light, Brake Light, Rear Number Plate, Lucas No. 207, 6 watt; Reversing Light, Lucas No. 1, 24 watt.

Ref. B/55/47

Temple Press Ltd., Bowling Green Lane, London, E.C.1. 3111—48

The same number of limousines were also made by Windovers (design no. 116, see p. 154); these were:

Body no.	Chassis no.	Date chassis received
6677	51164	November 1946
6678	51166	November 1946
6686	51165	December 1946
6692	51180	1947
6699	51179	July 1948

On the majority of post-war Straight-Eights, the spare wheels were housed under the covers mounted on the wings and displayed on the bonnet sides were chromium plated slats. These features would normally distinguish a DE 36 from a DE 27 but the practice concerning the side grilles was not always consistent. There were instances where Straight-Eights had none and in some cases they were fitted to 'Twenty-Sevens'.

Freestone and Webb made, in their time, some very elegant bodies. Six of the style illustrated, top p. 163, were mounted between 1946 and 1948 on to DE 36 chassis, as under:

Body no.	Chassis no.	Body no.	Chassis no.
1358	51167	1362	51210
1360	51703	1366	51234*
1361	51198	1370	51739

* exhibited at Earls Court

In addition to those listed, Freestone and Webb constructed two special bodies of very similar appearance to each other.

The first, body no. 1461, was built to the specification and order of Mr Ivan R. Hendricks of Jamaica, who during the 1939–45 war had worked in the Daimler factory.

It was well balanced and possessed a definite character. The well proportioned lines and curves gave a grace and dignity of their own and few chromium or other embellishments were required to give the car a strong appeal to the discerning eye.

From the time the idea was conceived and first implemented, nearly two years elapsed before the completion of the car early in 1949. At the time it was a matter of conjecture as to whether the vehicle might have represented the most expensive car built since the then recently ended war. The exact cost was not publicly disclosed.

The Freestone and Webb body was a full six-seater with adequate headroom and did not look as large as it really was. The exterior was painted in a soft pastel

Razor-edge styling – a post-war Straight-Eight limousine by Freestone and Webb

The specially designed Close-coupled Sports saloon by Freestone & Webb exhibited at the 1949 London show

shade of grey – described as 'silver birch'; – enhanced by a discreet use of a fine gold line. A slightly darker shade of grey was used for the leather upholstery. The cabinet work was made from a special Jamaican wood called 'Yellow Sanders' and which was finely figured with a very close grain.

The chassis no. 51238 was in standard form except that it had received special attention, particularly under the bonnet where all metal parts were highly polished, and the steering was some 4 inches lower than standard.

Composite construction according to normal coachbuilding traditions was employed. The doors were mounted on concealed hinges on the centre pillars. The front seat was of the bench type; the spare wheel was carried underneath the luggage locker in a separate compartment and the hollow areas in the wings behind the front wheels were utilized to form cupboards accessible from inside the car.

The interior view of the Freestone & Webb 1949 London show exhibit

Underneath the headlamps, fresh air intakes were installed and provided adequate ventilation to the occupants via butterfly flaps fitted to the interior of the scuttle.

In the rear a folding table was mounted either side of a central cabinet and on the floor adjustable footrests were provided. All the tools were specially plated and were attractively fitted into a tray built into the boot lid.

For the controls on the fascia board and the steering wheel, ivory was used. To take account of the changed weight distribution the suspension was suitably altered and it was reported that the car handled beautifully.

The second of the two special cars, body no. 1541, was the one depicted on p. 163 and it was painted beige with the wings finished in a deep maroon. The interior of this London show exhibit was trimmed in beige Vaumol hide with contrasting maroon pipings. All the interior woodwork, including the instrument board, cabinet and folding tables was finished with walnut burr butt veneers in high gloss lacquer. A press button radio set was installed immediately below the instrument board with a second speaker built into the rear parcel shelf. The interior and boot lights were operated automatically or manually by switches and air conditioning and de-mister equipment was installed.

The overall length of the car was 18 feet 8 inches, the width 6 feet 2½ inches and the height only 5 feet 5½ inches.

At both the 1948 and 1949 London motor shows, Lancefield Coachworks, London exhibited a special invalid limousine. Similar vehicles had been shown before the war and although this one was not particularly elegant to look at, it was quite unique and worthy of a detailed description. In fact the Judges of the coachwork competition thought highly of the vehicle and awarded its makers with a Silver Gilt medal.

The vehicle had three full length doors with drop windows and ventilators, concealed luggage rail on the roof and good accommodation for trunks on the lid at the rear. The exterior was painted in blue and black.

Inside a full length stretcher was fitted and this was mounted on its own chassis and could be revolved on ball bearing sockets to align with the side door for loading and unloading. Medical equipment cupboards were installed and contained ample supplies according to the patient's needs and in another cupboard, spare linen was carried. A luxurious revolving chair was concealed in the division when not in use and also fitted in the division was a heater.

The division glass and rear blinds were electrically operated and a radio was set beneath the rear quarter window. All the window blinds were concealed in the roof by polished cornice mouldings. Upholstery was in brown Luxan grain leather with matching carpet laid over felt and rubber undermats. The roof was treated with anti-drumming compound and the interior was attractively lined in highly polished African walnut. Triplex toughened glass was used throughout. All the fittings on this unusual limousine were heavily chromium plated.

The car shown below was equally different – at least in its unusual appearance. It was specially constructed by the French coachbuilders – Saoutchik, in 1952

A Straight-Eight with coachwork by Saoutchik & Cie, France

165

for HM King Ibn Saud for use by his son Prince Talal in Saudi Arabia. The car was nearly 22 feet long and according to contemporary reports, it weighed about 3¼ tons!

Hooper & Co (Coachbuilders) Ltd, made a total of 114 bodies on the DE 36 chassis. Many of these were to a standard design but a considerable number of 'specials' were constructed. In a very real sense, the co-existence of the Daimler Straight-Eight chassis and Hooper's superlative coachwork made every car to leave their works, a 'special'.

The following were among the many illustrious customers who were fortunate enough to sample post-war Straight-Eights with Hooper coachwork:

The President of Czechoslovakia	(no. 9206)
HM King of Afghanistan	(no. 9225)
The Queen of Holland	(no. 9183)
The Governor of Cyprus	(no. 9184)
The Governor of Natal	(no. 9190)
The Prince of Monaco	(no. 9197)
HIH the Emperor of Abyssinia	(no. 9198)
HM King George VI	(nos. 9335, 9336, 9541 and 9542)
Government of South Africa	(nos. 9338–9342 inc.)
Sir Bernard Docker	(nos. 9345, 9352 and 9620)
Lord Beaverbrook	(no. 9382)
Government of Australia	(nos. 9427, 9428, 9494, 9495, 9496 and 9499)
Government of New Zealand	(nos. 9429, 9430, 9497, 9498, 9500 and 9501)
'Royal Stock'	(no. 9515)
HM King of Thailand	(no. 9563)
The French Ambassador to Peru	(no. 9881)

The Government of South Africa ordered in 1946 a number of cars to be used by the Royal Family on their proposed visit. The order – executed by Daimlers in conjunction with Hoopers; – was for five special Straight-Eights. Two limousines, two landaulettes and the remaining car was an open tourer with 'all-weather' head.

All five cars were finished in royal blue and black relieved by fine red lines. The interiors of the limousines and landaulettes were upholstered in grey ribbed cloth with a grey head lining and as can be imagined all were beautifully finished in a quiet dignified style. Occasional seats were fitted in all five cars. The division and door glasses were all operated electrically and in the landaulettes the roof was sliding but beneath it was a fixed transparent panel.

Another Royal tour, this time of Australia and New Zealand was planned for 1949 and a large fleet of Daimlers was prepared. Apart from a large number of DB 18 2½-litre saloons – mainly of standard specification, the most important cars were again Hooper built Straight-Eights – twelve in all. Half of this number were for New Zealand and the other six for the Australian Government. Of the total 'Thirty-sixes', five were landaulettes, four were four-door convertibles and

The five Royal tour cars at Stoneleigh Abbey

One of the open tourers built for the Royal tour of Australia and New Zealand

three were limousines. The general designs were similar to those made for the earlier tour. The limousines and landaulettes had twin radio speakers below the division – mounted one either side of the rear heater controls. In these cars the woodwork was walnut veneer but in the tourers Australian teak was the coach-builders' choice.

HM King George VI had four post-war Straight-Eights, all fitted with landaulette bodies constructed by Hooper & Co. Two were delivered in May

167

The 1949 Royal tour cars awaiting shipment

Royal tour of Australia and New Zealand

Sydney Racecourse – Australian Royal tour 1954

Car 9542 in the Royal Mews

1947 (chassis 51172 and 51177 with bodies respectively numbered 9335 and 9336) and then in June 1949 delivery was made of the other two (chassis 51740 and 51741 with bodies respectively numbered 9541 and 9542). The last mentioned car was, following the King's death, retained by the Queen Mother and in retirement, it is now kept at The Royal Mews and on certain days of the week, it is one of the several Royal Daimlers on display to the public. As a precaution against fuel starvation twin electric pumps were fitted to these Royal Daimlers.

Awarded the premier place in the Institute of British Carriage and Automobile Manufacturers' coachwork competition, was this fine Touring limousine

169

An example of the less common Four-Light Hooper limousine (1947)

HOOPER & C°
(Coachbuilders) Ltd
54 St. James's St.
London. S.W.1
Telephone-REGent 3242

"HOOPER" Touring Limousine
on New D E 36 H.P. Daimler Chassis.

by Hooper exhibited at the 1948 London motor show. The car (chassis 51256) was painted mistletoe green all over with a gold picking out line and was trimmed with light beige leather throughout. The price for the complete car was £4,195 with an addition of £2,332.1.2 for purchase tax.

A greater attraction at the show, was a magnificent streamlined drop-head coupé. The first and lasting impression was one of immense size – 20 feet long and 6 feet 5 inches in width. Of particular interest was the electro-hydraulically operated head which folded away under a power operated metal cover forward of the boot. The drop windows to the two doors were also electrically operated and the wide curved windscreen gave excellent forward vision. The screen's width necessitated the fitting of three wiper blades. The rear wheels were partially covered by aluminium panels fitted with spring balanced arms.

In the front an adjustable bench type seat for three was fitted with separate backs the outer two of which were hinged to facilitate access to the rear where

Another splendid example of Hooper coachwork on the DE 36 chassis – the All-Weather tourer, South African Royal tour, 1947

Hooper & Co, Straight-Eight touring limousine (chassis 51256) – 1948

The 'Green Goddess' drop-head coupé by Hooper & Co, Earls Court Motor Show 1948

Another view of the 'Green Goddess' Straight-Eight

The ample accommodation within the special drop-head coupé

two more separate seats were provided. These were so positioned that rear passengers had a clear forward view between the heads of those in front.

About eight of these cars were built and differed in detail only slightly from each other. The apparent variations concerned the treatment of the head and side lights and the rear wheel covers. In one instance the covers were diagonally louvred.

The car exhibited was on chassis 51233 and was painted in pastel jade green and fitted with beige upholstery – hence the unofficial Christening – 'Green Goddess' or, in at least one motoring journal – 'Chariot of the Sun'.

The Daimler fluted motif was repeated along the top edge of each chromium frame to the 'Perspex' covers over the head and pass lights. An H M V Radio-mobile was installed and the standard steering column gear selector was extended

Hooper landaulette on D E 36 Straight-Eight chassis for H M King of Siam, 1949

173

This style of Six-Light limousine coachwork by Hooper was the 'standard' design when first the post-war Daimler Straight-Eight was put into production. This particular car was delivered to the Governor of Cyprus

A revised rear-end styling was then adopted as shown by the above car exhibited at the New York show in February 1949 priced at $22,000

almost to the rim of the ivory plastic steering wheel giving finger tip gear control. Although no official road test of the car was ever recorded it is understood that the maximum speed was around the 90 mark.

At a total price of £7,001 the car was the most expensive exhibited at the show. That figure consisted of approximately 36 per cent purchase tax, 35 per cent for the cost of coachwork and the remaining 29 per cent the basic cost of the chassis.

In 1949 at both the London and Scottish shows, further Straight-Eights were exhibited by Hoopers and by The Daimler Co. At London the Coachbuilders had on their stand a Sedanca painted in metallic silver grey and black. Apart from all the usual luxurious fittings there was of course a folding de ville extension over the front seat and Daimlers on their stand had in addition to their products an example of Hooper's standard type Straight-Eight limousine seating eight passengers including driver.

A car like the one exhibited at the Scottish show is illustrated below – this version being known as the 'Spey'.

Yet again in 1950, a Hooper bodied Daimler Straight-Eight found favour with the judges and gained (joint) first prize in Section 1 of the Coachwork competition. This Sedanca body (no. 9620 on chassis 52823) was painted in off white and black. White cloth was used for the rear compartment and black leather in the front. With no occasional seats fitted, five passengers could be

The 1950 exhibit by Hooper & Co at the London Motor show

The front compartment of the 1950 show car

carried in addition to the driver. A de ville extension patented by Hoopers was a notable feature and another point of particular interest was the cocktail cabinet. This was so designed that at a touch of a button the centre portion of the cabinet would extend back and upwards to the rear occupants – then the door opened to form a table and finally the interior was illuminated. The rear seat centre armrest contained the radio controls. At a later stage of its life the car was converted into a limousine.

Possibly the most magnificent and expensive Daimler ever to be made was shown at Earls Court in 1951. To assert that it was the 'star of the show' would be an understatement. Needless to say it was the premier award winner!

Built for Sir Bernard and Lady Docker, this touring limousine represented the ultimate in every detail. The huge but graceful body was black and gold – above the waistline, black and on the side panels below, black with tiny gold stars, or in heraldic vocabulary – 'sable semée of mullets of six points, or'.

Each and every part of the car that would normally have been finished in chromium was plated with gold – even to the latch plates of the locks and stop light surrounds. Golden silk materials for the upholstery and head lining were

The 1950 Sedanca – rear interior

The Hooper limousine shown at Geneva 1951 (chassis 52821)

The Gold car on DE 36 chassis no. 52830, exhibited in 1951

The rear interior of the Gold car

specially prepared by Messrs Warners and woven by them on a handloom. The cabinet work was of course carried out by Hooper's own craftsmen and to give a warm golden colour Australian camphor-wood was used. The gold plating was entrusted to the Goldsmiths and Silversmiths Company and the gold and crystal picnic fittings were by Cartier of Bond Street, London.

Black suitcases made of crocodile hide, mounted in gold and lined with silk were fitted within the enormous boot. Black and gold china tea things, cut-glass decanters and cutlery and a table cloth and napkins of finest Irish linen were schemed to fit into the division. The Thermos tea-jug was gold plated all over as was also the handle and clip of the 'Perspex' sandwich box. Drinks were stored in the left hand cabinet in the division, a tea service in the right hand cabinet and the table linen in between the two. In the armrests were gold plated controls for the radio.

Careful attention to detail was also given to the body structure. A deep curved screen afforded excellent forward vision. Over the rear compartment a toughened glass roof panel was fitted with an electrically operated shutter. All

Another view of the Gold car

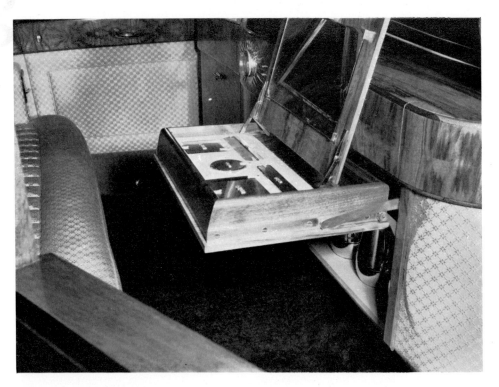

Interior fitments in the Gold car

windows and the division were similarly operated. Internally heated glass was utilized for the rear window to eliminate misting and to achieve a similar purpose double glazing was employed for the side windows. Separate heating and ventilation units were fitted for front and rear passengers. 'Perspex' covers were again used for the head and pass lights and flush fitting rear wheel covers with spring-balanced arms, similar to those on the 'Green Goddess' were used.

The undisclosed total cost must have been astronomical!

On ten to a dozen selected cars, the standard front shock absorbers were replaced by telescopic dampers and the radiator was pivoted on a centrally placed rubber chassis mounting. The idea was to isolate the front wings and radiator from the chassis so as to eliminate vibration and possible shake. The experiment proved to be successful. The work was carried out at Hoopers and one of the first, if not the first example to have the modification was the Gold car.

After five or six years service the resplendent car was destined for sale but not before it was rendered 'anonymous'. Most of the unique and special features were removed – the gold in particular! – and the front was remodelled so that the 'new car' eventually appeared as shown at the foot of p. 182.

*The front compartment
of the Gold Daimler*

The splendour of the 1951 Earls Court Motor Show

The Gold car

The Gold car – rendered anonymous

Daimlers are so versatile! Few would have chosen a 5·4-litre coachbuilt limousine for rally work and those who did had many doubts concerning their sanity.

A typically magnificent Hooper limousine, huge and stately, was the car chosen and driven by Tommy Wisdom, Lord Selsdon and Anthony Hume in the 1952 Monte Carlo rally. They started off from Lisbon and encountered ice in the streets of Madrid and light snow in the mountains near the French frontier. Some two thousand spectators lined the streets at Bordeaux and it was reported that there were gasps of admiration for the Daimler and the way in which it rode the icy roads with impressive steadiness.

1952 was the year, it will be recalled, that Mercedes made a comeback to rallying and they too used the Lisbon route. Apparently the German crew thought the Daimler a huge joke but it transpired that the considerable weight of the Straight-Eight proved to be its salvation.

Aided by the excellent traction in such arduous conditions, the mildly tuned Daimler superbly driven actually overtook the whole Mercedes team travelling at over 100 mph on sections of the route south of Paris. Although unplaced in the overall result, the Daimler Straight-Eight finished the course with honour.

Yet again a Daimler Straight-Eight was the leading Hooper exhibit at the 1952 Earls Court show. This was built to the order of Sir Bernard Docker and was primarily designed for long distance touring. It was capable of accommodating a considerable amount of luggage. The external lines of the body were quite simple with a roof sloping gently back from the highest point above the screen to merge into the top of the luggage compartment, with the front wings tapering on a gentle slope throughout the entire length of the car, their darker paintwork continuing at running board level past the rear wheels. Similar to some other Hooper designs, this car had no rear wings as such and the flush sides tended to accentuate the length and breadth of the vehicle. At the front a 'smooth' appearance was gained by blending the head and pass lights into the wings and covering them with shaped 'Perspex'.

Triplex laminated heat-reflecting safety glass was used for the curved and raked windscreen and also for the rear quarter lights. The paintwork was in dual

The special fixed head coupé constructed and exhibited in 1952

Fitting for all occasions: above the Monte Carlo rally car and below a special open tourer conveying His Excellency, the Governor General of Nigeria

For the open cars already in their possession, the Governments of Australia and New Zealand commissioned Hooper & Co to make detachable 'Perspex' tops which were used on the 1953–4 Commonwealth tour

tones of powder-blue and grey, the lighter panels being covered with a regular pattern of quatrefoil or four-leaf clover in the darker shade. The result was to give the car a graceful balance which prompted one contemporary writer to say of it – 'it is the most elegant thing at Earls Court'.

As an alternative to veneers, grey-blue lizard skin was used for the interior furnishings. With great skill the material was used for the steering wheel cover, door finishers and also for the cabinets flanking the 'arm-chair' type rear seats, for the instrument board and capping and for the armrests. To relieve what might otherwise have been a rather 'heavy' look, the skins were ingeniously matched (after the manner of veneers), so that texture variations were contrasted to great advantage.

The main windows and the rear quarter lights were all opened and closed electrically. A transparent sun-panel was set in the fore-part of the roof, with a cover on the under-side to blank off the light when desired.

Double glazing was again used to keep out heat, cold and noise, whilst thermal insulation was fitted to the roof. Nylon carpets were fitted throughout and when additional luggage space was required, the rear seats could be folded to provide the room.

Birmingham City Corporation were the recipients of this fine example

A masterpiece of coachbuilding and engineering combined! The Hooper Sedanca de ville, 1949 London show exhibit

Royal splendour – the visit to Coventry, 1956

Queen Elizabeth II and Prince Philip visiting Coventry, 1956: DE 36 Straight-Eight

CHAPTER 4

The Three-Litre Models

Prototypes chassis numbers 57000–57009
Type DF 300/1 chassis numbers 80000–80007
Type DF 302   chassis numbers 82000–82027
Type DF 303   chassis numbers 82400–82404

IN October 1950 a new Lanchester was announced. This was the 'Fourteen' –
(later, and with a number of modifications known as 'The Leda'). The purpose
of referring to this car is to note the dimensions of its 'new' 2-litre engine –
76·2 × 107·95 mm (1,968 cc). Whilst production of the Lanchester got under
way, development of another power unit of the same bore and stroke measurements was progressing. The result was an enlarged unit with six instead of four
cylinders and giving a capacity of 2,952 cc. This was placed into an entirely new
Daimler saloon which was completed in time for the 1951 Paris and London
shows.

The 'Regency', as the new arrival was named was a most attractive car and
the first of the series of 'modern Daimlers'.

At this time the 'Consort' 2½-litre was still in production and although there
were many similarities between the two engines, the 3-litre incorporated a number of new developments. Moreover, there were changes in the chassis and track
(the wheelbase remained unchanged at 9 feet 6 inches); and of course the body
owed but little to the well proved 'Consort'. To accommodate the larger engine
and provide an increase in leg room, the engine and gearbox were moved well
forward. Although ground clearance was increased by one inch to seven, the
chassis side members were actually slightly lowered.

For the express purpose of providing good low speed performance and consistent with the then prevailing inclination, the new bore-stroke ratio manifested
an approach towards the 'square' characteristic which ensued. It was claimed
that the 'Regency' performed some 10 to 15 per cent better than the 'Consort'
with a maximum speed in the region of 80 mph.

Following previous Daimler practice, the overhead valves were push-rod
operated and inclined slightly. The angle of the inclination, however, was
increased over earlier models by approximately a further five degrees. The
combustion chambers were of the same lozenge shape but were nevertheless,

The 3-litre 'Regency' saloon – (1952–3)

Mudguards disappear!

appreciably modified. The new unit produced 90 bhp at 4,100 rpm and the chassis for the saloon was designated 'DF 300' and 'DF 301' for left hand drive.

Considerable care was taken in the design of the new cylinder head to avoid distortion. The head bolts were placed well clear of the bores and of course ample cooling was provided. The water pump was so arranged as to direct coolant into the top of the block and from thence the flow was directed by jets on to the exhaust ports and sparking-plug bosses.

Separate ports were provided to all the valves and Brimachrome inserts were used for the exhaust valve seats. These were to ensure that there was no possibility of their becoming loosened even in the event of severe overheating caused by neglect. Brivadium cylinder liners were another feature making for longevity. Water-jacketing to the induction manifold was provided as on earlier models and

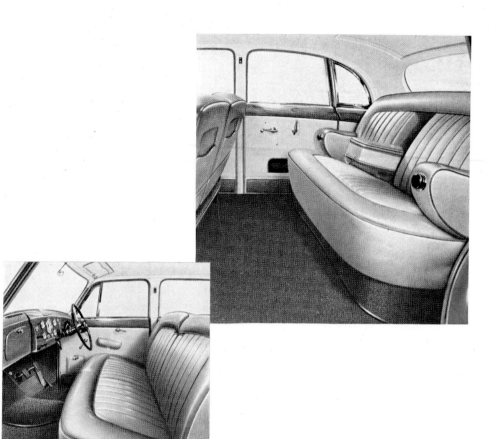

Catalogue illustrations

an interesting arrangement was incorporated for pressure balancing the two s u horizontal carburetters. From the air intake manifold, balance pipes led to the tops of the float chambers to eliminate excessive fuel consumption should the air cleaner become choked and further balance pipes lead to the area of the jets the object there being to prevent aeration of the fuel which might have occurred under certain conditions.

A four-bearing crankshaft, statically and dynamically balanced, was used and an innovation for the gearbox was the use of needle-roller bearings for the planetary gears. The ignition system incorporated not only the usual centrifugal advance and retard mechanism coupled to an overriding vacuum control, but also a manually operated control to enable adjustments to be made according to the grade of fuel available.

L

With the engine and gearbox well forward it was found to be desirable to use a divided propeller shaft of the Hardy Spicer open type with a flexible support in the centre. With worm-drive axles about to be rendered obsolete by the termination of the DB 18 models, hypoid bevel was the natural choice for the 'Regency'.

The chassis frame was of very robust design with deep box-section side members trussed by a channel-section cruciform structure in the centre, two tubular cross members at the rear, a similar cross member at the front and the massive pressed-steel structure at the front which also supported the suspension. Minor points of interest, were the lateral extensions for the four-point jacking system, a cradle just forward of the axle on the nearside carrying the battery and the very thorough silencing and exhaust system which passed through the cruciform member on the offside and incorporated two expansion chambers.

The front suspension system was basically similar to that employed on the 'Consort' – that is to say, it was of the independent coil type with single upper and lower transverse links of unequal length on each side supplemented by a stout radius arm running back to a pivot point on the chassis side member. A notable difference, however, was the use on the 'Regency' of telescopic dampers situate within the coil springs. To complete the arrangement there was a torsional anti-roll bar.

At the rear, long semi-elliptic springs were used but the width of these was increased to 2 inches as opposed to $1\frac{1}{2}$ inches as used on the 'Consort' with Newton telescopic dampers.

Girling hydro-mechanical brakes were used, as on the 'Consort' but these too were now increased in size giving a friction lining area of 202 square inches. The thermal automatic chassis lubricating system as previously employed was again used for this new model. The various points requiring lubrication were connected up to a central distribution system which incorporated an expansion chamber adjacent to the engine exhaust. Each time the engine warmed up from cold a supply of oil was pumped from the reservoir – the only items not covered by the system were the propeller shaft joints, water pump and the steering box.

The more modern body (built at Radford Works, Coventry, under the name of Barker & Co) – was designed to offer increased passenger comfort and space. When required three could be accommodated on the front seat and a similar number in the rear. The front seat was of the divided bench type and provided an internal width of 52 inches. The maximum width measurement in the rear was 56 inches. The seats were carefully shaped to provide full support both to the thighs and shoulders and were deeply upholstered and covered in best quality leather. In the front, adjustable armrests were fitted on the doors and in the rear fixed armrests at the sides (incorporating ash trays) were provided and in the centre there was a substantial folding armrest.

Due principally to the positioning well forward of the engine, the amount of leg room was generous and all occupants were seated within the wheelbase. Opening quarter lights were fitted to the front and rear windows and there was

SPECIFICATION

ENGINE: Six-cylinder o.h.v.; bore 3 ins. (76.2 mm.), stroke 4¼ ins. (107.95 mm.), capacity 2952 cc.; Coupé has aluminium cylinder head, compression ratios Saloon 6.7 to 1, Coupé 7.5 to 1; maximum b.h.p. Saloon 90, Coupé 100. Statically and dynamically balanced 4-bearing crankshaft; big-ends fitted with steel-backed white metal liners; four-ring pistons; full flow oil filter; thermostatically controlled engine cooling; twin horizontal S.U. carburettors; A.C. mechanical fuel pump; air-silencer (oil-bath air cleaner on export models); ignition by distributor with automatic advance and vacuum control, with overriding hand adjustment for varying grades of fuel.

TRANSMISSION: Daimler fluid transmission with pre-selective four-speed gearbox; hypoid bevel rear axle. Overall gear ratios Saloon: 17.54, 9.98, 6.71, 4.3 to 1, reverse 23.2 to 1. Coupé: 14.68, 7.76, 4.89, 3.46, reverse 15.46 to 1.

STEERING: Right- or left-hand drive; Marles worm and double roller; adjustable steering column.

SUSPENSION: Independent front by coil springs, half-elliptic rear; torsional stabilising bar at front; hydraulic telescopic shock absorbers.

BRAKES: Girling hydro-mechanical on 12 ins. (30.5 cm.) drums; pistol grip handbrake.

FRAME: Robust cruciform braced boxed type.

CHASSIS LUBRICATION: Thermal automatic chassis lubrication system.

WHEELS AND TYRES: Disc-type bolt-on wheels; 6.50 x 16 tyres; spare wheel and tyre under luggage boot.

ELECTRICAL: 12 volt, voltage controlled system; built-in headlamps; separate wing lamps; twin fog lamps; wind tone horns; combined tail and stop lamps in each rear wing; number plate lamp and reversing lamp. Dual windscreen wipers and trafficators with internal warning lamps.

INSTRUMENTS: Speedometer, fuel gauge, water temperature gauge, ammeter, oil and ignition warning lamps, clock. (Coupé has Rev. counter.)

FUEL TANKS: Saloon, capacity 16 gallons (19 U.S. gallons, 73 litres) including 1½ gallons (7 litres) reserve. Coupé, twin rear-wing tanks 7½ gallons (9 U.S. gallons, 34 litres) each.

AIR CONDITIONING: Built-in heater and demisters.

JACKING: Bevelift mechanical jacking system.

DIMENSIONS

REGENCY SALOON

	A	B	C	D	E	F	G	H	I	J
Saloon Ins.	114	191	70½	56	54½	1½	3½	19	13	38
Saloon Cms.	290	485	179	142	138	4	9	48	33	96.5
Coupé Ins.	114	194½	70½	56	51	2½	2½	18	13	39
Coupé Cms.	290	493	179	142	132	6	6	46	33	99

	K	L	M	N	O	P	Q	R	S
Saloon Ins.	13	19	56½	48	39½	57	71	—	
Saloon Cms.	33	48	143	122	100	145	180	—	
Coupé Ins.	13	18	50	43	35	57	71	45	
Coupé Cms.	25	46	130	112	86	145	180	107	

Overall height: Saloon 65 ins. (165 cms.), Coupé 61 ins. (155 cms.). Ground Clearance: Saloon and Coupé 7 ins. (18 cms.). Weight unladen: Saloon 4,100 lb. (1860 kg.), Coupé 4,140 lb. (1878 kg.).

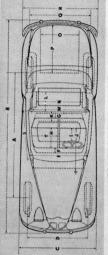

CONVERTIBLE COUPÉ

THE DAIMLER COMPANY LIMITED · COVENTRY · ENGLAND

The 3-litre Convertible coupé – 1952 and 1953

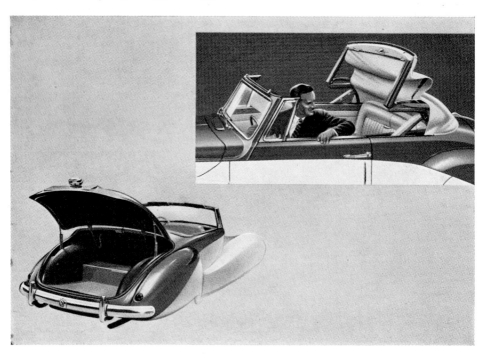

The 3-litre 'Regency' convertible coupé   The power-operated hood in action

a combined ventilating and heating unit built into the dash and so arranged as to draw fresh air from a fixed scuttle ventilator, with a reverse facing aperture to avoid water entering during driving rain. The usual demisting arrangements adjacent to the windscreen were provided. The screen itself was exceptionally wide, deep and sloped, thereby making the interior particularly light and forward vision above average. The rear window was also curved and of a reasonable size and all the pillars were comparatively narrow.

The Motor said of the fascia board that it

is in the typical Daimler tradition in that it sets off the air of luxury about the whole interior without any touch of extravagant ornamentation or departure from utility.

It was carried out in walnut, and the instruments were grouped on a central portion which protruded slightly from the rest. Equipment was particularly comprehensive and included a speedometer, fuel gauge, clock, ammeter and thermometer (all with round, clear faces), together with indicator lights for the trafficators, headlamps, engine lubrication system and ignition; neatly arranged were knobs and switches for the wipers, panel light, heater, lights, ignition, petrol reserve, mixture, hand throttle and starter. In the centre of the panel, provision was made for radio controls and there was also provision for one concealed speaker behind the head cloth above the windscreen and a second below the parcel shelf behind the rear squab.

The boot was of generous proportions and was covered with a spring loaded lid, hinged at the top and a separate compartment housed the spare wheel and tools.

Other notable details included twin fog lamps – recessed into the coachwork beneath the headlamps, pockets neatly concealed into the doors, a lockable petrol filler and a ball-bearing seat adjustment for ease of operation. The steering column was also adjustable for height. The basic cost of the car was £1,500, and with tax, a total of £2,334.16.8 was charged.

AND then . . . ! A year later in October 1952, at the Paris show, a most attractive derivation from the Regency made its debut. This was a 3-litre coach-built (by Barker & Co) Convertible coupé, in appearance very nearly identical to the highly successful 2½-litre Special Sports, but perhaps, even more elegant.

As standard equipment a power-operated hood was provided together with electric windows and a luggage boot lid which rose automatically when the opening handle was turned. The two-door body was fitted with bucket type front seats with centre armrests and in the rear a full width seat with central armrest was provided. The brochure asserted that the new model had been specially built for long distance high speed travel. To provide added impetus, the engine was given an aluminium head and a raised compression of 7·5 to 1 and the power output was increased to 100 bhp at 4,400 rpm. Further differences will be apparent from the specification. Like its 2½-litre predecessor, this convertible was given overdrive for the top ratio in the epicyclic box. This developed version was distinguished from the standard unit, DF 300/1 by the chassis type number DF 302/3.

An interesting arrangement was adopted for the spare wheel. First, twin fuel tanks were provided, one in each rear wing. The space thus made available under the boot was utilized to accommodate the spare wheel which was placed in a retractable cradle and by using the wheelbrace this could be lowered to the ground. In this manner a wheel could be changed whilst the boot was full of luggage.

No road test report for the Convertible coupé was published but visualise a little more power to the 2½-litre Barker sports. . . . To have sampled the car must have been a delightful experience. It was priced at £1,710 basic and £2,661.10.0 with tax.

Very few 3-litre chassis were built – certainly less than fifty and of those the greater number were DF 302's and went to Hooper & Co for special coachwork to be mounted. One Regency saloon was retained by the Company at Coventry and for many years used as a 'hack' around the factory premises and another – retaining its frontal originality but adapted to a truck, is at the time of writing still in use at the Company's London depot, although the original power unit has been replaced by a 3½-litre engine from a later model.

The 'Empress' on the 2½-litre special chassis (85 bhp) had proved so popular that Hooper & Co continued the model on the new 3-litre special series chassis (DF 302/3). The coachwork was slightly enlarged to conform to the new chassis and it now became a Six-Light sports saloon and in all respects a very desirable carriage. Clearly shown by the illustration are the well proportioned body, the graceful lines and distinctive appearance of the 'Empress'.

One such car, finished externally in two tones of green and mounted on chassis 82002 was exhibited by Hooper & Co at Earls Court in 1952 and like its 2½-litre predecessor, was highly commended by the Judges who awarded The Institute's silver medal.

The show Empress was trimmed in grey-green leather throughout, and with separate adjustable bucket seats at the front and a full width rear seat, five passengers could be carried in great comfort. Special features were included as in the earlier Empress. Of a total of some thirty-three Mk II 'Empresses' built on the Special Series 3-litre chassis, two were different in having only two doors.

On the same coachbuilders' stand at the 1953 show, there appeared a special two-seater fixed head coupé of entirely new design. The car,* made for Lady

*The motor show guide published by The Society of Motor Manufacturers and Traders and the contemporary journals described the car as being on a 'Daimler Special Series chassis'. Throughout Hooper's records pertaining to this car, reference is not only made to 'Special Series' but also specifically to a 3-litre chassis and moreover original photographs of 'Silver Flash' were similarly captioned. Had the chassis number been 82001 no difficulty would have arisen but the number recorded is in fact 85001 and although it creates a conflict of evidence, it should probably be concluded that the car was not constructed on a 3-litre DF 302 chassis as hitherto assumed, but on one of the prototype 2½-litre Century chassis; see also the footnote at commencement of Chapter 6.

The Daimler Empress Mark II (3-litre) by Hooper & Co

Front and rear views of 'Silver Flash' – 1953

*The front compartment
of the 'Silver Flash'*

The rear of 'Silver Flash'

Century, Empress, One-O-Four and Sportsman exhibited at the 1955 Paris show

Docker – wife of the BSA group chairman, and herself a director of Hooper & Co – was first painted dark green then shortly before the opening date of the show it was repainted in metallic silver. Lady Docker 'christened' this model 'Silver Flash'.

The specially constructed aluminium alloy body (no. 9966) was comparatively light and the overall height was kept as low as possible. A large one-piece curved windscreen and 'Sundym' glass roof panel were fitted and a shutter was provided to cover internally the roof panel when so required.

The whole car was of somewhat unusual appearance but notably the front end where the traditional Daimler radiator surround was completely restyled in a manner not so very different from the style adopted for the Jaguar–Daimler $2\frac{1}{2}$-litre v 8 production saloons to appear several years later.

Black leather with fine red piping was used for the trimming but the instrument board and all other interior finishes were covered with red crocodile.

The suitcases built into the rear compartment were also covered in red crocodile and were held in position by matching straps with floor attachments. In a shallow sliding tray in the nearside of the instrument panel there was a hinge-over mirror, silver powder compact, cigarette case, lighter and clothes brush. Other features were: the spare wheel was carried in a 'screw-down' cradle, as on the Regency saloon; detachable covers partly concealing the rear wheels; radio, demister, screen wash equipment; heating and ventilating unit; special instruments – the speedometer was calibrated to 120 mph, although it is rather unlikely that the needle ever pointed very accurately to this figure!

The car measured 16 feet 8 inches in length and 6 feet in width and weighed about 36 cwt.

A rather similar looking two-door two-seater saloon had, in March 1952, been constructed for Lady Docker by Hoopers (body no. 9856 on the 3-litre prototype chassis 57004).

CHAPTER 5

The 'Regency Mk II', 3½-litre 'Sportsman', 'One-O-Four', 'Lady's Model' and 'Empress' IIA and III

Type DF 304/5 chassis numbers 88000–88010; 88250–88633*
Type DF 306/7 chassis numbers 91450–91474
Type DF 308/9 chassis numbers 91475–91507
Type DF 310/1 chassis numbers 88700–89057;
90000–90016 (One-O-Four model);
96850–96898 (Lady's model)
Type DF 314 chassis numbers 90100–90234

In October 1954, the Company announced for the following year a production programme to include no fewer than ten models. Among these was the Regency Mk II (DF 304/5). Although mechanically very similar to the 3-litre 'Regency', the new power unit was enlarged to 3½ litres (3,468 cc) by increasing the bore from 75·2 to 82·55 mm. The compression ratio was actually slightly reduced to 6·5 to 1 but the net power output was raised from 90 to 107 bhp.

Notwithstanding the retention for the new car of track and wheelbase dimensions identical to those used for the obsolete version, the Mk II appeared to be and was in fact a much bigger car. A more elongated and sleeker body design was conceived and this accounted for an extra 5 inches in the overall length (16 feet 4 inches). The impression of length was accentuated by a reduction of 2¼ inches in the height of the car. As can be appreciated from a comparison of the photographs, the frontal appearance of the new car differed considerably from its predecessor. Deeper bumpers added to the overall pleasing appearance of the car – undoubtedly a Daimler – and yet conforming to the contemporary style.

As before the camshaft was carried on four steel-backed, white-metal bearings and was driven from the front end of the crankshaft by a triplex roller chain. Steel-backed white-metal bearings were also used for the big ends and the four main bearings. Integral balance weights were fitted to the crankshaft and of course it was statically and dynamically balanced and torsional vibrations were mitigated by a Metalastic bonded rubber type of damper combined with the

*It is believed that the DF 304/5 chassis bearing the under-mentioned numbers were re-categorized and given new numbers, when the high performance units were introduced: 88541, 88543, 88555–7, 88582–6, 88591, 88593, 88595, 88597/8, 88600, 88602/3, 88605, 88607/8, 88610–16, 88618, 88621/2, 88624–31

The 'One-O-Four' Lady's model

pulley for the fan and dynamo drive. The big ends of the H-sectioned connecting rods were split diagonally and the gudgeon pins were located in the little ends by pinch bolts. The carburation and induction arrangements followed the usual post-war Daimler practice and were almost identical to the layout of the 3-litre unit. Other engine and suspension details do not merit particular mention for in most respects they differed but little from the earlier example.

From the epicyclic gearbox, the drive was taken by a divided Hardy Spicer open propeller shaft with a centre steady-bearing to a Hypoid rear axle.

Apart from extensions to cope with the added length the chassis frame was also virtually a replica of the DF 300. Braking was on the Girling hydro-mechanical system working on 12-inch drums with a pistol grip handbrake. Tyres, $6·50 \times 16$ were fitted – as on the previous model. On the Mk II the fuel tank capacity was enlarged from 16 to 18 gallons.

The interior of the new Regency was replanned to give a little more room all round and picnic tables were added to the back of the front seats as standard equipment.

£1,640 was the basic price of the car but with purchase tax the model cost a total of £2,324.9.2 (January 1955). Radio was offered as an optional extra.

The Motor, when testing the car compared it with the 2½-litre Conquest and noted that the mean maximum speed of both varied by only 1 mph, the speed on gradients of 1 in 10, 1 in 15 and 1 in 20 also differed by only 1 mph and the zero to 50 mph acceleration time favoured the 3½-litre car by the narrow margin of 0·9 sec. It might therefore be concluded that the larger car was specifically designed for those customers who had experienced the satisfaction afforded by the Conquest, but who now expressed a preference for a larger and more dignified car with greater luggage accommodation and who were prepared to pay for such benefits in terms of greater weight and insurance costs and less fuel economy.

202

The Regency (like other models at the time), differed somewhat from other contemporary cars in having its engine and gearbox set comparatively well back in the frame with the result that the load was equally distributed, with a full tank and two passengers, over front and rear wheels. The fuel tank was mounted transversely over the rear axle. The steering characteristic was almost neutral but responded quickly and safely. *The Motor* praised the car in this respect and commented that it was a particularly safe car in extreme conditions such as their test staff encountered with the car on the Continent. The test itself contained the following paragraph:

There is also the pleasing feeling that should the highest possible speed on a corner be over-estimated the ensuing quickly-corrected tail slide will reduce the speed almost immediately to a stable figure and in a wholly safe manner. The experience of driving the car over many hundreds of miles of ice and snow during the course of the continental tests, stood in direct contrast to these considerations. Even under conditions in which a number of other cars could be seen travelling backwards or leaving the road altogether, the Daimler never once gave any indication of getting out of control, and forward speeds of 30 mph or over could be maintained steadily. The Regency is, in fact, a car with handling characteristics which will be enjoyed by all critical motorists, but especially by experienced buyers who may find the powerful understeering qualities of many modern cars unsettling. A woman might find the parking effort high.

The report continued with a description of the interior design and appointments giving high praise for the generous passenger accommodation, driving position, comfort and general quality. *The Motor* found there to be very little roll, a complete absence of pitch and no noise from the tyres when cornering. At a mile a minute the car proved to be exceptionally smooth and quiet.

No road test of a post-war Daimler produced before 1957 would be complete without special mention of the Daimler transmission. Without exception the unique features of the epicyclic gearbox coupled with the fluid flywheel never failed to receive a special mention by the testers and invariably one finds in contemporary reports well deserved complimentary remarks. In the case of the 'Regency Mk II' the report author recalled that the system had been in use for more than a quarter of a century and was the pioneer of all subsequent automatic transmissions, but, said the writer, – 'this should not lead to the conclusion that it is now outmoded. On the contrary, it retains one or two desirable features which are not offered by any alternative arrangement. One is that the engagement of any ratio is entirely under the control of the driver and as a corollary, direct drive in top can be retained over the whole speed range. Thus, in heavy traffic, unwanted gear changes (such as are provided by automatic systems) are eliminated and on slippery roads the car can be started from rest without developing wheelspin, and the speed discreetly checked by engaging third or second gear.'

The established practice of including automatic chassis lubrication (of the thermal type) was continued. Single or duo-tone colours were available over quite a large range.

SPECIFICATION OF THE NEW *Daimler Regency Mk II* WITH 3½ OR 4½ LITRE ENGINE

3½ Litre ENGINE—Six-cylinder; O.H.V.; bore 3¼ in. (82·55 mm.); stroke 4¼ in. (107·95 mm.); capacity 3468 c.c.; compression ratio 6·5 : 1; cast-iron cylinder head; 4 bearing crankshaft, statically and dynamically balanced; big ends fitted with steel backed white metal liners; heat treated aluminium alloy pistons; triplex chain driven camshaft supported in 4 bearings having steel backed, white metal liners; lubrication by gear type pump driven from camshaft by skew gear; full-flow oil filter incorporates safety by-pass valve while a pressure relief valve is fitted in the gallery; all main bearings pressure fed, metered feed to overhead valve gear; cooling by water pump and fan, system is thermostatically controlled and cools exhaust seats and sparking plug bosses; two horizontal carburettors; mechanical petrol pump with hand priming lever; 12 volt coil ignition, distributor has automatic advance with overriding vacuum control for part throttle operation, also vernier adjustment for varying grades of fuel.

4½ Litre ENGINE—Six-cylinder; O.H.V.; bore 3¾ in. (95·25 mm.); stroke 4¼ in. (107·95 mm.); capacity 4617 c.c.; compression ratio 6·53 : 1; other 4½ litre engine mechanical details as for 3½ litre engine.

TRANSMISSION—Daimler fluid transmission to latest design incorporating fluid flywheel and pre-selector epicyclic gearbox providing four speeds forward with ratios 4·08 : 1, 2·32 : 1, 1·56 : 1, 1 : 1 and reverse speed ratio of 5·4 : 1 for the 3½ litre engine, and 4 forward speeds (including overdrive) with ratios of 3·00 : 1, 1·62 : 1, 1 : 1; ·709 : 1 and reverse speed ratio of 3·39 : 1 for the 4½ litre engine; two open propeller shafts with needle roller universal joints flexibly supported at centre; hypoid rear axle with ratio of 4·3 : 1 (3½ litre engine) and 4·27 : 1 (4½ litre engine).

STEERING—Cam and roller mechanism with 18·7 : 1 ratio; telescopic adjustable steering column with 18 in. diameter spring spoked wheel.

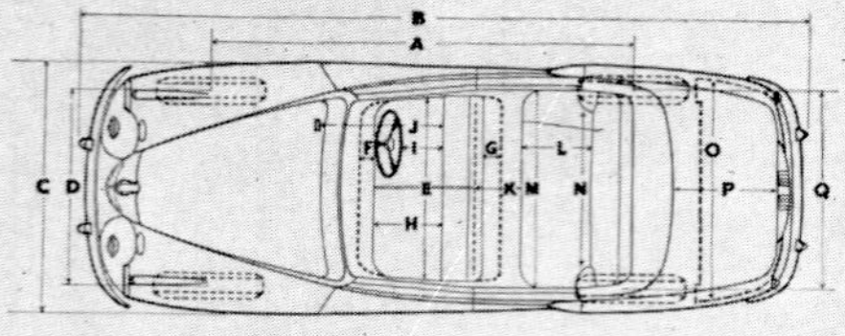

	A	B	C	D	E	F	G	H	I
Ins.	114	196	70½	56	55½	2½	2½	18	13
Cms.	285	490	176·25	140	139	6·25	6·25	45	32·5
	J	K	L	M	N	O	P	Q	
Ins.	38	14	19	57½	48	63	22½	57	
Cms.	95·0	40	47·5	144	120	161	56·25	142·5	

Note:—Dimension D is 57¼" (143 cm.) on 4½ litre chassis.

SUSPENSION—Independent front suspension using coil springs; half-elliptic springs at rear; hydraulic telescopic shock absorbers front and rear; torsional stabilising bar at front.

BRAKES—Hydro-mechanical operation on 3½ litre engined chassis, vacuum servo assisted hydraulic operation on 4½ litre engined chassis; 12 in. diameter drums; pistol grip hand brake mounted on dash.

FRAME—Cruciform braced box section for rigidity and strength; automatic thermal chassis lubrication system; built-in jacking points.

WHEELS AND TYRES—Disc bolt-on type wheels 16 in. x 5½ in. K; 6·5 in. x 16.00 in. tyres on 3½ litre chassis; 16 in. x 6 in. L; wheels and 7·00 in. x 16·00 in. tyres on 4½ litre chassis.

ELECTRICAL EQUIPMENT—Starter motor; 12 volt voltage controlled dynamo; 64 amp./hr. battery; headlamps and flasher direction indicators built into front wings; separate wing lamps; foot operated dipper switch; wind-tone horns; tail/stop/flasher direction indicator and reversing lamps built into each rear wing; rear number plate illumination lamp; dual windscreen wipers, two-speed and self parking; interior roof lamp.

INSTRUMENTS—Petrol gauge; revolution indicator; speedometer; water temperature gauge; ammeter; clock.

FUEL—Petrol tank situated in rear boot with reserve control on fascia board; capacity 18 gallons (81·9 litres) including reserve.

BODY—Six light, four door, six seater saloon; luggage boot at rear with spare wheel in separate tray below; pivoting front ventilators and rear quarter lights; curved windscreen and rear screen; exterior and interior fittings finished in chromium; separate, adjustable front seats with walnut folding tables in rear squabs; real leather upholstery; high quality, toning carpets with felt underlays; built-in fresh air heater and demister unit; cool air ventilation to front compartment.

COLOURS—

DUO-TONE

Body above waist	*Body below waist*	*Upholstery*
Silver	Black	Grey
Silver	Maroon	Red
Silver	Blue	Blue
French Grey	Light Green	Beige
French Grey	Dark Green	Beige

OR ALTERNATIVE SINGLE COLOUR

Body	*Upholstery*
Silver	Red or Blue
Black	Red, Green, Beige
Maroon	Red
Blue	Blue
Light Green	Beige
Dark Green	Green

GENERAL DIMENSIONS—

3½ Litre Chassis		
Ground clearance (unladen)	6 in.	(15·24 cm.)
Overall height	5 ft. 2¾ in.	(159·38 cm.)
Weight (dry)	1 ton 15 cwt. 2 qrs.	(1805 kgs.)
Kerb weight	1 ton 17 cwt.	(1880 kgs.)
Turning circle	42 ft.	(12·8 metres).
4½ Litre Chassis, as above except:		
Weight (dry)	1 ton 17 cwt.	(1880 kgs.)
Kerb weight	1 ton 18 cwt. 2 qrs.	(1955 kgs.)

CONDITIONS OF SALE

Daimler cars are offered subject to the Conditions of Sale set out in the Company's Purchase Agreement Form. The right is reserved to alter any detail of price, specification or equipment without notice.

THE DAIMLER COMPANY LIMITED · COVENTRY · ENGLAND

PRINTED IN ENGLAND BY J. HOWITT AND SON LTD.

PUBLICATION NO. R27/010/169

The Regency Sportsman

The 'Sportsman' or 'Four-Light' saloon

The new Regency was generally well received but with 84–85 mph as its top speed it was inevitable that it should be subjected to modification.

Therefore, almost from the inception of the new range, a slightly more powerful version (D F 306/7) was produced as the basis for the continued Empress – now the Mk IIA. In this form the power yield was 114 bhp at 4,000 rpm and like the unit previously employed to power the Empress Mk II, the additional urge was obtained by using an aluminium head and increasing the compression from 6·5 to 1 to 7·6 to 1.

Then followed D F 308/9, which with further slight modifications, produced 130 bhp at 4,200 rpm and was the basis for the 'Regency Sportsman' as illustrated above. This differed from the standard saloon in a number of respects.

First as regards external appearance – the 'Sportsman' was a Four-Light saloon of Mulliner design and construction but finished by The Daimler Co. The most notable distinguishing features were to be seen at the rear. A large curved wrap-round rear window blended in well with the body shape, the boot lid was angled more sharply than on the Regency saloon, detachable covers were fitted over the rear wheels and the back wings terminated in 'fins' each housing separate rear and turn indicator lights, reversing light and reflector. A continuous line was created by flowing the front wings into the body with a gradual sweep through the doors and down to the extremity of the tail. Two inches were added to the overall length.

Without being flamboyant, the Sportsman's appearance was individualistic, well pleasing to most, and yet once again, unmistakably a Daimler.

Whereas the Regency saloon had a normal four speed gearbox, the arrangement on the Sportsman (and on the Empress IIA) was to make third the direct gear and top (in effect) overdrive with a ratio of 0·706 to 1. Moreover, the hypoid rear axle on the Sportsman had a reduction ratio of 4·89 as compared with 4·3 on the standard Regency. Vacuum servo assisted Girling hydraulic brakes were fitted.

Internally the layout was very similar to that in the saloon. In some, special insulation material was placed above the roof head lining. Picnic tables were of course fitted and the fascia in most instances, but not all, differed from the standard layout in that it was of the style adopted for the subsequent 'Lady's Model'. In October 1954, the inclusive price of the Sportsman 3½-litre was £2,650. It may be mentioned that various models in the 'Regency' range were at this time offered with an alternative 4½-litre engine but these are described in a separate chapter.

Where specialist coachwork was to be mounted, it was normal to have either a DF 306/7 or DF 308/9 chassis in preference for the standard DF 304/5 type. Apart from 'Empresses', Hoopers made only one body no. 10023 – a two-door saloon on a 3½-litre DF 306 chassis no. 91452.

One or two 3½-litre chassis went abroad to have non-standard coachwork mounted. The car illustrated opposite was built to special order by Beutler of Switzerland. It was a full four–five seater convertible coupé with a power-operated hood.

Announced for the 1955 London show, were a new series of faster Daimlers. In the 3½-litre range the Regency was renamed the 'One-O-Four' (104 mph was the maximum recorded speed of the prototype – hence the name!) but this represented more than a mere change in nomenclature. The modified frame (DF 310/1) was fitted with a new I-beam cruciform member and improved body mountings at the front to provide a more rigid structure. In addition vacuum-servo assisted two trailing shoe hydraulic brakes were standard equipment and the rear axle ratio was raised to 3·92 to 1 or optionally a high axle ratio of 3·64 to 1 could be specified – principally for fast touring work. From 107 bhp the power was raised to 137 bhp at 4,400 rpm.

Beutler coachwork on the 3½-litre chassis

The 'Empress' by Hooper & Co in its ultimate 3½-litre form (1956–7)

M

An aluminium head was employed with improved porting and manifolding together with a quick-lift camshaft and the latest diaphragm type su carburettors. A substantial pull-up handbrake was given a place on the floor to the right of the driver's seat (similar to the arrangement on the 1935 Daimler 'Fifteen'!). Other detailed improvements concerned a modification to the rear side armrests to facilitate easier access, the fitting of tread plates on the door steps, the provision of courtesy lights operated on any door being opened and a light within the boot also automatically operated when the lid was raised. In the boot the tools were now carried in a specially designed wing recess within a good quality case, and other small changes within the boot gave an additional $2\frac{1}{2}$ inches interior length. A new material was used therein to enable easier cleaning and the spare wheel tray was also modified to render it virtually invisible from the rear of the car. From that viewpoint it would also have been observed that a 'D' medallion with traditional Daimler fluting appeared in a central position on the substantial bumper. A further visible change concerned the fitting of a flatter style of hub cap. The front side armrests were omitted to give extra width but the central rests were retained. Burr walnut was used for the fascia, door cappings and picnic tables in the 'One-O-Four' and flush fitting lids were fitted over the storage recesses in the doors.

All these improvements combined to transform the attractive 'Regency Mk II' into an outstandingly good 'One-O-Four'. The maker's claim of 100 mph was found on test to be justified with a small excess!

When announced in October 1955 the basic price of a 'One-O-Four' was £1,885 and with the addition of tax the final figure was £2,671.10.10. When in production the inclusive figure was adjusted to £2,395, at one stage it fell to £2,260, and at the other end of the scale, the highest price was probably £2,828 in June 1956.

In its final $3\frac{1}{2}$-litre form the Empress (Mk III) was built on the DF 308 chassis but fourteen only were produced. When the 'One-O-Four' appeared the 'Sports-man' continued as the 'Four-Light' saloon and was built on the DF 310/1 chassis. Just as it had been suggested that the 'Regency' was the $3\frac{1}{2}$-litre equivalent to the Conquest so a like analogy may be claimed between the 'One-O-Four' and the 'Century'.

THE LADY'S MODEL   The Maker's brochure acclaimed:

The special $3\frac{1}{2}$-litre One-O-Four Lady's Model is lavishly equipped especially for the Lady motorist and yet – by ingenious design – retains the appearance and performance of the standard One-O-Four which make it eminently suitable for business occasions. In company with other models included in the 'One-O-Four' series this car is capable of 100 mph, has vivid acceleration, servo-assisted brakes and excellent road holding properties to match its high speed. However, by virtue of the Daimler fluid transmission it will glide along leisurely, in and out traffic, uphill and downhill without the need to change gear – in fact the simplest one-gear drive. All the unique features of the standard One-O-Four described on earlier pages, are retained in the Lady's model and in addition the special fittings illustrated overleaf are incorporated.

The 'traditional' interior of the
'Empress' Mark IIA

A 3½-litre Empress but with rounded rear quarter window. Shown on the Hooper stand at the
1954 Paris show

The illustrations which follow, reproduced from the brochure are self explanatory.

At the 1955 London exhibition this model (chassis 96851) painted in silver and black was shown and earned the Institute's silver medal (in Section 7) for standard enclosed coachwork – group D, i.e. enclosed British built cars costing between £1,550 and £3,500.

The 'thin end of the wedge' – so to speak, appeared in the autumn of 1956 in the guise of automatic transmission. Although Daimler transmission had been in

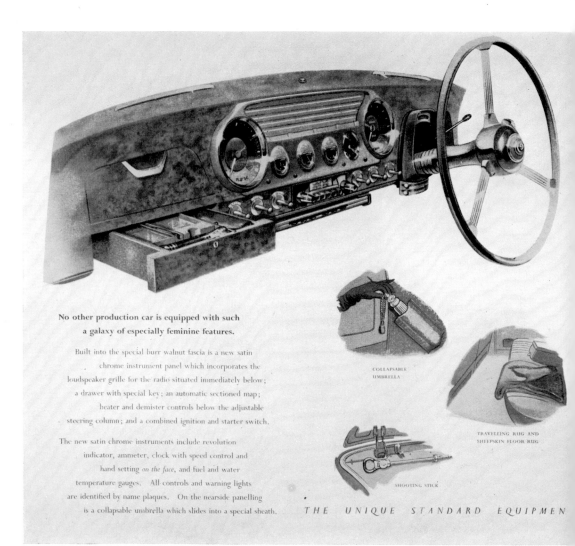

No other production car is equipped with such a galaxy of especially feminine features.

Built into the special burr walnut fascia is a new satin chrome instrument panel which incorporates the loudspeaker grille for the radio situated immediately below; a drawer with special key; an automatic sectioned map; heater and demister controls below the adjustable steering column; and a combined ignition and starter switch.

The new satin chrome instruments include revolution indicator, ammeter, clock with speed control and hand setting *on the face*, and fuel and water temperature gauges. All controls and warning lights are identified by name plaques. On the nearside panelling is a collapsable umbrella which slides into a special sheath.

COLLAPSABLE UMBRELLA

TRAVELLING RUG AND SHEEPSKIN FLOOR RUG

SHOOTING STICK

THE UNIQUE STANDARD EQUIPMEN

use for over twenty-five years it was still most satisfactory and ought not to have been regarded as obsolete. Nevertheless, automatic transmission was becoming fashionable in this country and it was accordingly considered to be expedient for this form of transmission to be offered – first as an alternative, but in a short space of time as 'standard'.

Traditional Daimler devotees both then and now lament the passing of the fluid flywheel and epicyclic gearbox with its distinctive whine in neutral. With the gratification of being able to note that of the two One-O-Four models tested,

ROLLED GOLD PENCIL,
NOTEPAD, TORCH, SUNGLASSES,
CIGARETTE PACKET HOLDER

VANITY CASE

Max Factor cosmetics comprise: dry rouge, foundation cream, lipstick, cleansing lotion, cologne, powder compact. Also included is a comb and cleansing tissues.

In the rear centre armrest is an ivory finish cosmetic case and, also in the rear compartment, a sheepskin floor rug and a double-texture all-wool travelling rug. On all doors, the windows are "push-button" power operated, whilst in the spacious luggage boot are ladies' and gents' aero-weight suitcases, a complete picnic case, an ice box and a shooting stick— additional to the attractive portable cabinet of cadmium plated tools.

PATENT, COLOURED,
SECTIONED MAP

POWER OPERATED
WINDOW BUTTONS

RIM EMBELLISHERS
AND TUBELESS TYRES

F THE LADY'S MODEL

the version with traditional Daimler transmission was slightly the faster, we can consider what *The Autocar* had to say on the matter:

Preselective gear change in the form of a fluid flywheel and Wilson gear box has been associated with the name of Daimler for many years. This enables the driver to select in advance the ratio required, and is still available on all the models produced by the company.

Since last year's London Show, however, the 3½-litre One-O-Four saloon has been produced with the Borg-Warner fully automatic system as an alternative bringing the Daimler in line with cars in a similar class. The new combination is a good and logical one and the automatic transmission

Wide doors which open to their fullest possible extent and a flat floor entirely free of obstruction combine to give you complete freedom of entrance and exit. Note how the new handbrake is out of the way, yet very accessible and easy to pull on hard.

The split bench type front seat—of generous proportions—is luxuriously upholstered in first quality leather and is equipped with folding centre armrests to provide additional comfort when the seat is used by two persons only. Each half is separately adjustable, running on rollers.

Burr walnut is used for window cappings and front screen surround, whilst the windows themselves are electrically controlled by push-buttons.

SPACIOUS,

is well suited to the 3½-litre engine. When compared with the last One-O-Four tested, the figures recorded for the latest car are slightly inferior. This discrepancy undoubtedly is caused by the greater proportion of engine power absorbed by the fully-automatic transmission. There is little difference in weight, and the fuel consumption is more or less unchanged.

Borg-Warner-equipped cars have featured in a number of recent Road Tests, but a brief description of the transmission as applied to the 3½-litre Daimler is justified. Basically the unit consists of a single-stage hydraulic torque converter with two epicyclic gear sets in series. There are three forward speeds — low, intermediate and direct drive. The driver selects the drive ratio by a

The rear interior includes all the refinements of the One-O-Four Saloon—upholstery in first selection leather; burr walnut occasional tables; ventilator windows; courtesy light in roof with over-riding switches; deep pile carpeting.

Special features of the Lady's Model are:

Exquisite vanity case which is concealed in centre arm rest but can be lifted out;

Sheepskin floor rug;

All-wool double texture travelling rug;

Polished burr walnut for the *entire* window surrounds;

Power operated windows to *all* doors.

LUXURIOUS AND ELEGANT

small lever which works in a quadrant mounted just below the steering wheel. The lever positions are marked with the now familiar symbols of P, N, D, L *and* R.

For normal driving the control is placed in the fully automatic position D, *and the gear changes are controlled thereafter by load and speed – but the driver can modify the change points by operation of the throttle. Take-off is in first gear which like second, is subject to modification of the mechanical gear ratio by the torque converter. The range thus varies in first between 9·1 and 19·5 and in second, 5·65 to 12·1. In direct drive the torque converter is out of circuit, the coupling between engine and output shaft being through a single plate clutch which is operative in this ratio only.*

There is a link between the ignition switch and the gear selector lever which permits the engine to be started only when the lever is in the 'park' or 'neutral' positions. When in 'park' the lever mechanism allows a pawl to engage with a notched ring on the gearbox output shaft – a useful provision when stationary on steep gradients. A safety device prevents engagement at speeds above walking pace. A similar system protects the mechanism if reverse is selected inadvertently.

On the car tested the engine gave a consistently easy start from cold, and the hand throttle control on the fascia enabled a fast tick-over to be used for warming up. This obviated, to a great extent the annoying stalling which can occur sometimes with a car equipped with automatic transmission, when moving off with a cold engine.

Driving a car – especially one of the Daimler's size – with automatic transmission is comparatively simple. Once the selector has been placed in 'drive' and the throttle depressed, changes take place progressively and smoothly between low, intermediate and top.

Normal acceleration from rest with the Daimler allowed changes to take place between approximately 10 mph and 20 mph from low, and from intermediate to top between 20 mph and 40 mph. Occasionally, and mostly in town traffic, there seemed to be a reluctance to change to top.

This was readily overcome by releasing the throttle, when the change would take place. In comparison with other identical transmissions, the gear box of the Daimler tested produced a slight but not unpleasant whine which was noticeable only when other noises were at a minimum.

Maximum speed on low was 45 mph, limited of course by engine speed; the maximum for intermediate is governed by the automatic change point, which occurred in this instance at 57 mph. The car's maximum speed was slightly below that of the similar model tested with the pre-selective change. A true speed of 98 mph was held for some five miles of high-speed road, with the car speedometer steady at 100 mph.

This is a very creditable figure for a full five-seater saloon which makes no pretence at being a sports car. During the test many miles were covered on the Continent at the maximum possible speed. The Daimler proved itself capable of cruising at 85 to 90 mph without fuss and in a manner expected of this class of vehicle. The owner of such a car is more likely to be interested in comfort at a cruising speed which can be used on trans-Continental journeys, than in a very high maximum speed figure.

As is customary with the Borg-Warner transmission, the accelerator pedal of the Daimler is coupled to a kick-down switch. Pressure on the pedal past the full throttle opening at speeds below approximately 50 mph produced good acceleration from the consequent automatic change from drive to intermediate.

The car was comfortable, and the suspension in the main was good. There were one or two occasions during the hard driving on the Continent when rapid vertical movement of the wheels could be felt; this was only when driving fast on uneven cobbled roads with a severe camber. On all other surfaces the suspension behaved very well. There was little noticeable roll when cornering at speed; it was evident that the manufacturers had decided upon the right compromise between sports car tautness and the high standard of comfort associated with their products.

A unique fixed-head coupé by Ghia–Aigle of Switzerland on a 3½-litre Daimler chassis – 1955

Another view of the Ghia–Aigle car

So far the assessment has been on the 3½-litre's behaviour at speed. This Daimler is equally good when driven quietly. The freedom from wind and road noises is very noticeable. It was found that the Daimler was as easy to handle in country lanes and in city traffic as when driven fast on a trunk road. The driving position is very good. Separate front seats, with folding central armrests, are provided; slightly more support for the driver's legs was thought desirable. The comparatively upright position proved comfortable at all times and there was favourable comment on the forward visibility.

From the driving seat, the top of each side lamp can be seen, and at night the minute red pilot lens in each lamp acts as a guide to the width of the car. The screen pillars are not over-thick, and *slope so that they tend to be out of the driver's eye line. There is telescopic adjustment of the steering column, which with the seat can be set quickly to suit drivers of most heights and arm lengths.*

The steering was quite light at speed but heavy in manoeuvring – a good case for power assistance. Neither under nor oversteer characteristics were noticeable. It was found necessary to make frequent corrections of course at maximum speed, and this may have been to some extent attributable to a strong wind. There are four and a quarter turns of the wheel from lock to lock, but the turning circle is such that there is little difficulty in parking the car in a space just over its own length.

The brakes, which are vacuum servo assisted, are well up to the performance and weight of the car. Similar systems have produced a lighter feel at the pedal, but in general the results achieved with the 3½-litre Daimler equipment leave little to be desired. The system was smooth in action, showed no sign of fade during severe testing and was progressive at all times. The handbrake lever is well placed by the side of the driving seat.

The interior is well equipped for long-distance touring. There is a deep pocket with hinged cover in each door, a picnic table fitted in the back of each front seat, and there is a full complement of ashtrays. There is no cigarette lighter. A compartment in the left side of the facia has a lockable lid. There is an efficient heating and demisting system which can be supplemented by a blower fan. Hinged front and rear quarter lights can be opened to increase ventilation. On the car tested, there was a draught from the bottom of the front passengers' door.

The car is especially suitable for touring. There is good all round visibility and the large windows let plenty of light into the car. The winding handles are well placed and the handle on the right side front door does not interfere with the driver's movements. There is a commendable amount of leg room in the rear compartment, and the angle of the backrest and depth of the seat cushion were found to give a smooth, restful ride.

The Daimler is one of the few cars which have built-in chassis lubrication.

Maintenance is simplified by the accessibility of the ignition system and the petrol pump. The battery is housed in a compartment beneath the rear seat cushion, but a two-pin socket in the engine compartment allows a charger to be connected to the battery when required.

Inside the luggage locker – wide and deep, but short fore and aft – is ample room for several suitcases. The interior is lined and a lamp operates when the lid is opened. Luggage has to be lifted over the rather high rear edge of the locker. In addition to small tools fitted in a shaped case, the jack and wheel changing tools are stowed in the locker.

Comfort and conservative good looks are built in this Daimler. It is designed for the owner–driver who requires quality with a better than average performance, and the automatic transmission will help to widen its market.

(In April 1957 the total price of the car was £2,580)

As above mentioned, the 'One-O-Four' with Daimler transmission was known as the type DF 310 or 311 if fitted with left hand steering. There was no production model which was ascribed the serial nos. 312/3, but the automatic transmission version of the 3½-litre 'One-O-Four' was given the type number 'DF 314'. One or two – probably not more, automatic versions of the 'Sportsman' or 'Four-Light' saloon were made.

The unique Hooper two-door 'Continental' saloon shown opposite was painted green all over except for the roof which was in light biscuit. The car was shown at Earls Court in 1956.

When first the car was conceived, those responsible for its design had in mind

The Hooper bodied Daimler 'Continental' saloon – 1956

the possibility of it being a competitor to the highly esteemed and more expensive Bentley Continental.

The first proposal was to use the 4½-litre Four-Light chassis (DF 402) and in fact such a chassis was allocated and delivered to the coachbuilders but in the event opportunity was taken to demonstrate the new type DF 314 with automatic transmission.

The special body (no. 10205) was as light and strong as possible and so far as practicable it incorporated a number of the features to be found on the corresponding Bentley. For example, the treatment for the exclusion of draughts and dust and insulation against noise and fumes were exactly as specified for the 'other' car.

The overall length of the completed car was 17 feet 3 inches, its width 5 feet 11½ inches and was only 5 feet 1 inch in height. To accommodate the extra length, the chassis frame was specially extended and because of the lower bonnet line a modified radiator was fitted and a special long starting handle had to be made! Notwithstanding the increased dimensions, the actual total weight – 35 cwt 2 qr, was considerably less than that of the standard 'One-O-Four' saloon.

Two bucket type seats were fitted to the front with hinged backs, adjustable for angle and in the rear, seating for two in extreme comfort, or occasionally for three passengers was provided. When not in use the rear seats could be folded to accommodate extra luggage. As part of the design more leg room was afforded within the Daimler than in the Bentley.

No occasional tables were provided. The instrument board was specially designed to avoid all sharp edges and corners and was well padded. Black faced instruments were used and radio, cigar lighter and ashtrays were included. No chromium mouldings were fitted, but instead untarnishable fitments were specified. Lightweight window lifts were installed and in the bottom of each door was a large open recess.

Triplex 'Sundym' heat reflecting laminated glass was specified for the back light and windscreen. For the woodwork, Eucalyptus burr walnut was used. The head and side lights were built into the nose of each wing, hooded at the top to minimize the upward throw of light beams in mist or rain. Above the lights, but still within the hood were housed specially designed air intakes.

Although in the design stage it was contemplated that the model might be put into limited production, the project, unfortunately, did not materialize.

CHAPTER 6

The Conquest and Century models

Type DJ 250/1 chassis numbers 82500–84999; 84500–84540; 85050–87076
Type DJ 252/3 chassis numbers 87550–87781; 87798/9
*Type DJ 254/5 chassis numbers 90450–90497; 90850–90866 (Roadster);
    90500–90553 (Drophead Coupé)
Type DJ 256/7 chassis numbers 90950–91349; 91350–91416; 91700–92699;
    92975–93974; 95000–95999; 96500–96849; 97050–97303
Type DJ 260/1 chassis numbers 97550–98049; 98050–98296

Any new model from the old established Daimler Company constitutes an event of considerable note. The new 2½-litre Daimler Conquest, which is being publicly announced today, will command widespread attention for the way in which traditions established in the earliest days have been blended with current ideas and requirements.   (*The Motor* – 6th May 1953)

The new model, which was fairly small by Daimler standards, was designed for the professional and business man who required high quality and good finish, coupled with accommodation for the family and good performance but who did not want an unduly large car nor one too expensive to run. Contemporaneous reports mentioned that the car was designed and brought into production within a period of four months. However, the basic chassis frame, suitably adapted, together with most of the body pressings were identical with those used for the Lanchester Leda.

The main item that was entirely new, was the engine. The unit was of the typical Daimler layout and post-war design with cylinder dimensions of 76·2 × 88·9 mm (2,433 cc), the bore was the same diameter as that of both the 2-litre Lanchester Leda and the 3-litre Daimler Regency, but the stroke was considerably shorter resulting in a bore-stroke ratio of 0·856 to 1. The cast-iron cylinder block and crank-chamber were of very stiff construction and were well ribbed to support the four main bearings. The bores were completely surrounded by water jackets which extended well below the exposed portion when the piston was at the bottom of its stroke. Dry liners were used and they were fine bored and honed into position. Great care was taken in positioning the cylinder head stud bosses so that no distortion was caused to the bores when the head was tightened down.

*The prototypes of the high-performance cars (92 bhp, later 100 bhp) were given chassis nos. commencing 85000, except for the two chassis upon which the Lanchester Dauphins were constructed, these being numbered 70006 and 70007 respectively.

The Daimler Conquest (1953)

The bottom of the crank chamber was enclosed by a deep cast light alloy sump with a baffle plate in the rear section around the oil pump. The crankshaft itself was of substantial construction. Balance weights were placed at the ends of the shaft, outside numbers one and six big end bearings and also on the outside of numbers three and four between the two centre main bearings. A Metalastik torsional vibration damper was fitted to the front of the crankshaft. Incidentally the crankshaft weighed $49\frac{1}{2}$ lb–26 lb less than that in the Consort!

All the four main bearings were $2\frac{1}{4}$ inches in diameter and had a bearing length of $1\frac{1}{4}$ inches and the steel backed white metal bearings were all interchangeable. Dowels were employed to position the main bearing caps, and thrust was taken by two semi-circular thrust washers placed in recesses, one on each side of the front main bearing cap.

The big end bearings were 2 inches in diameter and had a bearing length of $\frac{15}{16}$ inch. The H-section connecting rods measured $6\frac{1}{2}$ inches between centres and to facilitate assembly they were split on an angle so that the big end would pass through the cylinder bore. Like the main bearings the big end bearings were of steel-backed white metal and similarly the camshaft was supported in four main bearings. Chilled cast iron was used for the shaft itself and the cams were of a special design that provided a uniform acceleration; they permitted fast valve opening to ensure good breathing. The cam form also helped to reduce spring surge; the valve gear was quiet in operation and only one spring per valve was used. The camshaft was driven by duplex chain. The remainder of the overhead valve gear was quite conventional, $\frac{7}{8}$ inch diameter piston-type tappets (with an escape hole to prevent oil becoming trapped) used with tubular push rods, which had hardened end plugs and case hardened rockers pivoted direct on the rocker shaft.

The lubrication system was fed by a double gear pump placed low down and towards the rear of the engine and driven by a spindle geared to the camshaft. From the pump, oil passed through an outlet drilled in the crankcase into the full-flow filter bolted on the nearside of the engine. After passing through the filter (fitted with a by-pass valve) the oil passed through another drilling in the crankcase to the main oil gallery – a $\frac{5}{8}$ inch diameter hole running the length of the block.

Oil to the overhead valve gear was metered by a cast-in groove running half way round the rear camshaft journal. This allowed an intermittent supply to pass through a drilling in the bearing and block to an internal pipe connected by means of a banjo to the hollow rocker spindle. This was cross-drilled to lubricate the rockers.

Following the usual practice employed by Daimlers, a warning light operated by a pressure switch was used in place of a gauge and a relief valve was incorporated in the system and was set to blow at 40 lb per square inch.

The valves were inclined at 7° to the vertical (compared with 10° on the Consort), with the inlets of larger diameter ($1\frac{7}{16}$ inch) than the exhaust ($1\frac{5}{16}$ inch). The heads of the exhaust valves were of greater thickness in the interest of good heat absorption and Brimachrome was used for the valve seat inserts. The combustion chambers were lozenge-shaped, the flat portion of the head overlapping the bore on one side to provide a 'squish' turbulence effect as the piston approached the top of its stroke. The long reach 14 mm plugs were inserted at an angle on the nearside of the head.

Special attention was given to efficient gas flow both by careful valve positioning and by the design of the porting. The inlet manifolding cast in aluminium alloy and anodized to prevent corrosion was notable in two respects both of which followed the practice adopted on the 3-litre Regency engine. One was the use of separate porting to each cylinder and the other was that the manifold was water-jacketed throughout. The advantages claimed for this arrangement have been previously noted. A downdraught Zenith carburettor was used and two silencers fitted in series were employed in the exhaust system which was carried on rubber insulated brackets.

The cooling system employed a belt driven two-bladed fan and an impeller and the whole system was slightly pressurized by means of a spring loaded overflow valve in the filler cap. The bores were separated by water jackets and the delivery from the pump was to the upper portion of the block, whence the water was directed upwards to the exhaust valve seats. The cylinder block casting extended to the centre line of the crankshaft and pressed-in Brivadium dry liners were used and these could be renewed after extended service and as an interim measure, reboring up to a maximum of 0·040 inch oversize was permissible.

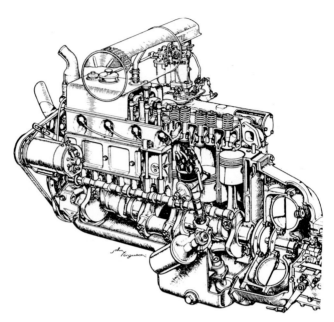

The 'Conquest' engine

In the design of the new engine considerable attention was also given to the elimination of all unnecessary weight. This object was achieved with a saving of approximately 1 cwt compared to the Consort engine – not by extensive use of light metals but by the discriminate elimination of surplus metal whenever possible without interfering with safety factors.

The maximum power derived from the engine was 75 bhp at 4,000 rpm and the compression ratio was (when announced) 6·6 to 1 but was later increased to 7 to 1.

The transmission incorporated the usual fluid flywheel and epicyclic gear box and a Hardy Spicer open propeller shaft with Salisbury hypoid bevel axle. The normal axle ratio was 4·56 to 1. Only three grease nipples on the propeller shaft and one on the fan bearing required attention from a grease gun. All the other points, twenty-one in all, normally requiring such attention were serviced automatically from a Girling Bijur lubrication system of the thermal type which delivered its product at approximately 4 lb per square inch pressure.

A conventional but sturdy chassis frame was used with box section longitudinals linked by channel section cruciform bracing and massive cross members at both front and rear. The front cross member which passed beneath the forward end of the crankcase, also served to carry the front suspension comprising laminated torsion bars and forged wishbones of unequal length – a layout initiated on the post-war Lanchester Fourteen. Long semi-elliptic springs were fitted at the rear and at both front and back there were Girling telescopic dampers.

Girling hydro-mechanical brakes operated in 11 inch drums with $1\frac{3}{4}$ inches wide linings providing a friction area of 148 square inches. The drums were machined all over (to eliminate squeak), and the webs of the shoes were slotted; whilst another unusual point was that each drum had eight $1\frac{1}{8}$ inches diameter holes drilled near the periphery at points which were clear of the dished wheel hub flange. On some other Daimler models this arrangement had been found to provide ventilation resulting in a reduction in maximum drum temperature of nearly 50 per cent.

Another illustration of thoughtfulness on the part of the designer, concerned the provision of a hole in the bottom of the sump just below the pump intake, enabling an external oil supply to be piped to the pump intake when the engine was on the test bed and permitting the engine to be very thoroughly flushed and cleaned during the initial running in. Thereafter the hole was sealed by a flush-fitting plug.

The body was of pressed steel construction, examples of which have stood the test of time and the elements better than some of the steel bodies on later models.

Interior furnishings conformed to traditional Daimler standards of quality, with walnut veneer being used for the fascia board and door cappings. The upholstery was carried out with simplicity and was devoid of superfluous ornamentation. High grade leather was used for all the wearing surfaces. The front seats were of the close-up separately adjustable style. A notable feature (common to all Daimlers of this period) was the absence of a transmission tunnel protruding into the car with only a small 'hump' for the gearbox cover. With the gear selector lever traditionally positioned to the driver's right, there were no obstructions in the 'cockpit' and on occasions three persons could be accommodated in the front and three in the back.

All four doors were provided with armrests – those in the front being adjustable and in the rear a centre folding rest was also fitted. The doors had concealed hinges fitted to their leading edges and also consistent with Daimler fashion was the arrangement that only the nearside front door was externally lockable by key. Both front and rear quarter lights were made to open. A Clayton heater and demister were built into the dash and this drew fresh air from a scuttle vent which was positioned backwards so that its aperture faced the screen.

Other items of equipment included – flush-fitting sun visors; small pockets in the doors, separate ashtrays for all four occupants, a lockable glove box on the passenger's side of the instrument panel, and a pair of small built-in fog lamps. The boot lid was hinged at the top and sprung to stay up when in the open position. Within, the spare wheel and tools were stowed beneath a luggage platform.

The model was given the chassis type DJ 250 (DJ 251 – left hand drive) and fitting for the 'Conquest', the basic price was fixed at £1,066! – with purchase tax the total price was increased to £1,511.5.10.

The similarity in performance between the $2\frac{1}{2}$-litre Conquest and the $3\frac{1}{2}$-litre Regency Mk II has been noted elsewhere. The mean maximum speed was just

223

over 80 mph together with a fuel consumption of almost 20 mpg. When driven hard the car could be cruised at around 70 mph for considerable periods without the engine showing any sign of stress.

After describing the suspension, *The Autocar* continued:

This results in a fairly firm and well controlled ride and over all types of road surface the car handles well, although noise from regularly placed bumps in the road (such as cats' eyes) is quite noticeable, and tyre squeal can be produced at comparatively low cornering speeds. The road-holding is very good and the car has a feeling of general stability that inspires confidence. This is augmented by a slight understeer characteristic that is present even when the car is fully laden. There is very little roll on corners, and passengers remain almost unaffected by brisk cornering methods. This Daimler hugs the road in a manner that enables particularly good averages to be made even over twisty road sections. The steering is not specially low geared and does not feel dead; it gives the driver a good idea of what the front wheels are doing, without being excessively heavy or transmitting shocks to his hands. The turning circle is good.

The *Financial Times* (London) 14 March 1955 carried the following testimony:

A visit to the Geneva Show provided an excellent opportunity of trying out a model on the 500-odd-mile journey across France and a Daimler Conquest saloon used for this trip proved to be a very pleasant car for fast, long-distance Continental touring. There were three persons, and a full load of baggage aboard, and it would have been easy to accommodate a fourth.

Crossing by the Dover–Dunkirk ferry overnight, snow was falling heavily when France was reached and the roads on the first stretch of the journey were distinctly tricky. The Daimler is, however, a car that handles with a marked degree of sureness, and rode the drifts, which in places were in a semi-frozen condition, in a manner that imparted a reassuring feeling of mastery to the driver. Later on, when the snow had been left behind in mid-France, the same impression of roadworthiness was present at speeds up to the 80 mph on the speedometer, which seemed to be the car's useful maximum.

It would be difficult to speak too highly of the Daimler's engine, a 6-cylinder unit of $2\frac{1}{2}$ litres, which ran with the most commendable smoothness and silence throughout the thousand-mile journey. Sometimes it was not easy to realize that the engine was, in fact, still running when the car was stationary, but when in action there was no doubt at all about its presence.
Transmission System:
Except on the mountainous section in the Jura there was seldom an occasion when a change down from top gear was necessary unless it were to gain extra acceleration, while only in built-up areas was the car overtaken. The British driver has an inbred desire to slow down when passing through a village or town; the average French driver has no such inhibitions.

The transmission on the Daimler Conquest includes the fluid flywheel and pre-selector self-changing gearbox, as has long been standard practice with this make. It proved entirely satisfactory and certainly has much to recommend it, including smoothness at low speeds and simplicity of changing from any gear to any other. The sole criticism is that there is a tendency for the car to 'creep' when, for example, waiting at traffic lights with gear engaged, and this is more marked when the weather is cold, especially in the early mornings.

We encountered some chilly weather on this trip, and would have been glad of greater output of warmth from the heater in the car. Nevertheless, we completed the journey with a high regard for the capabilities of the Daimler Conquest, and on working out figures, found that our running average speed had been no less than 48 mph and petrol consumption just over 21 mpg.

Conquest Roadster

One of the sensations at the 1953 London Motor Show was a striking new two-seater coupe known as the 'Roadster' (DJ 254/5). A lightweight body construction was achieved by using aluminium alloy castings panelled in aluminium and the traditional Daimler radiator was reduced 5 inches in height from that on the standard Conquest saloon.

This version utilized the basic Conquest chassis with a few modifications but the greatest innovations were concerned with the power unit. Despite having two horizontal SU carburettors, high lift cams, an aluminium head giving a compression ratio of 7·75 to 1 and modified timing, the Roadster offered notable fuel economy and moreover the total weight of the engine, compared to the saloon version, was actually some 30 lb less! *The Motor* found that at a constant 30 mph the fuel consumption was 34½ mpg and over a full road test an average of 21·4 mpg was obtained. The performance was quite exciting with a maximum recorded speed of 101·7. The maximum power output on production models was 100 bhp given at 4,400 rpm (some sources state, 4,600 rpm); and a few early examples gave an output of only 92 bhp. The four forward speeds provided ratios of 3·84, 2·21, 1·47 and 1·00 to 1 with a hypoid bevel final drive with a final reduction ratio of 4·11 to 1 or optionally 3·73 to 1.

Road speed tyres (6·00 × 15) were fitted and the car was equipped with a hood which folded down neatly behind the rear squabs but the operation of raising or lowering the hood was best carried out by two persons. Side screens

The Motor Road Test No. 21/54 (Continental) —

Make: Daïmler   **Type:** Conquest Roadster

Makers: The Daim'er Co., Limited, Coventry

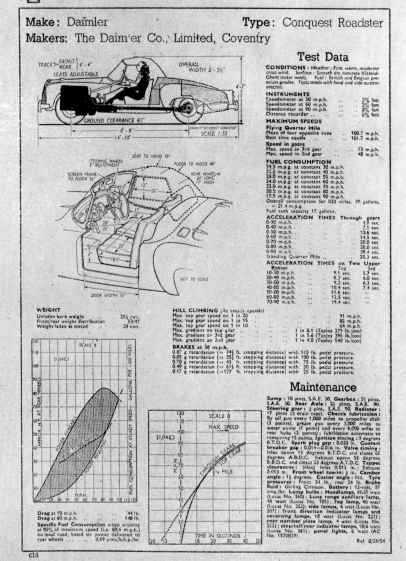

Test Data

CONDITIONS: Weather : Fine, warm, moderate cross wind. Surface : Smooth dry concrete (Ostend-Ghent motor road). Fuel : British and Belgian premium grades. Tests made with hood and side screens erected.

INSTRUMENTS

Speedometer at 30 m.p.h.	..	2% fast
Speedometer at 60 m.p.h.	..	2% fast
Speedometer at 90 m.p.h.	..	2% fast
Distance recorder	..	5% fast

MAXIMUM SPEEDS

Flying Quarter Mile

Mean of four opposite runs	..	100.7 m.p.h.
Best time equals	..	101.7 m.p.h.

Speed in gears

Max. speed in 3rd gear	..	72 m.p.h.
Max. speed in 2nd gear	..	48 m.p.h.

FUEL CONSUMPTION

34.5 m.p.g. at constant 30 m.p.h.
32.5 m.p.g. at constant 40 m.p.h.
28.0 m.p.g. at constant 50 m.p.h.
24.0 m.p.g. at constant 60 m.p.h.
22.0 m.p.g. at constant 70 m.p.h.
20.5 m.p.g. at constant 80 m.p.h.
17.5 m.p.g. at constant 90 m.p.h.
Overall consumption for 833 miles, 39 gallons, = 21.4 m.p.g.
Fuel tank capacity 15 gallons.

ACCELERATION TIMES Through gears

0-30 m.p.h.	..	4.7 sec.
0-40 m.p.h.	..	7.1 sec.
0-50 m.p.h.	..	10.6 sec.
0-60 m.p.h.	..	14.5 sec.
0-70 m.p.h.	..	20.0 sec.
0-80 m.p.h.	..	28.0 sec.
0-90 m.p.h.	..	39.4 sec.
Standing Quarter Mile	..	20.3 sec.

ACCELERATION TIMES on Two Upper Ratios

		Top	3rd
10-30 m.p.h.	..	9.1 sec.	5.7 sec.
20-40 m.p.h.	..	9.3 sec.	6.0 sec.
30-50 m.p.h.	..	9.2 sec.	6.3 sec.
40-60 m.p.h.	..	10.4 sec.	7.4 sec.
50-70 m.p.h.	..	11.6 sec.	—
60-80 m.p.h.	..	13.5 sec.	—
70-90 m.p.h.	..	19.4 sec.	—

WEIGHT

Unladen kerb weight	..	25½ cwt.
Front/rear weight distribution	..	53/47
Weight laden as tested	..	29 cwt.

HILL CLIMBING (At steady speeds)

Max. top gear speed on 1 in 20	..	91 m.p.h.
Max. top gear speed on 1 in 15	..	85 m.p.h.
Max. top gear speed on 1 in 10	..	64 m.p.h.
Max. gradient on top gear	..	1 in 8.1 (Tapley 275 lb./ton)
Max. gradient on 3rd gear	..	1 in 5.6 (Tapley 395 lb./ton)
Max. gradient on 2nd gear	..	1 in 4.0 (Tapley 540 lb./ton)

BRAKES at 30 m.p.h.

0.87 g retardation (= 34½ ft. stopping distance) with 115 lb. pedal pressure.
0.85 g retardation (= 35½ ft. stopping distance) with 100 lb. pedal pressure.
0.70 g retardation (= 43 ft. stopping distance) with 75 lb. pedal pressure.
0.49 g retardation (= 61½ ft. stopping distance) with 50 lb. pedal pressure.
0.17 g retardation (=177 ft. stopping distance) with 25 lb. pedal pressure.

Maintenance

Sump : 10 pints, S.A.E. 30. **Gearbox :** 5½ pints, S.A.E. 30. **Rear Axle :** 2½ pints, S.A.E. 90. **Steering gear :** ½ pint, S.A.E. 70. **Radiator :** 17 pints (3 drain taps). **Chassis lubrication :** By oil gun every 1,000 miles to propellor shaft (3 points), grease gun every 3,000 miles to water pump (1 point) and every 6,000 miles to rear hubs (2 points); lubrication automatic to remaining 15 points. **Ignition timing :** 9 degrees B.T.D.C. **Spark plug gap :** 0.020 in. **Contact breaker gap :** 0.014–0.016 in. **Valve timing :** Inlet opens 13 degrees B.T.D.C. and closes 65 degrees A.B.D.C. Exhaust opens 55 degrees B.B.D.C. and closes 23 degrees A.T.D.C. **Tappet clearances :** (Hot) Inlet 0.013 in. ; Exhaust 0.013 in. **Front wheel toe-in :** ⅛ in. **Camber angle :** 1½ degrees. **Castor angle :** Nil. **Tyre pressures :** Front 24 lb., rear 24 lb. **Brake fluid :** Girling Crimson. **Battery :** 12-volt, 51 amp./hr. **Lamp bulbs :** Headlamps, 45/35 watt (Lucas No. 360); Long range auxiliary lamp, 48 watt (Lucas No. 185) ; fog lamp, 48 watt (Lucas No. 323); side lamps, 6 watt (Lucas No. 207); front direction indicator lamps and reversing lamps, 18 watt (Lucas No. 221); rear number plate lamp, 4 watt (Lucas No. 222) ; stop/tail/rear indicator lamps, 18/6 watt (Lucas No. 361); panel lights, 6 watt (AC No. 1570839).

Ref. 8/25/54

Drag at 10 m.p.h. .. 44 lb.
Drag at 60 m.p.h. .. 148 lb.
Specific Fuel Consumption when cruising at 80% of maximum speed (i.e. 80.6 m.p.h.) on level road, based on power delivered to rear wheels .. .. 0.69 pints/b.h.p./hr.

c16

were provided and when not in use these were stowed in an 'envelope' behind the seats. There was ample luggage space in the boot.

Very good visibility was afforded through the wide curved windscreen although this was apt to produce reflections from the instruments. The fascia board was leather covered and a rev counter was included in the instrumentation. Praise was earned by the good and precise steering and by the excellent road holding afforded by the suspension arrangements which were ideally matched to the performance and characteristics of the car. Similarly the Daimler transmission was found to be well suited – *The Motor* commented:

what does need emphasizing is the excellent way in which its characteristics harmonize with the sporting qualities of this car, not only enabling very quick changes to be made, but also making it possible for the driver to preselect a desired ratio before entering a corner or negotiating an obstacle and then, by a mere kick of the pedal, achieve the desired change at the exact moment required leaving both hands free.

The brakes were as on the Conquest saloon but with 11-inch drums and 2¼-inch linings the friction areas was increased to 184 square inches. The Roadster exhibited at Earls Court (pre-production chassis 85004) was painted in red and was awarded the Institute's Silver medal for coachwork. It was said that the Roadster was designed and produced within six weeks!

When production of the Conquest got into its stride the Company showed initiative as regards sales and service by adapting two ambulances, Daimler D C Twenty-Sevens, and fitting each of them with a special Brockhouse trailer. These units toured principal towns in the north and south of England displaying a complete chassis and component parts and the exhibits were explained and demonstrated by a Supervisor and two service representatives from the Company.

Two-seater sports cars are not everyone's cup of tea and The Daimler Co was quickly sensitive to the demand for a 'traditional' saloon but with outstanding

The 100 bhp Daimler Conquest Century

The Mk. II Chassis frame is built of specially lightened "U" section side members cruciform braced, resulting in an immensely rigid construction devoid of unnecessary weight — the perfect structure for withstanding the strains and stresses of high speed performance.

THE RIGID CHASSIS OF THE 100 BHP MODELS

performance and roadholding. In the spring of 1954, such a car to be known as the 'Century' saloon was announced and a further addition to the Conquest range was a drop-head coupé.

First, the Conquest Century: The selling price was £1,661.9.2 (basic – £1,172) and, like the Roadster, the Century engine had an aluminium cylinder head in place of the cast iron head fitted to the standard Conquest saloon, which was of course continued. It also had the Roadster's 7·75 to 1 compression ratio, the larger inlet and exhaust valves, the twin SU horizontal carburettors and high lift camshaft. The output was 100 bhp at 4,400 rpm. To take account of the increased power, a propeller shaft of increased diameter ($2\frac{3}{4}$ inches instead of $2\frac{1}{2}$ inches on the Conquest saloon) and a four star type differential were specified, and as on the Roadster, the brake friction area was increased to 184 square inches. In other respects the chassis (type DJ 256/7 for the Century saloon) was almost identical to the standard DJ 250. The new chassis features were severely tested under arduous conditions when in the 1954 Monte Carlo Rally, seven Conquests (conforming, more or less, to the Century specification) were entered. Five of the

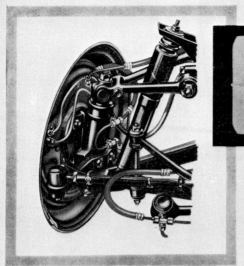

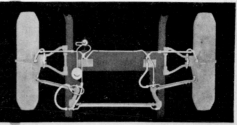

The lubricant feed pipes are shown in red on the left and in yellow on the right.

seven cars finished in the first hundred and the performance and handling of these five during the five lap high speed test on the difficult Monaco Grand Prix circuit greatly impressed the many knowledgeable spectators present.

External differences between the Conquest and Century were few. The windscreen surround on the new model was chromed metal instead of black rubber; similar treatment was applied to the rear window surround and at the rear of the front door windows, vertical strips of glass intended to act as draught excluders were added and the rear light surrounds were also chromium plated. Either side of the boot handle and placed horizontally across the lid were chromium flashes. On some but not all Centurys the name 'Daimler' also appeared on the boot lid. These were probably the first cars from Daimler to carry the manufacturer's name. Both Conquest and Century saloons and other models in the Conquest range displayed on the rear bumper a 'D' medallion but this was no innovation – the practice having been instituted, mainly on the 2½-litre cars from about August 1937.

Inside the car there were also several differences. First, and perhaps most important was the re-positioning of the rear seat further back to provide 4 inches more leg room – although this arrangement was also common to later Conquests. The fascia was re-arranged to accommodate a rev-counter and the central panel was inclined slightly upwards. A welcome addition was a telescopic adjustable steering column and to add to the feel of steering precision, an 18 inch diameter wheel (17 inches on the Conquest) was fitted. The front seats were re-shaped and redesigned giving considerably more comfort and support. Windscreen washers were included as standard equipment and some cars had two-speed wipers. There were in addition other detail differences but particular mention should be made of the two suitcases which were supplied with the car as standard equipment.

The Century saloon would cover a standing quarter mile in 20·7 seconds (remember this was in 1954!) and the maximum speed was above 90 mph but for a better appreciation and assessment of the car's attributes, consider the following:

From its inception, acclaimed for high performance

"COUNTRY LIFE"—6th June, 1953 (J. Eason Gibson).

"CONQUEST" SALOON.

"There are only three grease nipples on the car; two on the propeller shaft and one on the fan. The rest of the car is automatically lubricated; this is a feature one would like to see more generally adopted.

The car's eagerness on the slightest opening of the throttle was most noticeable, even during the initial stages when I was driving in rather heavy West End traffic . . . . .

The Daimler has, in many ways, a dual character. The advantages of the type of gear-change and the good brakes urge one to drive it as one would a car of sporting type. This is both possible and safe, because of the car's surprising good road-holding and cornering . . . .

Driving after dark was particularly pleasing, because of the very good driving light provided and the sensible lighting of the instruments from behind, so that the moving needle shows as a silhouette . . . . .

The large individual front seats are well shaped, so that the driver is retained in a comfortable and efficient position; there is no tendency, even when one is driving very fast, to use the steering wheel to avoid sliding about on the seat . . . . ."

"THE FIELD"—3rd September, 1953.

(S. C. H. Davis writing of the "CONQUEST" SALOON).

"The high-backed seats are soft and springy, the suspension soft so that the road surfaces are of no importance. But once out on the open road you realise that the machine also has a startling acceleration, can corner fast without roll, and can cover 40 to 50 miles in an hour without sense of stress, a most valuable characteristic.

Running out of a city amidst the crowd of other cars inevitable in the circumstances the Daimler put 36 miles in an hour, then, as the traffic thinned, 44 and then 46, mainly by reason of its acceleration. Ten seconds after leaving a 30 limit on top gear the car can be back at 50, or 7 seconds if you use third. Useful maxima are 15 on first, 30 on second, 50 on third, and the claim that the car can cruise at 70 is true."

"MANCHESTER GUARDIAN" on the "CONQUEST CENTURY"—May, 1954.

"A Car to Captivate the Driver and His Womenfolk . . .

Internally the car will captivate a driver by its controls and his wife by its furnishings, both soft and hard.

All these refinements are standard equipment; only a radio (for which space is provided) will cost extra. Temperature and ventilation are excellent and vertical glass panels fitted to the front door windows would seem to have cured that common nuisance of draught at the back of the car.

The engine layout is a pretty piece of designing, and considering all that has been packed under the bonnet a high degree of accessibility has been achieved—certainly to those components requiring regular attention and adjustment, among them the oil reservoir for the automatic chassis-lubrication system. At the other end there is a roomy luggage boot in which are strapped two suitcases . . . . ."

"AUTOSPORT"—21st January, 1955 (J. Bolster).

"Daimler 'Century'. A 90 m.p.h. 2½ litre 'quality' saloon with first-class brakes and excellent handling characteristics. I would go so far as to say that this car handles a great deal better than some 120 m.p.h. sports models.

The brakes are worthy of great praise. They are very powerful but entirely progressive, so there is no fear of locking the wheels accidentally; nor is fading experienced. This must be one of the safest cars on the road, and high average speeds may be put up in ease and comfort."

"THE SYDNEY MORNING HERALD"—March and July, 1955

The 'Conquest Century'

"On the open road the most noticeable characteristic of the 'Century' is the ease with which it climbs and accelerates in top, and with which it maintains a high average touring speed . . . . .

The gearshift, through the pre-selector gearbox, provides the simplest and quickest mechanical gear-change available today. The fluid flywheel ensures smooth starting under any conditions.

Hill Climbing: Even difficult main-road hills can be climbed in top, and the simple selection of third speed is necessary only for mountain passes, or when baulked . . . . .

Engineering: The design of the Daimler engine is most modern, and workmanship is on the top line . . . . .

Another valuable feature is an automatic chassis lubrication system, operated by engine heat, which reduces greasing to three points every 1,000 miles.

Body: The characteristic of the body is interior spaciousness.

On the touring highway I was most impressed by the manner in which the 'Conquest' handles rough going at speed. I drove her hard through some mountain byroads as bad as one usually finds, and the car sailed through them in quite unruffled style, going very fast indeed."

"SPORTS CARS"— 1955
New York City,
Daimler 'Conquest Century'

"A really fine example of craftsmanship, the Daimler 'Conquest Century' is another example of the auto building art that has no counterpart in this country . . . .

The very highly developed chassis and a good fore-and-aft weight distribution enable this 100-horsepower car to corner like something akin to an all-out sports car . . . . .

However, steering is light and very responsive and, although the wheelbase is 104 inches, the car manoeuvres

The 100 bhp Conquest drop-head coupé (DJ 252/3)

nd luxury . . . .

in no more space than many smaller sports jobs. The interior leg room and luggage capacity of the trunk are unusually large for this size automobile . . . . ."

"THE AMBASSADOR"—July, 1955

The Daimler 'Conquest Century'

" . . . . but the number which really fall into the high speed luxury class is relatively small.

The new Daimler 'Conquest Century' is one of these comparatively rare examples . . . . .

In appearance it is a happy blend of traditional and modern styles; the interior is luxurious and the ride smooth; indeed, the car is as comfortable a 'town carriage' as ever graced the Royal Parks. Once well clear of the town, however, the 'Conquest Century' displays the gait of a greyhound; in our far from fast conditions of motoring it can be flung about congested roads and thrust through overcrowded miles as few sports cars can. Meanwhile the occupants continue to enjoy the restful ease of a well-insulated drawing-room. As evidence of its capabilities I can reveal that during our test the 'Conquest Century' carried three passengers nearly 500 miles in a day, to attend and return from a sporting event, which in itself took up six hours of winter daylight . . . . .

It is fitted with Daimler's own type of semi-automatic transmission; the pre-selected gears and a fluid coupling in the drive make for virtually two-pedal control while still leaving the choice of ratio to the driver. As I have said before, this seems to be among the best solutions to the desire of most drivers to be relieved of some of the tedium imposed by the conventional gearbox; and it is worth remembering that since it has been a standard fitment to Daimler cars for twenty-three years, the wrinkles have been ironed out—indeed, it is hard to recall ever having seen a Daimler halted involuntarily beside the road."

"THE TIMES"—16th August, 1955.

"The Daimler 'Conquest Century' Saloon . . . . .

Although it is a lively car capable of cruising at 70 m.p.h. without much effort, it does not depend upon sheer speed for its attraction. The real charm of the car

lies in the sense of fine engineering it conveys in its quiet but powerful 2½-litre, 6-cylinder engine, the positive action of its steering, its quite exceptional springing, and the good taste of its interior finish.

It is particularly helpful with such slow manœuvres as parking, because the car can be moved slowly forward inch by inch without recourse to the clutch pedal . . . .

It would be difficult to find a car with better springing than the Daimler, not only in its ability to absorb the shocks of poor surfaces but in the level ride it provides when travelling fast. The steering is positive and gives the driver confidence; and for a car of this size the lock is excellent."

"COURIER"—August, 1955.

The Daimler 'Conquest Century'

"I found the visibility and precise steering enabled me to thread my way through gaps which stopped apparently smaller cars. Once out of London, I cruised quietly westwards, for three hours, at sedate speeds, it seemed, arriving in Bristol still fresh and relaxed.

There was fog, there were floods in some parts. The secure feeling imparted by the Daimler greatly endeared it to me, as did the magnificent brakes . . . . .

It proved capable of cornering, accelerating, and climbing like a sports car, and in fact, laughed off several small sports cars which their owners thought could run rings round the bigger car. Yet the comfort, luggage capacity, and especially the silence of the 'Century', are in true Daimler tradition, up to limousine standards. All this with a maximum speed around the 90 m.p.h. mark, and a truly classic line."

"THE AUTOCAR"—12th August, 1955

(Michael Brown's feature entitled 'Alpine Conquest')

"The 'Conquest Century' is one of those cars that is right, absolutely right . . . . .

The 'Conquest' has the famous fluid flywheel transmission with the epicyclic gearbox, and this plays no small part in the delight of Daimler driving . . . . .

In the narrow Alpine towns there could be no easier mount. A Daimler will trickle when other engines have begun to gulp; it will turn a prop-shaft steadily when other cars want a slipped clutch, and for anyone to whom engagement of first gear in motion has terrors, a fluid flywheel is the answer . . . .

As one who likes driving for its own sake, I appreciated the array of instruments—a full one including a rev. counter, though the oil pressure indicator is only a warning lamp. Ash trays are big, sensible, and mounted on the doors; there are arm rests all round."

"SUNDAY TIMES"—29th August, 1955

"Here is a very lively car with 100 h.p. under the bonnet and an exciting road performance.

The fluid flywheel, plus the high power-to-weight ratio, makes driving delightfully easy. The driver gets away from a standstill smoothly on third gear, simply by pressing the accelerator and the car rapidly gets up to 50 m.p.h. and more without changing gear at all.

On the open road, top gear is high enough for fast Continental touring . . . . , I much like the ample space allowed for getting into and out of the driving seat."

"COUNTRY LIFE"—22nd December, 1955.

(J. Eason Gibson)

"The interior finish and comfort of the body are very good, the separate front seats in particular being luxuriously upholstered and the squabs very well shaped, so that one is held in a comfortable position, without any tendency for the passenger to slide about, or for the driver to use the steering wheel as a support on corners. The steering wheel is telescopically adjustable, which feature, combined with a wide range of adjustment on the driving seat, allows drivers of very different sizes to find a comfortable position. Swivelling ventilators are fitted to the rear quarterlights, as well as in the front doors; the rear ones act most effectively as extractors of the used air.

Combining the traditional smoothness of the Daimler with a new liveliness, the 'Century' should appeal to many motorists. The advantage of incorporating an automatic system of chassis lubrication is a point that will appeal to many busy drivers."

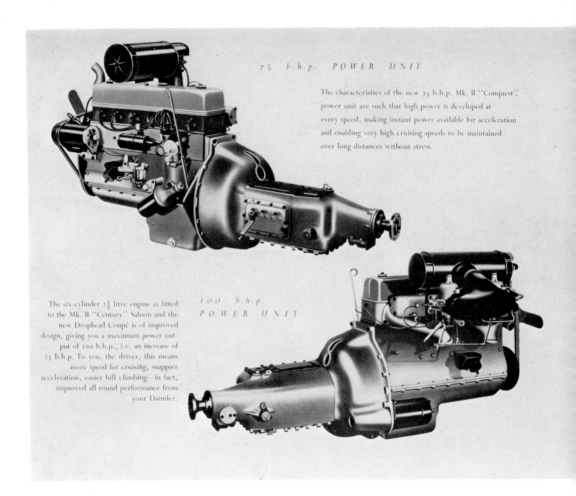

75 b.h.p. POWER UNIT

The characteristics of the new 75 b.h.p. Mk. II "Conquest" power unit are such that high power is developed at every speed, making instant power available for acceleration and enabling very high cruising speeds to be maintained over long distances without stress.

The six-cylinder 2½ litre engine as fitted to the Mk. II "Century" Saloon and the new Drophead Coupé is of improved design, giving you a maximum power output of 100 b.h.p., i.e. an increase of 25 b.h.p. To you, the driver, this means more speed for cruising, snappier acceleration, easier hill climbing—in fact, improved all round performance from your Daimler.

100 b.h.p. POWER UNIT

At the 1954 International Touring car race at Silverstone, two Centurys driven respectively by Reg Parnell and George Abecassis gained first and second places in their class. For competition purposes, the Works engines were developed to produce about 116 bhp at 5,800 rpm.

Later the same year, at the London show another surprise; a fixed head coupé version of the Roadster was exhibited. Although hundreds of brochures were printed and the car was listed for some months, probably no more than two or three were produced. £1,750.14.2 was the total price asked for the model (basic £1,235).

With the Conquest, Roadster and Century already announced and in production by June 1954, another variant was added. This was the Conquest drophead coupé (DJ 252/3) – a two-door four-seater with power operated hood. It will be recalled that the 3-litre special coupé (DF 302/3) also had a power hood.

An exclusive Mk. II "Century" Saloon feature is the vertical glass edging to the front windows. Rear seat passengers are entirely free from the nuisance of draughts although the windows may be wound down for full ventilation.

DRAUGHT-PROOF VENTILATION

The rear compartments of both Saloon models are equipped with ventilation windows which, when used in conjunction with the heater, provide perfect air-conditioning. There are ventilation windows in the front as well, of course.

The front seats of the Mk. II "Century" Saloon are shaped to provide full support for high speed driving. Foam rubber over the cushion springs, and in the back rests, assures lasting comfort during long journeys.

TELESCOPIC STEERING

The Mk. II "Century" Saloon is equipped with a telescopic adjustable steering column which can be locked in any desired position by a simple clamping lever. The three inches movement of the column together with the front seat adjustment assure a relaxed driving position for any driver.

Almost certainly The Daimler Co had the honour of being the first manufacturer in this country to offer such a hood as standard equipment. The drop-head coupé had the Century specification and differed but little in performance. Surprisingly perhaps, no rev-counter was fitted. The hood could be left in the 'de-ville' position with the furled part and cant rails held up by the straps provided. As with most coupés at that time visibility rearward was restricted by the small back window. When the hood was erected, the car was remarkably free from draughts. When announced the basic price was £1,225 – with tax, £1,736.10.10.

At the 1955 London show further changes throughout the Conquest range were made. The Conquest and Conquest Century saloons were up-graded to the rank of Mark II and although no significant changes in the mechanical specification resulted, many minor improvements were incorporated. Revisions were made to the rear suspension and a new Smiths heating and ventilation system was

233

Silverstone 1954

installed; burr walnut was used for the fascia and cappings; separate fog and spot
lights were mounted above the front bumper and air intakes occupied the apertures previously reserved for the auxiliary lights. Later black faced instruments
replaced the white faced ones previously used. In the course of production there
were also variations in the style and layout of the fascia and controls.

The principal change, however, concerned not the saloons but what might
be termed an 'amalgamation' of the DJ 252 and DJ 254. The two-door four-
seater coupé was discontinued after about 234 had been made and the name
Roadster was abandoned. Thereafter the DJ 254 continued in a revised form
being in effect a much improved version of the Roadster with three seats arranged
as shown in the brochure. The new version was known as the 'new drop-head
coupé'. The body was produced by Carbodies Ltd and now boasted wind-up
windows and the revised waist-line added an improvement to the good looks of
its predecessor. At the 1955 and 1956 London shows the car earned the gold and
silver coachwork awards in its class, respectively. The new coupé continued to
use the Century engine and chassis and although a rear axle ratio of 4·11 to 1
was common to both saloon and coupé an alternative high ratio of 3·73 to 1 could
be specified.

Two special Lanchester cars were produced utilizing early Century power
units and chassis (which were designated types LJ 252). These two were the
'Lanchester Dauphins' and they looked rather like two-door versions of the
Empress. They carried special Hooper coachwork of composite construction in

234

light alloy and English Ash completely panelled with aluminium. Four seats were provided and one of the two cars was exhibited at Earls Court in 1953. The Dauphin had a price tag of £2,830 (with purchase tax – £4,010.5.10). The power output was 92 bhp at 4,400 rpm. The overall length of the Dauphin was 15 feet 5 inches, 5 feet 7 inches in width and the overall height was 5 feet. The two cars were really Daimlers in disguise! One, on chassis 70007 was destined to reveal its true identity. This 'Dauphin' was first registered on the 17th March 1954 and was owned by Mr R. E. Smith, General Manager of The Daimler Co but early in its life, a Daimler radiator surround and grille was substituted for the Lanchester frontispiece. Seventeen years later, both cars still existed in excellent condition and were seen together at the 1970 National rally of The Daimler & Lanchester Owners' Club at Woburn Abbey.

With effect from the 1st May 1956, considerable price reductions applied to the Mark II Conquest and Century saloons. The total prices with tax were

THE NEW DAIMLER · CONQUEST ROADSTER
FIXED HEAD COUPÉ

*T*HIS alternative style of the renowned open Roadster with folding hood and side screens has been designed to meet the requirements of those who, while requiring a car which will give them "Roadster" speed and performance, prefer the protection offered by a fixed head coupé

235

ENGINE: Six-cylinder, o.h.v., bore 76·2 mm., stroke 88·9 mm., capacity 2433 c.c., compression ratio 7·75 : 1, maximum b.h.p. 100 at 4,400 r.p.m., aluminium cylinder head, statically and dynamically balanced four bearing crankshaft, big ends fitted with steel-backed white-metal liners, four bearing camshaft (high speed) with steel-backed white-metal liners. Lubrication by submerged gear type pump; full-flow oil filter with safety by-pass; pressure relief valve easily accessible; engine flexibly mounted to isolate torque reactions. Cooling by water pump; thermostatic temperature control. Two horizontal S.U. carburettors with air silencer. 12 volt coil ignition; distributor has automatic advance and vacuum control with over-riding hand adjustment for varying grades of fuel.

TRANSMISSION: Fluid transmission with fluid-flywheel and pre-selective 4-speed epicyclic gearbox; selector lever on steering column. Overall gear ratios: 1st 14·32 : 1, 2nd 8·24 : 1, 3rd 5·48 : 1, Top 3·73 : 1, Reverse 19·43 : 1. Open propeller shaft with needle roller universal joint. Hypoid bevel rear axle with ratio 3·73 : 1 reduction.

STEERING: Right-hand or left-hand drive, high efficiency cam gear with ratio 14-12-14 : 1; 18″ (45·7 cm.) diameter spring spoked telescopic adjustable steering wheel.

SUSPENSION: Independent front by laminated torsion bars; half-elliptic rear springs; torsional stabilising bar at front; hydraulic telescopic shock absorbers at front and rear.

BRAKES: Hydro-mechanical operation on 11″ (27·94 cm.) diameter drums; frictional lining area 184 sq. ins. (1187 cms.).

FRAME: Box section cruciform braced.

DIMENSIONS

Track 4′ 4″ (132 cms.)
Wheelbase 8′ 8″ (264 cms.)
Overall length 14′ 10″ (447 cms.)
Overall width 5′ 5″ (165 cms.)
Height 4′ 9¾″ (147 cms.)
Ground clearance (unladen) 4¼″ (10·4 cms.)
Turning circle (left and right) 34′ (10·2 metres)

COLOURS AND UPHOLSTERY
DUO-TONE

Above Waist	Below Waist	Upholstery
French Grey	Red	Grey
Ivory	Blue	Blue
Racing Green	Ivory	Green

CHASSIS LUBRICATION: Thermal automatic chassis lubrication system, delivering to lubrication points whenever engine warms up.

WHEELS AND TYRES: Disc-type bolt-on wheels with 4½″ (11·430 cm.) base rims; 6·00 × 15 road speed tyres with one spare.

CONDITIONS OF SALE

Conditions of Sale set out in the Company's Purchase Agreement Form. The right is reserved to alter any detail of price, specification or equipment without notice.

ELECTRICAL: 12-volt system voltage controlled; battery in luggage boot. Headlamps (fitted with "Le Mans" type glasses) in front wings; side lamps on top of wings; fog lamps (where fitted) on front over-riders; anti-dazzle dipping control operated by foot switch, twin combined tail and stop lamps; separate rear number plate illumination lamp; twin reverse lamps; twin rear reflectors; dual wind tone horns; dual windscreen wipers; flasher type direction indicators beneath headlamps and in stop/tail lamps.

INSTRUMENTS: Speedometer; revolution indicator; clock; oil, ignition, main beam and direction indicator warning lights; water temperature and petrol gauges; ammeter.

FUEL TANK: 16 gallons (19·2 U.S. gallons or 72·6 litres) capacity, including 1½ gallons (1·8 U.S. gallons or 6·8 litres) reserve operated from dash.

JACKING SYSTEM: Mechanical with built-in attachment points at front and rear of car.

BODY: Two-door, two-seater fixed head coupé body of light metal construction; rear luggage boot housing spare wheel, leather covered instrument board; chromium plated fittings; separately adjustable seats upholstered in leather with high grade toning carpets and felt underlays; cubby hole in dash; full width pockets in doors; cold air ventilating system; heater and de-mister optional at extra cost.

Daimler Fluid Transmission licensed under Vulcan Sinclair and Daimler Patents

THE DAIMLER COMPANY LIMITED
COVENTRY · ENGLAND

Printed by L. Bell & Co., Ltd., Guildhall Press, Leicester

Publication No. R27/010/161/S

Conquest Roadster Fixed head coupé

reduced by £186 and £198 respectively. Then later in the same year it was announced that the Century could be had with Borg Warner automatic transmission.

Basically this transmission consisted only of a hydraulic torque converter and two epicyclic gear sets in series; it gave three forward speeds: Low, Intermediate, and High as well as Reverse. For low gear the three units operated in series while for the intermediate gear a multi-disc clutch locked up the front epicyclic gear set so that it rotated as a unit. The drive was then taken through the torque converter and reduction of the rear epicyclic set only. For High or top gear a single plate clutch operated to couple the engine output direct to the gearbox output shaft, thus giving a direct one to one ratio and by-passing both the torque converter and the gear system.

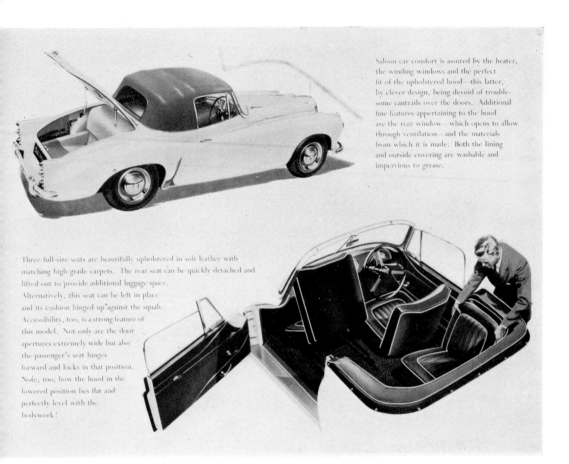

Saloon car comfort is assured by the heater, the winding windows and the perfect fit of the upholstered hood—this latter, by clever design, being devoid of troublesome cantrails over the doors. Additional fine features appertaining to the hood are the rear window—which opens to allow through ventilation—and the materials from which it is made. Both the lining and outside covering are washable and impervious to grease.

Three full-size seats are beautifully upholstered in soft leather with matching high-grade carpets. The rear seat can be quickly detached and lifted out to provide additional luggage space. Alternatively, this seat can be left in place and its cushion hinged up against the squab. Accessibility, too, is a strong feature of this model. Not only are the door apertures extremely wide but also the passenger's seat hinges forward and locks in that position. Note, too, how the hood in the lowered position lies flat and perfectly level with the bodywork!

new Drop-head coupé

The whole mechanism was hydraulically operated from two oil pumps, one located at the front end of the gearbox and directly driven by the engine so that it supplied pressure at all times when the engine was running. The second was located at the rear of the box and directly driven off the output shaft so that it only supplied pressure when the vehicle was moving in a forward direction. The output from these pumps was controlled by a special valve unit which not only acted as a relief valve, but also caused the front pump to discharge freely when the output from the rear pump was sufficient, thus improving the mechanical efficiency of the system. The arrangement enabled the car to be push-started if necessary.

In addition to the quadrant positions of Neutral, Drive, Low and Reverse there was 'Park'. In that position a pawl engaged with a notched ring on the

237

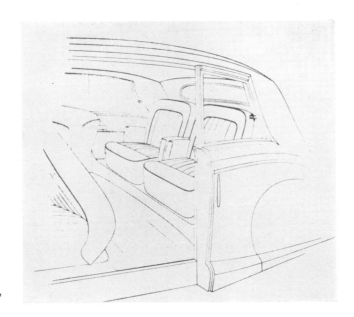

The interior of the 'Dauphin'

The Lanchester Dauphin

output shaft effectively preventing movement on the steepest gradient. The car could only be started when the selector was positioned in Neutral or Park.

The automatic Century was given a new type no. – DJ 260 and had as standard, a rear axle ratio of 4·1 to 1 . Including tax the extra cost of the Borg Warner

Originally the 'other' Lanchester Dauphin – chassis 70007

A special 'Empress' style Hooper body mounted on the 2½-litre Century chassis

transmission was £185 but until September 1957 customers were offered a choice of transmission systems – preselector and fluid flywheel or automatic. Thereafter, only cars equipped with the latter were produced and the last of the very success-ful Centurys was made in January 1958.

'Century' fascia (type DJ 260)

A few estate versions were made

CHAPTER 7

Prototypes DJ 258/9 and DF 312/3

THE introduction by The Daimler Company in 1930 of the fluid flywheel and epicyclic gearbox represented the beginning of another chapter of Daimler history and tradition. The system was not only an immediate success from the time of its inception but it remained outstandingly popular and successful throughout the twenty-six or twenty-seven years of its production.

Some form of epicyclic gear is common to almost all automatic gearboxes and it is perhaps to be regretted that Daimler were not enabled to establish a lead in this direction, at least so far as concerned the British Motor Industry.

A year or two prior to the outbreak of the second world war, a gentleman named Millar (who subsequently joined the staff of The Self Change Gear Company), devised an automatic system. The Daimler Company experimented with this and carried out the following modifications to an ordinary preselector gearbox:

1   An overriding control was linked to the throttle,
2   To the pre-selector control there was fitted a 'notching-up-and-down' solenoid,
3   The gear-engaging pedal was connected to a solenoid controlled vacuum cylinder, and
4   The fitting of a speed control switch to operate each of the above mentioned devices in sequence.

A Wilson gearbox so modified was installed in a DB 18 Daimler car which served for some while as personal transport for the Chief Engineer, C. M. Simpson. The system worked on the two-pedal principle but it was not possible to override the control, although no doubt this could have been overcome had the activities demanded by the outbreak of war not intervened.

During the blitz on Coventry the Company's premises received more than a fair share of devastation. The damage suffered was very great indeed and the entire engineering department was lost. With it were totally destroyed both the automatic gearbox and the technical details and drawings pertaining thereto.

After the war was over, every effort was made to get back into private car production as soon as possible and it was not found to be practicable for some time to think again seriously about automatic transmission systems. Later many experiments were carried out and some were satisfactorily developed beyond the

241

embryonic stage. The Board of the Company favoured the Hobbs system and as developed by the experimental department, this was adopted for the new Lanchester Sprite which made its debut at the 1954 Earls Court show (£1,077.15.10 with purchase tax).

The Lanchester Sprite (1·6-litre engine producing 60 bhp) was the first British light car offered with automatic transmission and it also represented a radical departure from Daimler–Lanchester practice in that it was of lightweight unitary construction employing no chassis in the conventional sense. Full production of the Sprite was about to be implemented when owing to management changes, the entire project was abandoned.

The design of the Hobbs gearbox employed a pair of friction clutches, a compound epicyclic gear and a series of friction brakes which in conjunction with the clutches, controlled the selection of the four forward ratios and reverse. In its functioning the box was entirely mechanical so that there was no power absorption such as occurs with the use of a torque converter, but its operation was carried out hydraulically.

The Hobbs transmission, as utilized in the Sprite provided two-pedal control with a 'kick down' arrangement. Moreover, the selector control had six positions, namely: Reverse, Neutral, First, Second, Third and Automatic, and at the volition of the driver any ratio could be manually selected and automatically engaged.

Other versions of the Hobbs gearbox were devised and it was envisaged that suitable units would be standardized. Experiments with both Centurys (DJ 258) and One-O-Fours (DF 312) were made, very often in the West Country after daylight. On the descent of Porlock Hill, considerable difficulties manifested themselves, particularly in second gear. These problems were not considered to be insuperable and no doubt with further attention they could have been resolved but it was decided not to waste further time and money developing the Hobbs automatic gearbox for Daimlers but instead to utilize the well proven Borg-Warner system.

However, not all the experiments were to no avail, for the original pre-war system – much developed in later years, formed the basis of the semi and fully automatic epicyclic electro-pneumatically-operated 'Daimatic' gearboxes used very successfully on the majority of Daimler buses and coaches from about 1957.

CHAPTER 8

The 4½-litre – Saloons and limousines

*Types DF 400/1/2 chassis numbers 92725–92785
†Type DF 403 chassis numbers 92965–92969
Type DK 400/1 chassis numbers 92700–92724; 96000–96106

PRODUCTION of the DE 27 ceased in 1951 and the last Straight-Eight was made in 1953. The reader will need no reminder that Daimler's policy was always to include in their range models of considerable size. By the autumn of 1954 new models in the 2½- and 3½-litre class had been introduced and the programme was completed with the announcement of two new 4½-litre 6-cylinder chassis.

In an earlier chapter the 3½-litre Regency Mk II engine was fully described and it will therefore suffice to say that the new 4½-litre was in layout and design basically the same. The smaller version in standard form (DF 304/5) produced 107 bhp at 4,000 rpm. The 4½-litre engine had the same stroke but a larger bore and slightly higher compression – 6·53 to 1 and produced 127 bhp at 3,600 rpm. The displacement of the new unit was 4,617 cc. (95·25 × 107·95 mm) and the chassis was listed as 'DF 400' (or '401' for the left hand drive cars).

The Regency Mk II saloon could be had in both 3½- and 4½-litre forms and a similar choice was available in respect of the Sportsman (already described in Chapter 5). Where, however, the bigger engine was fitted, this was coupled to a gearbox in which the gear trains were re-arranged so that the third gear was direct and top was, in effect, an overdrive. By comparison the ratios were:

Gear	3½-litre	4½-litre
Top	1:1	0·709:1
3rd	1·56:1	1·00:1
2nd	2·32:1	1·62:1
1st	4·08:1	3·00:1
Reverse	5·40:1	3·39:1

The Regency 4½-litre saloon was priced at £1,960 (tax £817.15.10) and the corresponding figures for the Sportsman were – basic £2,190 and tax £913.12.6. A 4½ Regency Sportsman painted in French grey over light green with a beige interior was exhibited at the 1954 Earls Court show – on Mulliners' stand and

*For the reason mentioned later in the text, the following saloon chassis were cancelled: Nos. 92733, 92735/6, 92741–5, 92749, 92751–55, 92760–68, 92770–74, 92777 and 92779–85.
†Of perhaps, five left-hand drive chassis made, nos. 92965 and 92968 were probably cancelled.

243

The 4½-litre Four-Light saloon – October 1955

The 4½-litre Daimler Hooper Regina limousine (1954), body no. 10058 on chassis no. 92701

Daimler DK 400 limousine (1955)

The Daimler Co Ltd displayed another on their own stand. On the Hooper stand the following year, a $4\frac{1}{2}$-litre Empress appeared. It was painted most attractively in royal blue and silver and the trimming was in matching deep blue.

For both the Regency saloon and Sportsman, the standard chassis (as used for the $3\frac{1}{2}$-litre cars) with a wheelbase of 9 feet 6 inches was used but the $4\frac{1}{2}$-litre engine was also installed into an extended chassis with a wheelbase of 10 feet 10 inches. Upon this was constructed a new limousine called the 'Regina'.

The power unit was as used for the other $4\frac{1}{2}$ models – producing 127 bhp but for the limousine a normal type preselective gearbox without overdrive was employed, with ratios of 4·00 to 1, 2·286 to 1, 1·511 to 1 and 1 to 1 and reverse 5·555 to 1.

For all the $4\frac{1}{2}$-litre versions, a full Girling hydraulic braking system was used in conjunction with a vacuum booster. A non-return valve was incorporated in the pipe line between the engine and the booster and a vacuum reserve tank was installed to minimize fluctuations and to provide a residue of power after the engine stopped. If the system should fail with a complete depression in the vacuum reserve tank, a warning light appeared on the fascia. Linked to the booster was a breather which, in order to receive clean fresh air, was positioned below the rear seat.

In addition to the increase in wheelbase on the limousine version, there was also a broadening of the track. At the front the measurement was 5 feet and at the rear 5 feet 3 inches. Rubber bushes were used for the rear springs and the

The Daimler DK 400 $4\frac{1}{2}$-litre limousine

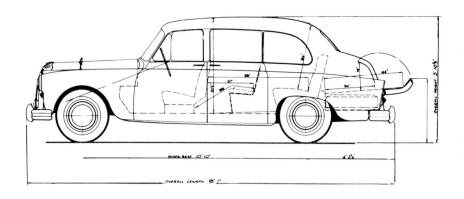

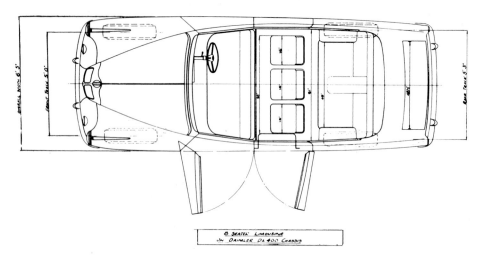

8 SEATER LIMOUSINE
ON DAIMLER DX 400 CHASSIS

steering was of the Burman re-circulating ball type instead of Marles-cam, and the turning circle was 45 feet. The fuel capacity was also increased to 20 gallons to include $1\frac{3}{4}$ gallons in reserve.

On the $3\frac{1}{2}$-litre saloons the tyre size was 6·50 × 16, whereas on the $4\frac{1}{2}$-litre saloons, tyres were 7·00 × 16 and on the limousine 7·50 × 16. Another change concerned the brakes. On the saloons the drum diameter was 12 inches but on the Regina this was increased by 1 inch so that the total friction lining area was 247 square inches as compared to 200 square inches.

The Regina painted blue and black was at Earls Court in 1954. Hoopers constructed the body and the overall length of the car was 18 feet 1 inch. A fixed bench-type seat was installed in the front and with occasional seats there was room for seven or eight passengers in addition to the chauffeur. There was an electric division, a built-in heater, ventilator and defrosting unit, two roof lamps

246

DK 400 rear compartment and boot

in the rear compartment – operated automatically on the opening of doors or by hand switches and another roof light illuminated the front compartment. Flashing indicators were included and so also was a rev-counter. A veneered fascia carried all the other normal controls and instruments. Only the one coachbuilt 'Regina' was made. For a while it was retained by The Daimler Company, but in 1956, it was used by the Royal Family during a tour of Sweden and much later the car came into the author's ownership.

As already noted, the 1956 programme of the Company was announced in the autumn of the previous year and all existing models in both the $3\frac{1}{2}$- and $4\frac{1}{2}$-litre categories were continued but in more potent forms. The standard wheelbase $4\frac{1}{2}$-litre chassis was re-designated DF 402/3 and modifications to the engine yielded a total of 167 bhp at 3,000 rpm. Unfortunately, the torque proved too much for many of the $4\frac{1}{2}$-litre overdrive gearboxes, and the chassis listed in

247

the preceding footnote were withheld or recalled. In all probability smaller power units and normal gearboxes were substituted to enable the 'rejects' to be utilised as 3½-litre chassis.

Similar alterations were incorporated into the engine for the limousine and the same power output was achieved at 3,800 rpm. A revised limousine known simply as the DK 400 was built and the name Regina was dropped. This had a body from Carbodies Ltd Coventry and was exhibited at the London show in 1955. The length remained at 18 feet 1 inch and the width was 6 feet 4½ inches with a height of 5 feet 9¾ inches. The interior layout and appointments differed but little from the first 4½ limousine. The selling price of the coachbuilt Regina was advertised (May 1955) at £6,213.4.2 (basic £4,385) as against a total price for the 'Carbodies' version a year later, of £3,957.17.6 (basic £2,793).

Before the next show, in the autumn of 1956, further revisions had been made to the coachwork. It now appeared more bold and modern and incorporated many changes from stem to stern. The width overall measured 6 feet 5 inches and ⅝ inch was added to the height. The turning circle was improved to 44 feet.

The Daimler coachwork specification for the new DK 400 limousine read:

The limousine has a four-door six light-body with fixed head and curved, one-piece front screen. The body is of composite construction and is built with special attention to weight saving and the elimination of dust and noise. All four quarter lights are hinged for use with the heating and ventilating systems fitted in front and rear compartments to provide perfect air conditioning. The doors are fitted with push button locks, those on the nearside being private locks; those on the offside being operated from catches on the inside. The front doors are fitted with pull-to handles, and ashtrays; pull-to handles fitted to rear doors. Ashtrays are conveniently situated in the side armrests of the rear compartment and division. All door hinges are concealed and a spring-operated check device holds open the doors. The limousine interior has division windows which are arranged to slide horizontally.

Seating accommodation for eight people is provided by a bench type front seat; a rear seat with ample room for three people when the centre arm-rest is raised; and three occasional seats which fold into the division. Best quality hide is used to upholster the front seat with a choice of colours from the standard Daimler leather range of Blue, Green, Red, Beige, Grey and Black (Any other leather required for the front compartment would be the subject of special quotation). Best quality West of England cloth is used to upholster the rear and occasional seats with choice from Dark Fawn, Medium Fawn or Light Fawn (Any other cloth required would be the subject of special quotation). Best quality hide can be provided for the upholstery of the rear compartment as an alternative to cloth upholstery at extra cost. The head lining may be carried out in cloth or plastic. Polished veneered walnut woodwork is used for the finishing panels on the doors, also for the instrument board, this latter incorporating speedometer, revolution indicator, petrol gauge, water thermometer, ammeter and clock. In the fascia panel there are two open cubby holes for gloves and incidental articles. The large lid of the luggage boot hinges at the base. A light in the boot is operated by a hand switch incorporated in the lamp itself. The spare wheel is carried under the luggage floor and is accessible through a separate lid.

The normal finish for the exterior of this car is Black with Gold lining, but if required, the car can be produced in any of the other standard Daimler single colour schemes, i.e. Silver Grey, Maroon, Dark Green or Navy Blue. Any colour required outside this range would be the subject of special quotation upon application.

Occasional seating in the 'DK 400 B'

For all the long wheelbase 4½-litre cars an impressively large and deep radiator surround was specially evolved. For the 1957 show, the DK 400 was shown with three abreast-type occasional seats but for users requiring maximum comfort for all occupants an alternative arrangement could be had. In this alternative form the car was known as the 'DK 400B' and in place of the occasional seating for three as in the 'A' model, there was a pair of greatly improved folding seats. These were each 2 inches wider and were arranged to disappear completely into the recesses in a re-designed division. A special feature was a telescopic spring strut which not only counterbalanced the weight of the seat but was also arranged to swing up a hinged flap which closed the upper part of the aperture to give a neat flush appearance when the seat was folded, without interfering with leg room when the seat was in use.

Above each occasional seat was a handy shelf whilst between the two was a provision for radio and a useful cupboard, the front central panel pulled down to form a hinged table – convenient, although rather small. The cupboard also concealed the division glass winder mechanism since in the 'B' version, the glass was of the 'drop' type compared with sliding glass in the standard 'A' type limousine. Below the cupboard was an outlet for the rear compartment interior heater and on the sides of the division were grab handles. The additional woodwork was in matching burr walnut. As at the 16th October 1957 the DK 400A sold for £4,195 (basic £2,795.15.0) and the 'B' version for £4,315 (basic £2,875.15.0).

On road test, the standard DK 400B limousine was found to have a maximum speed of 93·8 mph and over a distance of 908 miles a fuel consumption of 12·3 mpg.

The 'DK' chassis is of interest, not because of any particular feature of outstanding engineering or mechanical merit, but simply because it was the last limousine chassis to have Daimler fluid transmission and to carry specialist's coachwork made according to traditional methods.

Following the practice established over the several previous years, Hooper & Co again prepared a special exhibit for the 1954 London show. The famous Gold car on the DE 36 chassis shown in 1951 was again, three years later, attracting much attention in Paris where it was on exhibition in the new Daimler showrooms in the Avenue Montaigne. Contemporaneously in London there was being displayed, 'Stardust' – a new car built on an experimental DK 400 chassis – no 92700. The wheelbase was shorter than standard by 2 inches and the track was also a little narrower.

Instead of gold and black as used on the earlier car, a combination of silver and royal blue was chosen for 'Stardust'. The roof, bonnet, rear quarters and wings were all in plain blue and the remaining side panels were covered with a multitude of silver stars. Hooper's Chief Designer – Osmond Rivers, described the starred appearance as 'sham caning in reverse'. The creation, like its predecessors, evoked very considerable comment, most of it favourable. *The Motor* said of the car –

it is the finest and most costly vehicle in the show; a 'masterpiece' in the old sense of that word, being a means of displaying all the artistry and techniques at its creator's disposal.

For the interior, the silver and blue scheme was continued. The upholstery and trimming were in a silver silk brocatelle – specially woven on hand looms for the purpose. For the cabinet work and cappings, pale blue crocodile was selected, and the elaborate cabinet itself was constructed not of wood but of aluminium, to

'Stardust' – the 1954 London show exhibit on Hooper's stand

eliminate excess weight; it was built into the division and served a threefold purpose. The central portion was fitted with double doors, which opened to reveal cut glass decanters displayed against a mirror background – (the mirror was also aluminium, electrolytically polished). Either side there was a further cupboard the doors of which lifted upwards to form a pair of tables. A most ingenious arrangement concerned a flap made in 'Perspex' and enclosing silk to match the upholstery, which was designed to lay from the nearside to the offside table tops to provide a continuous table platform almost the width of the car. In drawers built into the capping were stowed glasses, silver, cups and saucers, cutlery, plate and white linen and as a centrepiece, set in crocodile skin there was a silver 'Sunburst' clock.

The front compartment was trimmed in blue leather, piped with grey and on the floor in the rear was a nylon fur rug. The car was designed to carry three on the front seat and another three passengers on the rear seat. The driver's seat was adjustable. The roof, although fixed, was fitted with a glass panel in the rear portion – covered, at will, by an electrically operated sliding shutter. All four windows were double glazed and electrically operated. Separate and independent heating and ventilating units to front and rear compartments were installed.

The rear wheels were partially concealed with hinged covers, on spring balanced arms and in the large boot there was provided four matching crocodile suitcases and the spare wheel was mounted vertically. Naturally a radio set was fitted and this was controlled from the rear armrest.

After a comparatively short period of 'glory', this car also received the 'neutralizing' treatment and in about 1957 was sold and re-registered. At the time of writing, the car is owned by Daimler enthusiast, Alec Norman.

In furtherance of the Hooper–Daimler tradition, this splendid DK 400 (body 10094 on chassis 92707) was built for 'Royal Stock'. It was painted in the colours of Royal claret and black but in 1958 it was repainted black and then sold. The

'Stardust' – after modification (about 1957)

Hooper body 10094

Hooper body 10093

front was upholstered in black leather and grey West of England cloth was used for the rear compartment. All the finishers were carried out in burr walnut. Another almost identical car (body 10233 on chassis 92714) was delivered to the Governor of Sierra Leone. Another similar car, but in landaulette form and with power operated head (body 10093 on chassis 92704) was made in 1956 for Royal use.

Queen Elizabeth the Queen Mother still retains for her personal use this imposing Hooper bodied special DK 400 limousine which was built for her in 1955 – (body no. 10135 on chassis 92702). Since this is not a 'State car' it is not

The Queen Mother's DK 400-Hooper body 10135

253

painted in Royal colours but is finished externally in all black with West of England cloth in both front and back compartments inside.

The car has no occasional seats. Walnut was used for all the woodwork; radio was fitted and special detachable interior shields were provided to cover the rear quarter windows giving privacy to the occupants. The division and rear window blind were operated electrically.

The car is of course maintained in the peak of condition and still runs beautifully although the lack of power assistance makes for rather heavy steering.

As with the King and Queen's earlier personal cars, a 'Lion' surmounts the radiator.

From 1955 Hooper & Co offered a superbly appointed and luxurious alternative to the standard Daimler bodied DK 400 limousine. The eight-seater coachbuilt version (design no. 8434) was of all metal construction – using light alloys. A Triplex laminated screen was fitted, a radio was installed in the offside rear seat armrest and for the rear passengers a heater was included under the nearside front seat. Two occasional facing forward seats were fitted and when not in use these folded flush against the division. In October 1955 the basic price was £4,385 and with tax the total was raised to £6,213.4.2. Seven only of these elegant vehicles appeared. The first (body 10147 on chassis 92706) was exhibited by Daimler at the 1955 London show. The Lord Mayor of Cardiff was provided with the next one (body 10148 on chassis 92709) and in it was installed a special hidden case to hold the chain of office. The index number KG I on this car had at times previous been seen on Mayoral Daimlers in Cardiff. The third such limousine (body 10149 on chassis 92708) was in November 1956 supplied to HH the Sultan of Johore; another (body 10152 on chassis 92715) was delivered to the Princess Marina and the remaining three (bodies 10150/1 and 10153) were delivered between December 1956 and October 1958 to private customers.

Slightly different treatment over the rear wheels gave this limousine a distinguished appearance. It was made by and for Hooper & Co.

Hooper eight-seater limousine on Daimler 4½-litre chassis, design no. 8434 – interior view

The Hooper DK 400 4½-litre limousine

The 1955 annual set piece on the Hooper stand at the London show was a very striking exhibit and with the departure of Sir Bernard Docker from the board of the BSA Group before the next show, this car proved to be the last in the line of the exotic post-war 'Docker' Daimlers.

The outside of the car (body no. 10146 on chassis 92705) was cellulosed in perfectly plain ivory-white, with all the bright parts plated in gold. Gold plate was used throughout the interior for the fitments and genuine ivory was used instead of wood for the instrument panel and all the cappings and finishers – all set in a very slim gold-plated framework. The upholstery and door panels were quite striking in appearance, real zebra skins having been specially prepared for the purpose.

The bench-type front seat was made up with three separate panels and in the rear were two seats of the folding armchair type. The faces of the seat cushions and squabs were covered with zebra skin and for the borders, ivory-coloured leather was used. For the head lining a very special material was woven by Messrs

The 1955 London show exhibit of Hooper & Co – the last of the 'Docker' Daimlers

Fothergill & Harvey: it was the colour of ivory with a tiny gold spot. As with the earlier 'Docker' cars, this one was fitted with a 'Perspex' panel and shutter to the roof.

All windows were electrically operated and all had additional switches under the control of the driver. Other equipment included controlled variable heating and ventilating, head and pass lights built into the nose of each front wing – hooded at the top, and protected by 'Perspex' covers; automatic indirect lighting to the interior, cocktail and picnic equipment in two cabinets – one in each rear quarter containing cut glass decanters, glasses, Thermos jugs, 'Perspex' sandwich boxes, cups and saucers and linen. In the centre of the front seat was fitted one folding table and in the nearside door recess a manicure set was provided. In a lower part of the same door was placed an ivory and nylon umbrella and in a sliding tray positioned beneath the nearside of the instrument board there was a hinge-over mirror, clothes brush, comb, powder compact, cigarette case and cream jar, and in the boot were raw-hide suitcases fitted with gilt Bramah locks. The fluted radiator was surmounted by a miniature zebra, in gold, which was of course, removed when the car, like the earlier special exhibits, was rendered 'anonymous' prior to re-sale. It was then painted black.

Among the many thousands of admirers of the last mentioned car, at Earls Court was HH The Ameer of Bahawalpur who shortly thereafter placed with Hoopers an order for a special car to resemble the exhibit but with sufficient differences to render it unique. The result can be judged from the photographs and the striking similarity (especially below the waistline) between the new car and the Golden-zebra car, will be observed. The Ameer's car was built with body 10235 on chassis 92716 and being one of the last 'one-offs' it merits a detailed description.

The car was painted cream and the transparent 'Perspex' canopy was specially moulded. Within the car a light nylon blind was fitted beneath the canopy and this blind could be raised or lowered electrically. To provide rearward

Formerly, the Golden-zebra car

The special Hooper bodied Daimler built for HH The Ameer of Bahawalpur

view when the blind was in the erect position, an aperture was included. The body construction was in aluminium with alloy castings, some of which were specially fabricated. Special insulating materials were added to the floor and doors and above the exhaust system was fitted a barrier of aluminium and asbestos. The windows were all electrically operated but for use in emergency, a manual device was incorporated. Triplex 'Sundym' safety glass was used for door and quarter windows and three blades were employed for the windscreen wipers.

The seating arrangements were very similar to those in the Golden-zebra, but in the rear of the centre front seat, was built a cabinet containing three Thermos jugs, glasses and sandwich boxes. Either side of the centre cabinet were tables in the back of the front seats. The seats were all in cream leather and all the cabinet work and finishers were in birds-eye maple.

Two blowers were installed to pass unheated air along the ventilation ducts running the full length of the 'Perspex' roof. A chromium plated tubular rail connected the door pillars and served not only as a rug rail but also as a stiffener to the structure. All the internal metal parts had untarnishable finishes.

In the front of the car was a special ash tray designed for a pipe smoker; on the offside of the instrument board, provision was made for a pistol; 'Rolvisors' were fitted to the top screen rail; in the lower part of the front doors were recesses (capable of taking sandwich boxes) covered by sliding shutters and a radio was included in the comprehensive specification and an extension speaker was fitted to the rear parcel shelf with a volume control mounted in the offside quarter, and in the nearside quarter a cigar lighter was to be found. Special thick white carpets covered the floors, a fire extinguisher was placed accessibly on the nearside beneath the dash and flashing indicators and semaphore signals were placed in the rear quarter panels. A special box was constructed in which to carry tools.

The car was given the index number BWP 378 and if further distinction was required, this was to be found in the small crest which was added to each of the front doors. The car was completed in about April 1957.

Following the car built for The Ameer of Bahawalpur, the very next one – body 10236 was specially designed and constructed for The King of Afghanistan. Chassis number 92724 was used and in all probability this was the only drop-head coupé built on the DK series. Crests in silver were specially cast and fitted to the rear doors.

After the first two – Stardust and the Regina, all the Hooper bodied DK 400 cars had a common distinguishing feature, in the form of hooded headlamps. In fact, so far as Daimlers were concerned the arrangement, with one exception (the $3\frac{1}{2}$-litre Continental), was exclusive to the DK 400's although in a less pronounced style the feature did reappear on the later Sovereigns and Vanden Plas limousines.

The Hooper 'All weather' $4\frac{1}{2}$-litre car built for The King of Afghanistan

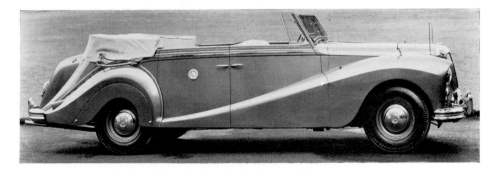

The King of Afghanistan's car with hood lowered

CHAPTER 9

Hooper & Co (Coachbuilders) Ltd

In 1959 Hooper & Co (Coachbuilders) Ltd, decided that it would be impracticable to continue their business which had been established in 1807 at the Haymarket, London, by George Adams and George Hooper. They were first granted the Royal Warrant in 1830 and retained that honour continuously until the end. The Company's work had always been of the highest order. They built the Royal State Landau for King Edward VII and prepared the State Landau for Queen Victoria's Jubilee on 22nd June 1897. They were also entrusted in 1901 and again after the second world war with the renovation of the fabulous gilt State coach built for George III in 1761 and used for Coronations.

The very special and close connections between Hoopers and Daimlers have been clearly illustrated in preceding pages. In no small or insignificant manner, Hoopers contributed more than other coachbuilders to the Daimler tradition. Special mention must be made of Osmond Rivers who for many years was Hooper's Chief Designer and a Director and who was responsible for the design of the many delectable and exotic post-war Hooper–Daimlers.

Between 1929 and 1959, Hooper & Co provided coachwork of the highest grade for a total of 691 Daimlers. Their closure marked the end of an era.

CHAPTER 10

The 3·8-litre Majestic

Type DF 316/7/8/9 chassis numbers 98300–98749 (R.H.D.); 98750–98769 (L.H.D.); 98770–99774 (R.H.D.); 99780–99794 (L.H.D.)

IN July 1958 another new model was announced as an addition to the then existing Daimler range. The Majestic was a direct development of the well established One-O-Four 3½-litre car.

The name Majestic was appropriate to the re-styled flush-sided body which offered considerably increased accommodation for six passengers and a more modern look was gained by lowering the radiator. Mechanically, the main changes concerned the engine, transmission and braking system.

The new power unit was enlarged to 3,794 cc (86·36 × 107·95 mm) (RAC rating 27·74 hp) but this was not achieved simply by boring out the One-O-Four unit. The cylinder block was itself sufficiently enlarged to permit reboring and a second rebore and the fitting of liners; dry liners were not in the first instance employed as they had been on the previous models. An aluminium head was again used giving a compression ratio of 7·5 to 1. An improved gas flow was obtained by modifications being made to the ports. These several changes brought about a gain of 10 bhp at the peak power speed of 4,400 rpm, to a gross maximum of 147 bhp. The torque characteristics were also much improved. Of lesser importance but of practical interest, the starter was repositioned more accessibly high up on the right side. To fit beneath the sloping bonnet, the radiator block was reduced 2 inches in height and to compensate for the loss of frontal cooling area, the depth of the radiator was increased.

Whereas for the 'One-O-Four' the customer had (towards the end of the production period) a choice of either the traditional Daimler transmission or Borg-Warner automatic, the purchaser of the 'Majestic' was provided with the automatic system without any alternative. This incorporated a torque converter which was locked out in top gear. On the two intermediate ratios the torque multiplication varied from 1 to 1 to 2 to 1 – providing a starting ratio of 18·095 to 1 rising to 9·047 to 1 as torque multiplication ceased. An intermediate gear lock was under the manual control of the driver. The propeller shaft was of the divided type and the final drive was by hypoid bevel rear axle.

The Company had experimented with disc brakes from about 1952 but the Majestic was almost certainly the first British saloon car to offer as standard

The DF 316 chassis (Majestic)

equipment disc brakes all round. These were of Dunlop design, operating on
12½-inch diameter discs at the front and 12-inch discs at the rear. A Lockheed
vacuum servo unit was installed and operated direct without the use of a vacuum
reserve chamber. The handbrake – with its lever positioned under the fascia to
the driver's right, worked on a separate pair of callipers at the rear.

The automatic chassis lubrication system used on the 3½-litre cars and in one
form or another on most of the earlier models from about 1937; was omitted from
the Majestic specification. The number of nipples requiring attention was therefore increased from four to seventeen but in answer to those who condemned this
as a retrograde step, it was pointed out that even the automatic systems did not
eliminate the need for attention to be given to the propeller shaft points and
further on a car of this sort it was considered that in most instances an owner
would not be too greatly inconvenienced as he would most likely have the car
serviced by a garage in any event. Moreover, where automatic lubrication systems
were fitted on other models, it was found that not infrequently some part or parts
of the system failed after a time and unless owners were sufficiently diligent to
observe and rectify the fault, they were liable to encounter further difficulties
with the passage of time.

The whole body was increased in width from the scuttle rearwards so that
the front wing contours were extinguished in the front doors from which point
the body sides were continued at full width to the rear. The lamp cluster at the

Majestic prototype (note the absence of wing-top sidelights)

The production model

No321

The Motor Road Test No. 21/58

Make: Daimler   **Type:** 3.8-litre Majestic saloon

Makers: The Daimler Co. Ltd., Coventry.

Test Data

World copyright reserved; no unauthorized reproduction in whole or in part.

CONDITIONS: Weather: Warm with light wind for maximum speed, constant speed fuel consumption and braking tests. (Temperature 69°-70° F., Barometer 29.7-29.8 in. Hg.) Remainder of tests carried out on cool day with some rain and little wind. (Temperature 55°-56° F., Barometer 30.10-30.15 in. Hg.) Surface: Tar macadam, dry for max. speed, constant-speed fuel consumption and braking tests; wet for remainder of tests. Fuel: Premium grade (approx. 95 Research Method Octane Rating).

INSTRUMENTS

Speedometer at 30 m.p.h.	accurate
Speedometer at 60 m.p.h.	10% fast
Speedometer at 90 m.p.h.	10% fast
Distance recorder	accurate

WEIGHT

Kerb weight (unladen, but with oil, coolant and fuel for approx. 50 miles) .. 35 cwt.
Front/rear distribution of kerb weight .. 52/48
Weight laden as tested .. .. 38½ cwt.

MAXIMUM SPEEDS

Flying Quarter Mile
Mean of two laps of banked circuit .. 100.6 m.p.h.
Best ¼-mile time equals .. 103.5 m.p.h.
"Maximile" Speed (Timed quarter mile after one mile accelerating from rest.)
Mean .. .. 99.5 m.p.h.
Best one-way time equals .. 100.0 m.p.h.
Speed in Gears
Max. speed in intermediate gear .. 58 m.p.h.
Max. speed in low gear .. .. 38 m.p.h.

FUEL CONSUMPTION

27 m.p.g. at constant 30 m.p.h. on level.
26 m.p.g. at constant 40 m.p.h. on level.
24½ m.p.g. at constant 50 m.p.h. on level.
22 m.p.g. at constant 60 m.p.h. on level.
19 m.p.g. at constant 70 m.p.h. on level.
16½ m.p.g. at constant 80 m.p.h. on level.
14 m.p.g. at constant 90 m.p.h. on level.

Overall Fuel Consumption for 1,018.5 miles, 54.5 gallons, equals 18.7 m.p.g. (15.1 litres/100 km.)

Touring Fuel Consumption (m.p.g. at steady speed midway between 30 m.p.h. and maximum, less 5% allowance for acceleration) 19.3 m.p.g.

Fuel tank capacity (maker's figure)
18 gallons (incl. 1½ gallons reserve)

STEERING

Turning circle between kerbs:
Left .. .. 39½ feet
Right .. .. 40 feet
Turns of steering wheel from lock to lock .. 4½

BRAKES from 30 m.p.h.

0.90g retardation (equivalent to 33⅓ ft. stopping distance) with 85 lb. pedal pressure
0.86g retardation (equivalent to 35 ft. stopping distance) with 75 lb. pedal pressure
0.74g retardation (equivalent to 40½ ft. stopping distance) with 50 lb. pedal pressure
0.40g retardation (equivalent to 75½ ft. stopping distance) with 25 lb. pedal pressure

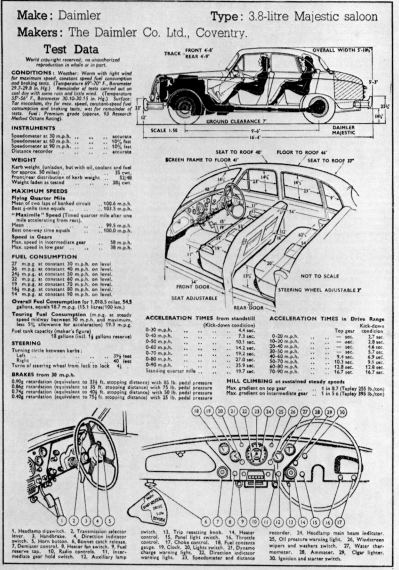

TRACK FRONT 4'-8" REAR 4'-9"
OVERALL WIDTH 5'-10½"
5'-3"
25⅜
14½
12"
GROUND CLEARANCE 7"
SCALE 1:50
9'-6"
16'-4"
DAIMLER MAJESTIC

SEAT TO ROOF 40"   FLOOR TO ROOF 46"
SCREEN FRAME TO FLOOR 41"   SEAT TO ROOF 37"

NOT TO SCALE
STEERING WHEEL ADJUSTABLE 3"
FRONT DOOR
SEAT ADJUSTABLE
REAR DOOR

ACCELERATION TIMES from standstill

(Kick-down condition)

0–30 m.p.h.		4.4 sec.
0–40 m.p.h.		7.3 sec.
0–50 m.p.h.		10.1 sec.
0–60 m.p.h.		14.2 sec.
0–70 m.p.h.		19.2 sec.
0–80 m.p.h.		27.0 sec.
0–90 m.p.h.		35.9 sec.
Standing quarter mile		19.7 sec.

ACCELERATION TIMES in Drive Range

	Top gear	Kick-down condition
0–20 m.p.h.	— sec.	2.7 sec.
10–30 m.p.h.	— sec.	2.8 sec.
20–40 m.p.h.	— sec.	4.6 sec.
30–50 m.p.h.	— sec.	5.7 sec.
40–60 m.p.h.	9.4 sec.	6.9 sec.
50–70 m.p.h.	10.3 sec.	9.1 sec.
60–80 m.p.h.	12.8 sec.	12.8 sec.
70–90 m.p.h.	16.7 sec.	16.7 sec.

HILL CLIMBING at sustained steady speeds

Max. gradient on top gear .. 1 in 8.7 (Tapley 255 lb./ton)
Max. gradient on intermediate gear .. 1 in 5.6 (Tapley 395 lb./ton)

1. Headlamp dipswitch. 2. Transmission selector lever. 3. Handbrake. 4. Direction indicator switch. 5. Horn button. 6. Bonnet catch release. 7. Demister control. 8. Heater fan switch. 9. Fuel reserve tap. 10. Radio controls. 11. Intermediate gear hold switch. 12. Auxiliary lamp switch. 13. Trip resetting knob. 14. Heater control. 15. Panel light switch. 16. Throttle control. 17. Choke control. 18. Fuel contents gauge. 19. Clock. 20. Lights switch. 21. Dynamo charge warning light. 22. Direction indicator warning light. 23. Speedometer and distance recorder. 24. Headlamp main beam indicator. 25. Oil pressure warning light. 26. Windscreen wipers and washers switch. 27. Water thermometer. 28. Ammeter. 29. Cigar lighter. 30. Ignition and starter switch.

The Majestic driving compartment

extremity of each rear wing was revised; the uppermost of the three lamps combined the functions of a stop-and-tail light and a built-in reflector, in the centre there was a reversing light and below that an amber flasher.

The result of the increased width was to provide very generous six seater accommodation. In the front the width over the seats at elbow level was increased from 56 inches in the 'One-O-Four' to 59 inches in the 'Majestic', whilst at the rear the difference was even greater – an increase of 5 inches to 62½ inches. Furthermore, the wheelarches were virtually eliminated and small separate armrests were fitted at elbow height. Central armrests were provided in both back and front seats and in the front further rests were fitted to the doors.

Consistent with Daimler tradition, the upholstery was deep and comfortable and by recessing the backs of the front squabs additional leg room was afforded to the rear passengers and for their feet a small angled floor rest was provided. Speaking of traditions, it has already been noted that this was the first Daimler for over a quarter of a century to be offered without a preselector gearbox and also that no automatic lubrication system was fitted – yet another departure from tradition was the omission of the characteristic rebate or ledge running along the bonnet edges from radiator to scuttle. Petrol stations did not exist when Daimler cars were first sold and so from the beginning, fuel was provided and then through succeeding decades the Company advertised the sale and recommended the use of its own lubricants. For many years the supply and blending of Daimler oil was the responsibility of Maxima Oil (Barrett, Tagant & Gotts). This facility terminated about the time when production of the Majestic ceased.

The Majestic was given the type number DF 316 for right hand drive and DF 317 for the left hand version. From about 1960 (r.h.d. chassis no. 99300) a new designation, DF 318/9 was ascribed. These later cars included improvements to

A Majestic, at one time owned by the Author

A Majestic interior by Hooper & Co

the front suspension including modifications to the shock absorbers and the instrument layout was revised; on the earlier cars the rear axle ratio was 3·92 to 1
but for the DF 318/9 this was changed to 3·77 to 1. Also on the later models the
tyre size was increased to 6·70 × 16 tubeless on 16 inches by 5½ inch K rims. A
number of other detailed improvements were made, e.g. a pre-packed needle
roller bearing assembly was used for the water pump fan spindle, thereby render-
ing unnecessary the use of a grease gun at that point; a larger aperture in the
floor was provided for access to the gearbox filler and slight alterations were
made to the rear brakes.

In the official specification for both the DF 316/7 and DF 318/9 the kerb weight
was given as 36 cwt and not 35 cwt as mentioned in some road test reports. A
minor detail concerns the separate side lights mounted on the wing tops – these
were identical to those used on contemporary Triumph motor cycles which were
of course also a product from within the BSA group.

Variation occurred in relation to the front seating; in some cars bench seats were fitted and in such cases extensible pockets were provided on the rear squabs but where separate front seats were installed, these incorporated picnic tables.

During the course of production (from chassis 99400 r.h.d.), power assisted steering was offered as an optional extra for less than £100. For a time during 1959 the total price fell to £2,355, returning to £2,495 for the next two years and then again fell to £2,352 during 1962 when production ceased.

Shortly before cessation of business, Hoopers did some work to special order on Majestics. This was mainly concerned with divisions, revised fitments, and special finishes, but there is no record of any specialist coachwork having been mounted on the Majestic chassis.

Stirling Moss writing for *The Sunday Times Magazine* (5.10.1959) concluded his test report on the Majestic:

To sum up, the Daimler is a very large car (I believe its back seat is one of the widest made), but because of its light steering and responsive handling it seems much smaller. Its excellent visibility also helps give the impression of compactness and manoeuvrability. If I were a chauffeur I would be pleased to drive it; but if I were the owner I should be tempted to take the wheel myself. It is a highly enjoyable car to drive and not unduly expensive for a luxury car at £2,495 (inclusive P.T.).

The SP 250

*SP 250 chassis numbers 100000–100005 (Prototypes); 100010–100569 (L.H.D.); 100570–100759 (R.H.D.); 100760–101324 (L.H.D.); 101325–101509 (R.H.D.); 101510–101585 (L.H.D.); 102510–102834 (R.H.D.); 103710–104456 (R.H.D.)

EDWARD TURNER, motor cycle designer within the BSA group, and a director of The Daimler Co, stated in *The Motor* for the 23rd April 1958:

I would plump for 8 cylinders, which on a 2½-litre gives a cylinder size of something over 300 cc. This size, at very high rpm would still keep bearing loads within reason, valve size down to manageable proportions and provide a unit of reasonably small package and light weight. Of the disposition of the cylinders, the obvious choice is a 90° V-8 as this provides a short crank with minimum torsional oscillation, good balance, a fairly symmetrical layout and provided one is justified with commercial rpm a convenient shape for push rod operation. Of course for a racing engine, a direct operated overhead camshaft for each bank of valves is de rigueur, but I often think too much emphasis is placed on this and considering . . . cost . . . and the fact that for a V-8 one would have to use four camshafts as compared with a neat disposition of a single camshaft, my choice would be for the push rod operation every time.

Mr Turner was not stating a purely hypothetical proposition, for under his direction, work was already well in hand for a new Daimler power unit. During the summer holiday of 1958 the first experimental engine was successfully run on the test bed and with few modifications it was considered to be satisfactory for production. Initially the test engine was fitted with a Solex double choke carbureter. One engine was installed in a Century saloon, first with an automatic gearbox and then with a conventional stick-shift box (borrowed from an Austin-Healey 100!). Much of the later prototype testing was carried out in Wales.

The Motor for 25th February 1959 commented:

The Daimler renaissance is being watched with particular interest, and the launching of the new 2½-litre V-8 is eagerly awaited, for it is on this car that the future of the old established concern will so largely depend. Moreover if all goes well, it will probably be produced in considerable quantity for the Daimler factory was equipped after the war with some of the most modern production assembly lines in the country.

---

*100010 was the New York show pre-production car and was subsequently dismantled.

SP 250 prototype on test

Christened the 'Dart', the new car made its debut in pre-production form at the International Automobile exhibition which opened in New York on the 4th April 1959 although full production did not commence before the autumn. By that time the name 'Dart' had been dropped and the car was simply called the 'SP 250'.

The chassis frame consisted of a pair of sturdy box-section side members, each formed by seam welding a deep and shallow channel-section member together with their flanges both facing inwards, the shallow member being inserted in the corresponding deeper member. At the front, the chassis members were supplemented by a flat plate welded beneath the flanges of the side and cross members and the centre of the frame was braced by a drilled channel-section cruciform member. At the front, coil and wishbone independent suspension was used and

The SP 250 chassis

the wishbones were attached to sturdy boxed vertical members attached to the chassis side members and braced to them by box-section diagonals at the rear. Further rigidity of the spring turrets was provided by a bowed detachable cross member running across ahead of the engine and fitted after the latter was in position.

Other chassis features included hydraulically-operated disc brakes on all four wheels, cam-type steering with the option of an adjustable column and as normal equipment, pressed steel disc wheels shod with 5·50 × 15 Road Speed tyres.

The power unit had a cast iron block, light alloy head and crankcase, with a short stiff dynamically balanced crankshaft carried on five bearings. On the nose of the shaft was a torsional vibration damper, a four-blade fan and the pulley for a triangulated thin belt drive for the dynamo and water pump, the former

Daimler 'Dart' 2½-litre V8

being neatly and accessibly mounted between the cylinder blocks. At the rear of the engine the drive was taken from the back end of the camshaft for the distributor which, being positioned high above the unit was commendably easy to reach. With over-square dimensions of 76·2 × 69·85 mm (2,548 cc) and a compression ratio of 8·2 to 1 the power output was 140 bhp (gross) at 5,800 rpm.

The basic price for the complete car (October 1959) was £1,395 which included £411.1.9 purchase tax. The undermentioned extras were listed:

Wire wheels £41.1.7, white wall tyres £11.13.9 (extra), adjustable steering column £5.13.4, leather covered steering wheel £12, front bumper £19.8.2, rear bumper £13.9.10, tonneau cover £15.11.8, detachable hard top £94.18.4, and Borg Warner automatic transmission £181.6.8.

The SP 250 was such a remarkable performer that two road test reports are warranted. First from *The Autocar* 2nd October 1959:

So different is the SP 250 from the mental picture of other Daimler models which people carry in their minds, that it may be regarded as a complete breakaway from tradition. Certainly our full description of the model last week showed it to be new in every respect, yet a glance at the 6-cylinder 2½-litre Conquest Roadster of 1953 reveals a family resemblance. There the similarity ends, because this new sports car, smaller and lighter, has an outstanding performance by any standards – conferred on it by its quite delightful vee-8 engine. If later we seem to dwell on the behaviour of the engine and the performance, it is because these two give the car its character and appeal.

First impressions: the SP 250 offered for test has the layout and equipment expected of the medium-priced modern sports car, and several luxury features as well. For example, an instrument panel with padded leather overlay – the two main dials immediately in front of the driver; a wide, curved screen, fixed and mating up with winding windows in the doors; and well-fitted leather-bound carpeting. The separate front seats, leather-covered, are bucketed to give lateral support and are of a size and resilience to offer comfortable support on long journeys. Leather is used also as the optional steering wheel covering, but the workmanship here is prototype-ish. The rear bench seat is of the two-small-children or one-adult-sitting-crosswise type. This, too is well upholstered. With the front seats in their fully back position to suit taller occupants, there is no leg room at the back, nor is there space to tuck toes under the front seats when they are moved forward.

It is an easy matter to slip into or out of the front seats with or without the hood up, and adjustment of steering column length and seat position should allow any driver to find a comfortable position; tall drivers may find their eye level rather near the top frame of the shallow screen. Although the doors extend down to floor level they do not usually catch on kerbstones when opened, though a little care is needed in this respect.

From the driver's seat vision is good; slim screen pillars, the absence of quarter lights and their frames, the slope-away nose, the separate side lamps, the rear wing tips and the wide transparent panel in the hood, all help to provide the aids and view a driver appreciates. When parking, allowance must be made for the extended nose and the optional front bumper mounted farther ahead.

All the controls are pleasant to use. Pedal pressures are light; the throttle pedal movement is smooth and progressive; the substantial floor-mounted brake lever to the right of the transmission hump is positive and – unusual for an all-disc brake system – it holds the car even on a 1 in 3 gradient. Most drivers might like to have the stubby gear lever about 2 in nearer to them; no doubt it could easily be cranked to suit individual choice. There is plenty of room between and around the pedals. The relative positions of the brake and accelerator pedals do not permit heel-and-toeing.

Glass-fibre bodies, though far from being new, are still something of a novelty, and that of this first production right-hand-drive SP 250 requires much greater rigidity and attention to detail finish. To judge from the creditably low all-up weight of the car and from lifting the boot lid, it is a very light body.

In the past weeks of summer weather the vee-8 engine was an instant starter, hot or cold. The pull-out choke also opens the throttle, and a half twist secures the control in any position – a convenient arrangement seen too infrequently today. The engine has a pleasing, deep, twin exhaust note which, over about 4,000 rpm develops into a throb or bark which is rather too loud for most British tastes. And speaking of high rpm this engine is remarkable for its readiness to leap to 6,000 rpm. The rev counter is marked to 7,000 rpm with a red limit line at 6,000 rpm. Performance figures were taken observing the 6,000 limit and it is left to the discretion of owners to use higher engine speeds occasionally if the circumstances demand. The instruction manual recommends that no gear change be made above 6,000 rpm.

But this does not mean that power only comes with high engine speed, for this unit is also unusually flexible, and pulls strongly down to 1,000 rpm in top gear. Top gear acceleration figures are interesting, the increments of 20 mph each taking very nearly the same time of around 8 seconds. At no time is the engine fussy, mechanically noisy or other than smooth. As one driver remarked, – 'Whether I were to choose the new Daimler or not, I should always be glad to have its engine in any car.'

Fuel consumption is light; the highest figures of 23 mpg was for one hard-driven journey of 69 miles, two up, with scarcely any straight stretches. On another rapid drive of 180 miles from the Channel coast to the Midlands, the figure was 30·1 mpg. For the whole test of 1,490 miles the consumption averaged 29·1 mpg and so with normal spirited driving 28–30 mpg would be a representative figure. On this particular car, oil consumption, using Visco-static as recommended, was high; 2 gallons were consumed.

Indications of the car's performance capabilities are given by its mean maximum of 121 mph, its standard quarter-mile of under 18 seconds and its zero to 100 mph in 26·3 seconds; these figures were obtained with the hood up and a test crew of two. With a competition clutch, the acceleration figures could be slightly improved because there was a fraction of clutch slip. In spite of the conventional rear suspension and live axle, there was never any axle hop during a fierce getaway, which is much to the car's credit.

Coupled with the high measured performance, there is an eagerness on the part of the car which makes for exhilarating driving and rapid eating-up of miles on a journey. Then the gear ratios are just about ideal for the car and engine. The gear box and change are far from attaining the same very high standard, and it is difficult to avoid a growl or grunt when making rapid changes up through the gears. Leisurely changes are satisfactory, but better syncromesh with bottom gear included would make for more pleasant handling.

Second and third gears are particularly rewarding when driving fast, for they give an unusually long pull before the next change must be made. Normal maximum speed in second gear is 72 mph at 6,000 rpm and in third, 106 mph. Maximum torque is produced at 3,600 rpm. Automatic transmission may be specified for the SP 250 and the manual change car can be fitted with a Laycock overdrive as an optional extra. The test car was not so fitted.

High performance is a liability unless there is braking to match. On this model the four Girling discs do their job very well indeed. They are smooth and very powerful bringing the car to a standstill in a straight line. Under test measurement the retardation figures are progressive up to a high 0·91 g at 100 lb pressure – near to the 1 per cent per lb push which many drivers regard as the right balance.

Front seat comfort, as we have said, is satisfactory; the ride which the car gives is firm and rather lively, without being harsh. It is of the kind familiar in live axle sports cars through a number of years. The rear wheels patter at times on non-smooth roads but there is no pitching, and when cornering there is only a negligible amount of initial roll. However, on all but the smoothest roads there is a considerable steering wheel shake and some body flexing. On two occasions of fast cornering to the left the driver's door flew open, although there did not appear to be any fault occurring in the latch.

At low speeds on dry roads the steering, of cam-and-lever type, is fairly heavy and an increase in tyre pressure, as used for high speed driving, has no appreciable effect. At higher speeds the steering load is lighter and the response is positive, though somewhat dead in feel. There is firm self-centring action, and on corners the car shows slight oversteer characteristics.

If, on a corner, the rear is purposely caused to break away with use of power, it can be checked instantly, and the driver feels quite confident when driving fast. On wet roads no more than the normal extra care is needed to avoid wheelspin or rear-end slide. The tyres do not squeal readily, but will do so, especially at the back, in fast cornering. On a straight road at speed the car holds a good steady line, and is little concerned with crosswinds. The minimum turning circle of 33 feet 11 inches is about average for a car of this size.

Although the SP 250 is compact and feels small to handle it has a good, big boot of convenient shape. It would hold much more luggage than the average sports car, even excluding the space behind the front seats. Beneath a false floor is the spare wheel, easily accommodated because the fuel tank is placed between the rear seats and the boot. Beside the wheel in its well are tucked the screw jack, a wheel mallet and a comprehensive roll of tools. The jack is operated through holes in the floor of the front compartment, normally covered by rubber cups and the carpet. Feeding directly into the tank, the fuel filler is centrally placed; a single fuel pump is found under a cover at the top left corner of the boot.

The bonnet is hinged at the rear, and its first catch is released by a toggle in the car. A simple stay is placed in position to hold it open (in similar manner to the boot lid). All engine components and equipment likely to require inspection or attention are accessible. The sparking plugs are sunk deep into the rocker covers, and the distributor is mounted high at the rear of the engine, away from any water which may be thrown up.

The SP 250

Weather protection on the *SP 250* is satisfactory, both draughts and rain (*so far as could be judged in two heavy showers*) being excluded. The hood frame and material are substantial enough to prevent flapping, so that wind noise is reasonable. Around the windows the sealing flaps are not the tidiest or best fitting. A hood cover, of novel wrap-round design, attaches neatly and firmly, and a tonneau cover with half-way zipper for the front seats was provided with the test car. With practice, the hood can be raised and secured in a couple of minutes, and folded away in the lowered position nearly as fast. There is a risk that the three clamps used to attach it to the screen top frame will soon rub through the cover while it is in the down position.

At night the head lamp beams have adequate reach for fast driving, and sufficient spread. Their dip switch is on the floor. Some drivers would prefer a hand dipper (preferably with signalling switch incorporated) in order to free the clutch foot. The screen is pleasantly clear of reflections.

Among the minor fittings, the wipers are silent, but because the screen is shallow the blades are necessarily short, and leave wide bands unwiped at the sides of the screen; the washers do their job as required. The twin horns, low-pitched, seemed to be out of tune on this car.

Stowage space in the car is limited to a lockable cubby hole in the panel, and small elastic-topped pockets in the doors. Passengers would welcome a grab handle. Smokers are provided with a lighter, and an ashtray built in behind the gear lever.

Warm weather makes it difficult to judge heating, but that on the *SP 250* seems good. Certainly the booster fan is quiet, and sends a powerful air stream over the windscreen. A thin rough-edged plastic instruction quadrant for the heater control immediately above the gear lever scratched the knuckles of two of the test drivers.

Keen drivers will be pleased to find, on the central panel, four clear instruments for fuel contents, water temperature, oil pressure and battery charge. Three tumbler switches operate exterior lamps,

275

panel lighting and wiper. The turn indicators have a switch on the steering wheel boss; they are self-cancelling and have amber warning blinkers in the rev-counter dial.

A comprehensive and well-illustrated handbook is available. It contains, at the back, a full lubrication chart which indicates that nine grease and three oil points need attention every 1,000 miles; others need servicing less frequently. There is no provision for a starting handle; the fan bolts directly on to the crankshaft extension and faces the centre of the large cross-flow radiator. The water header tank takes the form of a separate box carrying the filler cap. Frequent refilling was necessary in hot weather, and the temperature gauge was seldom below 200 deg. F.

With a compression ratio of only 8·2 to 1, the engine runs well on normal premium petrol, and this was used throughout the test. No undue pinking was noted on Continental premium fuel. The tank holds 12 gallons (14 US gallons), which allows an unusually good touring range of some 350 miles.

The test car, in bright red with beige hood, attracted a good deal of attention on the roads. Alternative colours are green, ivory and black.

In summary, this new 2½-litre Daimler sports car, of unusual appearance, has an open-road performance over which drivers can enthuse, yet it is docile and easy to handle in traffic. In either condition it is unusually economical in fuel consumption.

In February 1961, Borg Warner automatic transmission on this Daimler became available to the British public – previously it had been available for export models and for SP's used by the Police and not an inconsiderable number of SP's were put to the latter use.

In April 1961, the 'B' Specification became operative and from that time the chassis structure was greatly improved and the body was strengthened and there was included as standard equipment: adjustable steering column, front and rear bumpers, petrol reserve unit and switch, windscreen washers and exhaust pipe finishers, and then from April 1963 for the 'C' Specification further items were added as standard equipment and these consisted of a heater/demister unit, trickle charger socket and cigarette lighter. Furthermore from October 1960 customers had the choice of purchasing either a soft top model or one supplied with both soft and detachable hard tops. Where centre lock wire wheels were fitted, normally these were accompanied by tyres 5·90 × 15 in size.

Under the heading 'Who wants a turbine?' there appeared another road test report in *Cars Illustrated* for June 1961:

There can be few cars which have the characteristics of an ultra-high-speed sports car and limousine, all rolled into one. The Daimler SP 250 certainly has – it will throttle down to 10 mph in its high top gear (3·58 : 1), trickle along without any sign of fussiness, and accelerate strongly without snatch or pink. It will also behave like a projectile if it is given full bore through the gears and will in fact reach 100 mph from a standstill in little more than 25 seconds, also without fuss and with a very low noise level. When road conditions permit the Daimler will cruise at 100 mph with only a low growl from the V8 engine, and this is a speed which can be quickly reached – in third or top gear!

The unusually powerful yet silky V8 engine was designed by Edward Turner when the Daimler was still a product of the BSA Group. It is a remarkably simple yet cleverly schemed-out unit with pushrod-operated overhead valves and a single crankcase-located camshaft. In keeping with Turner's background the Daimler V8 has inclined valves operated 'motor cycle style' by fairly long rockers, a system which enables hemispherical combustion chambers to be employed – a feature usually reserved for the expensive-to-produce twin overhead camshaft type of engine. Thus a real power-pack is available at reasonable cost, and its simplicity makes it a natural for automation, and economical production.

Since the Jaguar Company bought the Daimler Company a great deal of work has been put into the SP 250 with a view to improving the finish, and roadholding. These have both quite definitely been improved, but the chassis cannot yet be described as 'fast enough for engine'. On good, smooth roads the Daimler can be driven very fast indeed but as soon as the surface deteriorates the rear axle will 'tramp', it becomes a handful and restraint must be exercised. Jaguar's have increased the rear spring travel and made many detail modifications but although the improvement over the early models is most marked the Daimler is undoubtedly at its best on a smooth road.

The immense performance of this unusual sports car is kept in check most impressively by the four-wheel Girling disc brakes, a fairly high pedal pressure being necessary but the results most satisfactory. Fade is non-existent.

The lines of the SP 250 are also unusual. A low-set air-intake with the crinkled Daimler motif incorporated in the front of the glass-fibre 2/3 seater open bodywork contributes to the modern appearance, although the tailfins do seem unnecessarily high. The car always draws admiring glances as it passes through a town, and a small crowd will usually collect when it is parked. The test car was fitted with the optional hardtop, and centre-lock wire wheels, and finished in a most attractive shade of green it was undoubtedly an 'eyeful'. Finish of the SP 250 both inside and out was to a very high standard. The moulded glass-fibre body was notable for a high-gloss paint finish and for the good fit of doors, bonnet, and bootlid. There were no rattles in the car even at high speed and nothing became deranged, or fell off during the 700-mile test.

The interior was in the true Daimler tradition with all seats, padded facia, and door trim carried out in the finest coach hide. Deep pile carpets accented the sense of luxury, and the easily removable glass-fibre hardtop converted the car into a snug coupé, with no draughts, leaks, or rattles. There were two good-sized doorpockets, a dash locker, and plenty of space on the rear seat for bulkier oddments – providing a passenger wasn't being accommodated there! The rear seat can only be assessed as a 'single' transverse but it is undoubtedly useful for children and extra luggage – and it is beautifully trimmed.

The hardtop, as already mentioned, can easily be fitted or removed, there being a normal soft hood as well but its height is not sufficient for a reasonably tall driver if brisk motoring is to be indulged in. The 5 feet 11 inches writer, who sat as far away from the steering wheel as possible to take advantage of the highest section of the hardtop (as well as to get the best possible driving position) found himself being struck on the head at speeds around 50–60 mph on second-class roads. It is undoubtedly a problem, for if the hardtop height was increased the lines of the car would be lost. The heater was very efficient but it was not possible to segregate deliveries to windscreen (for demisting) and cockpit. Consequently when heat was required for feet only the front seat occupants had to endure a stream of hot air on their faces.

The doors are wide, hinged from the front, and entry and egress are reasonably easy. The bucket seats have excellent backs which are well-shaped and provide good 'hold' on fast corners. The cushions however, although deep and well made, need extra length to provide ample thigh support – a most necessary feature on a car of this type. Driving position of the SP 250 was better than most, the adjustable steering wheel capable of being set down close to the dashboard, and the generous seat adjustment allowing the driver a passable 'long-arm' position. Unfortunately the clutch movement was such that it was necessary to fully depress the long-action pedal for a sweet gear change, and this necessitated sitting further forward than would otherwise have been the case.

All three pedals were of the pendant type and were positioned rather strangely with the necessity for the driver to keep his legs well bent for maximum control with consequent discomfort. Footwells, or even strip footrests would have made a great improvement. As it was the driver's feet were apt to slip under and forward of the pedals, and the insufficient length of the seat cushions necessitated a reshift to a natural driving position after every gear-change – not conducive to easy, fast driving. The situation was aggravated even more by the gearbox action which although equipped with a short 'floor' lever in exactly the right place, was stiff and not pleasing to operate. Full depression of the clutch pedal was essential to get a clean change, and this made the operation a chore. In addition the bad fit of the leather gear-lever 'sleeve' allowed a great deal of transmission hiss to enter the interior, and this spoiled an otherwise very quiet car. The sleeve, equipped with a rubber band at the lower, wider end, to retain it on the glass-fibre gearbox cover, would not stay in position, the groove cut in the glass-fibre being much too shallow.

In spite of this the Daimler was still fascinating to drive. The colossal torque of the engine virtually eliminated gear-changing, and there was enormous performance on tap using top gear only. On smooth roads the SP 250 could be driven very fast indeed, and it was possible to put 60 miles into the hour in normal traffic conditions due to its tremendous acceleration, high cruising speed, and wonderful brakes. The Daimler is a very safe car to drive for it has out of the ordinary acceleration and braking to get out of trouble.

Handling on reasonable roads is good enough for the performance to be exploited. It is an oversteering car, and this characteristic can be used to assist the cornering, use of the throttle bringing the tail round easily with a sensitive foot. Even driven hard its high gearing and torque ensure well over 20 mpg, and after 700 miles of fast motoring the Daimler had not used one drop of oil.

Bodywork of the SP 250 has good air-penetrating qualities, and in spite of a rather square-cut tail it cheats the wind as its top speed and fuel consumption figures indicate. It is not the most beautiful of cars when viewed from the rear but its shape has resulted in a really useful boot size with a capacity that must be rated as extra large by sports car standards. This in conjunction with the rear seat space makes the Daimler a first-rate proposition for the driver who likes to travel far, fast, and with his creature comforts aboard.

The V8 engine is completely unobtrusive in operation. It will tick over with just a murmur from the tappets in spite of the lack of soundproofing material under the glass-fibre bonnet. Accelerator response is immediate. There are no flat-spots at all, the two SU carburetters lifting the revs in a flash with only a slight hiss through the 'pancake' air-filters. To give the car full throttle in the gears is quite an experience – 50 comes up with a rush in first, then 80 in second, 100 in third, and 120 plus in top. Maximum revs are 6,000 and these are attained so quickly that a wary eye must be kept on the large rev-counter. The maximum power, 140 bhp, is developed at 5,800 rpm but even more remarkable is the maximum torque of 155 lb/ft at 3,600 rpm, a most impressive medium-speed figure which will waft the Daimler from 30 to 50 mph in top gear in $6\frac{1}{2}$ seconds. Another useful top gear acceleration phase was from 70–90 which the Daimler managed in 9 seconds. The car was run on Premium fuel throughout the test and no pinking was experienced even though the top gear performance was exploited to the full. Steep hills that have been known by the writer for many years just disappeared!

The ride was firm and no roll was evident at high cornering speeds. It was difficult to induce tyre squeal, and the car was completely steady at an indicated 120 mph. Steering was light when the speed had risen above 25 mph. The wind-up windows worked well, admitted no draughts but possessed the 'popular' fault of having a handle which fouled the driver's knee! Road view through the curved windscreen and rear hardtop window was first-class, the high-speed driver feeling that a

SPECIFICATION

PERFORMANCE

Through the gears:

0—30 m.p.h. ... ... 3 sec.	0—70 m.p.h. ... ... 11 sec.
0—40 m.p.h. ... ... 4.5 sec.	0—80 m.p.h. ... ... 15.1 sec.
0—50 m.p.h. ... ... 6.5 sec.	0—90 m.p.h. ... ... 19.5 sec.
0—60 m.p.h. ... ... 8.5 sec.	0—100 m.p.h. ... ... 25.4 sec.
	30—50 (top) ... ... 6.5 sec.

Maximum speeds: Top 124.2 m.p.h.; Third 101.2 m.p.h.; Second 80 m.p.h.; First 50 m.p.h.

Car mileage at completion of test: 4,500 miles.

ENGINE

Daimler SP 250 90 degree V8 water cooled. Bore: 76.2 mm. Stroke: 69.85 mm. Cubic capacity: 2,548 c.c. Compression ratio: 8.2: 1. Power-output 140 b.h.p. (gross) at 5,800 r.p.m. Maximum torque: 155 lb. ft. at 3,600 r.p.m. Two S.U. HD6 carburetters. Lucas coil and distributor (12-volt). S.U. electric fuel pump.

TRANSMISSION

Four-speed gearbox with remote "floor" control. Synchromesh on upper three ratios. Overall ratios: First, 10.5: 1. Second, 6.236: 1. Third, 4.41: 1. Top, 3.58: 1. Reverse, 13.5: 1. Final drive by hypoid bevel.

SUSPENSION

Independent front by coil springs, double wishbones and telescopic dampers. Rear suspension by live axle, semi-elliptic leaf springs and lever-type dampers. Cam and lever steering box.

BRAKES

Girling discs. Front 100 in. dia. Rear 10 in. dia. Hydraulic operation. Fly-off handbrake on rear wheels. Centre-lock wire wheels on test car, but bolt-on perforated pressed-steel wheels optional.

DIMENSIONS

Wheelbase: 7 ft. 8 in. Track: front 4 ft. 2 in., rear 4 ft. Length: 13 ft. 4½ in. Height (to top of hood): 4 ft. 2½ in. Width: 5 ft. 0⅛ in. Ground clearance: 6 in. Kerb weight: 1 ton. Turning circle 33 ft. 6 in. Fuel capacity 12 gallons (Imp.) including reserve. Average fuel consumption (mostly hard country driving): 24 m.p.g., Premium fuel. Tyres: 5.90 × 15 Dunlop RS5.

BRAKING FIGURES

Using Bowmonk Dynometer. From 30 m.p.h., 100 per cent, 30.2 ft.

PRICE

£1,355 including Purchase Tax. Hardtop and wire wheels extra. Basic price £1,121.

skinned eye could be kept on all quarters. Exhaust noise was low and the acceleration could be used quite freely in built-up areas with no fear of annoyance. Oil pressure kept to a reassuringly high figure even after two or three hours hard driving, and the engine seemed unburstable.

Starting was always instantaneous and little choke was needed before the engine settled down to working conditions. The engine finish was very easy on the eye, the twin polished aluminium rocker covers, and dynamo shield providing the enthusiastic owner with a source of pride. The engine remained clean after the long, hard test.

In spite of a recent price increase the Daimler SP 250 is the least expensive 120 mph car on the British market, and it is probably the most flexible 120 mph car in the world. It has fantastic acceleration, fabulous brakes, and a surprisingly light thirst for (Premium) fuel.

For an SP 250, painted white and shown at the 1962 Earls Court Show, the Daimler Company received the Institute's silver medal for open sports coachwork and a similar award was earned the following year.

First over the finishing line and class winner of Bathurst 6 hour Classic held on the tricky Mount Panorama Circuit, New South Wales, on the 30th September 1962, was the above illustrated SP driven by Geoghegan brothers Leo and Ian. The winning Daimler covered five laps more of the 3·78 mile circuit than the second car, a TR 4. The SP 250 was never extended during the six hours as its fastest speed for the flying 1/8th mile of the Conrod Straight was only 119 mph. Ian Geoghegan already held the fastest time for the flying 1/8th on this circuit in a Daimler SP 250 of 128·57 mph and fastest lap of 3·042 minutes for Production Sports Cars. Other successes were gained in sports car races all over the world, particularly in America

S. Oxton (car 51) and B. Merrett at Puke Kohe, North Island, New Zealand

The 'Felday-Daimler'

The Hooper 2-door special SP 250 sports saloon

The SP 250 power unit was quickly taken note of by enthusiasts and there were several examples of the engine being used to good effect in competition.

A young Surrey engineer, named Peter Westbury, finished seventh in the 1962 hill climbing championship – using a Daimler V-8 powered Cooper. During the ensuing autumn and winter Westbury built from scratch an entirely new car, which he called the 'Felday–Daimler'. This was powered by an SP 250 unit but with a simple 2 in SU carburetter and Roots supercharger. The power from this engine came in very smoothly and its range was so great that only two of the five ratios in the Lotus gearbox were needed in the final run of the RAC hill-climbing championship of 1963 held at Dyrham Park, Gloucestershire.

During an early run the crown wheel and pinion of the Felday–Daimler failed but Westbury's rivals sportingly agreed to postpone the championship runs until later on in the meeting and somehow the car was repaired in time. Westbury tore up the course on his first run faster than anyone had done before and his closest rivals, Boshier-Jones and Marsh could not approach his time, and it was Westbury with the Felday–Daimler who won the championship for 1963. Earlier with the same car, he had established a new record for the course at Craigantlet, Northern Ireland.

Possibly the last Daimler to have a Hooper body fitted to it was the one depicted overleaf and mounted on an SP 250 chassis no. 100571. It was exhibited at Earls Court in 1959 and had two doors and four seats and a metal body. The equipment included: wind-down side windows, hinged quarter windows, separate bucket-type front seats with hinged backs and fully upholstered bench seating in the rear. The spare wheel was stowed in a separate compartment below the boot. The instrument board was padded with leather. Flashing indicators were fitted to the front and rear with miniature repeater flashers on the side at roof level. A heater/demister unit was installed together with screen-washers and a radio. It is believed that the original car was later 'written-off' while on test at MIRA.

The Ogle–Daimler SX 250

One of the experimental Mk II SP 250's

When Hoopers closed, their Chief Designer, Osmond Rivers spent some months with the parent Company at Coventry. Under his direction about five further similar bodies were constructed, but in fibreglass and one additional prototype was completed. This incorporated a number of revisions to suspension and steering and the interior layout was also improved.

A decade or more ago, David Ogle, a young industrial designer with a passion for motor cars constructed a Grand Touring car using as its basis the chassis platform and mechanical parts from a Riley 1·5. Six of these cars fitted with glass fibre reinforced plastic bodies were made. These were sufficiently successful to prompt further experiments and in the course of time, a considerable number of Ogle-Mini-Coupés were built and sold. Tragically, David Ogle was killed in a road accident during 1962 but the Company – David Ogle Ltd and its enthusiastic staff at Letchworth, Herts, remained and at the Earls Court Motor Show in October 1962, there was exhibited the Ogle sx 250. Based on an sp 250 chassis, this sleek coupé, created a great deal of attention and favourable comment. The

283

The hard-top SP 250

body was moulded in glass fibre and the car exhibited was finished in twelve coats of sable brown cellulose. Its sound-insulated interior was upholstered in fine Suwide and deep pile luxury carpeting in contrasting shades of grey. The car was fitted with reclining seats, radio, heater and windscreen washers, twin sealed beam headlamps, twin horns and cigar lighter. Chrome wire wheels with 165 × 15 Pirelli Cintura tyres were fitted. The external dimensions were fractionally more than for the standard SP 250 – width 5 feet 11 inches and length 14 feet 2¾ inches. The total selling price was around £2,500. Incidentally the body styling was some time later adopted for the Reliant Scimitar.

Another attractive car was the SP 250 made by Daimler (see p. 283) and which, had it been put into production, would have constituted the mark II SP. Sir William Lyons was responsible for the modifications which were incorporated in the car and although quite numerous, quite the most important were alterations to the suspension, giving an improved ride, and even better handling and the fitting of rack and pinion steering in substitution for the cam type with which the earlier production cars were equipped.

CHAPTER 12

The 2½-litre v-8 and v-8 250 saloons

2½-litre v-8 saloon (Type XDM 2) chassis numbers IA 1001–IA 13377
(R.H.D.); IA 20001–IA 20622 (L.H.D.)
v-8 250 saloon chassis numbers IK 1001–IK 5780 (R.H.D.);
IK 30001–IK 30105 (L.H.D.)
The suffix 'DN' indicated overdrive
The suffix 'BW' indicated automatic

TOWARDS the end of the Conquest–Century production period (1958), the 2½-litre engine of Edward Turner's design was in the course of development for the SP 250 sports car and it was logical to expect the unit to be installed in a new saloon. During the experimental stage, the v-8 engine was, as already mentioned, fitted into a Century saloon with good results but in order to present a new image a lower and more modern looking body was envisaged. A Vauxhall Cresta (PAD type) was acquired with a view to ascertaining the feasibility of using the main structure as a basis for a new Daimler saloon which would, had it been developed, been much modified externally to conform to Daimler design concepts and of course to incorporate the famous fluted radiator. One prototype was actually made but whilst preliminary negotiations were in hand for the possible supply of body parts, Jaguar Cars Ltd – seeking more space for expansion, acquired The Daimler Co Ltd, Transport Vehicles (Daimler) Ltd, and their subsidiaries at a price of £3,400,000.

Sir William Lyons, in a paper entitled – 'The History of Jaguar and the Future of the Specialized Car in the British Motor Industry' – read to The Institute of the Motor Industry in 1969, gave a brief account of the takeover:

By 1960 our factory was once again 'bursting at the seams'. Unfortunately, this came just at the time when the Government was increasing its pressure on manufacturers who wished to expand, to move into distressed areas and, of course, no factory extensions were permitted in Coventry. It came to my knowledge that the Daimler Company, which occupied the very fine factory at Radford, within two miles of our existing factory at Browns Lane, was for sale. After some preliminary talks with Jack Sangster, who was then the chairman of BSA, having followed Sir Bernard Docker, we eventually agreed terms for us to acquire the Daimler Company. I do not recall a more amicable deal with anyone although, when we both thought everything had been settled, a matter of £10,000 arose between us. Since each of us was honestly convinced that this was in our own favour, we decided that the only way to settle the matter was to toss-up for it. I am pleased to say that I won.

The Daimler factory just about doubled our floor space and, in addition, we acquired a bus manufacturing company as well as a contract from the Government for the Daimler Ferret armoured fighting vehicle. Both were at a very low ebb – the output of buses being no more than three per week and the orders for Ferret showing a decline. In spite of the diminishing Government contracts for the Ferret when we took over, so good is the vehicle that it has not yet been replaced, and we have continued to make it in limited numbers. Indeed, it is one of the standard wheeled vehicles for NATO forces.

In October 1962 the first direct progeny of the new Daimler–Jaguar marriage appeared and at first sight it looked like a Jaguar Mark 2 fitted with fluted radiator but there was more to the new model than this.

The engine was the Daimler 2½-litre v-8 conceived and developed so successfully for the SP 250 and already described under that heading. Coupled to the power unit was a Type 35 Borg-Warner automatic gearbox which differed from the type fitted to the Jaguars in three particular respects: first it provided strong engine braking in each gear range, secondly it was smaller in size thereby giving increased interior room and thirdly the unit was considerably lighter. As the v-8 engine also weighed less than its Jaguar counterpart, the front spring rate and damper settings were suitably rearranged. At the front, wishbones with coils and and anti-roll bar were fitted while at the rear, the live axle was suspended on cantilever leaf springs and was located by a torque arm and a Panhard rod. Girling telescopic dampers were fitted front and rear and Dunlop disc brakes were fitted to all four wheels and this system was supplemented by a powerful vacuum servo unit.

Naturally, the Daimler was no match for the larger 3·4 or 3·8 Jaguars' acceleration or maximum speed, although for its modest engine size, it performed admirably. The car's particular metier was its sweet and near-silent running at almost any engine speed.

As with the SP 250, the maximum gross power was 140 bhp given at 5,800 rpm and there was a red quadrant marked on the tachometer suggesting that peak revs should be within the range 6,000–6,500. Nevertheless, when *The Autocar* road tested the car (report dated 31st May 1963), they reached 112 mph (approximately 6,800 rpm) whereas when the same car (index number 4545 VC) was tested by *The Motor* (report dated 17th April 1963), the maximum recorded speed was 110·2 mph.

An interesting device which contributed to the quiet running at speed was a Smith's viscous (fluid) coupling for the cooling fan. This coupling transmitted only a limited torque and slipped progressively as engine speed rose so that the fan speed did not rise directly with that of the engine. During a fairly rapid 400 mile journey made by *The Autocar* testers with four-up, including fast driving on the dual carriageways of the A1 the overall fuel consumption was 17·9 mpg. This figure was no doubt influenced by the automatic transmission and the comparatively low final drive ratio providing a top gear performance of 16·6 mph per 1,000 rpm.

For cold starts there was a very precise rich mixture control for the twin SU carburetters. This consisted of a lever in a long vertical slide, the use of which also slightly increased the engine idling speed. A warning lamp was fitted to indicate when the mixture device was in use.

Whilst giving praise for the generally satisfactory way in which the Borg-Warner transmission coped with the rather heavy duties imposed upon it by this model, *The Autocar* also noted a fundamental shortcoming of the particular installation. Although one could hold 'low' with the selector when accelerating from rest right up to maximum revs, it was found to be impossible to re-engage 'low' from 'intermediate' above about 5 mile per hour. This arrangement was intentional in the design in order to prevent a kick-down double change from top through intermediate into low, which could have been disconcerting and even dangerous if it occurred whilst say negotiating a roundabout. Such a feature of the system was thought to be a considerable disadvantage when in hilly country when engine revs in intermediate had fallen so low that there was little torque.

Upward changes in 'drive' with the accelerator flat occurred at 37 mph and 62 mph and it was found that the kick down from top could not be operated above 52–53 mph. As with all automatic transmissions equipped with torque converters, there was no difficulty in restarting the car on even the steepest gradient that could be found on a public road.

The optional power steering was well suited to the car which was directionally stable in all but the most forcible of cross winds. There was no loss of sensitivity from the power assistance but even without this extra, the steering was very satisfactory and not unduly heavy.

The Autocar road test (31st May 1963) contained the following comments:

On long runs the combination of mechanical refinement and light controls, together with good riding comfort and very fine handling characteristics, make things particularly easy for the driver; and two elderly people suffered remarkably little from fatigue after several hours' non-stop in the car. In this respect the only limitation is in leg space for those in the back. While it is quite adequate for average runs, a little more room for fidgeting or stretching would be welcome. The cushion, too, is a little short fore and aft. In the front there are no such complaints, although the folding armrests in the seat backs are rather high, and the driver's left elbow loses its freedom of movement. Except on straight roads, he is better off without the rest. On the test car the optional reclining front seats were fitted; the backrests are adjustable for rake, and can be let right down. Very ingenious are the seat runners which raise and slightly tilt the seat as it slides forward.

Generally speaking, the ride is much more than satisfactory. It is firm enough to hold the car steady on winding roads, allowing little roll, and does not become sloppy at high speed. When moving slowly one naturally feels the bumps a bit more, but the foam rubber cushions absorb minor shocks nicely without bouncing their occupants. Over the special test surfaces of washboard and pavé, the Daimler could be rated exceptional, not only for making light of these from the comfort angle, but also for the quietness of its wheel and suspension movements and the rigidity of its body structure.

One can dismiss the braking system quickly by remarking that it is in every way right up to the customary high standard now expected of British disc installations; a minor point is that considerably less load on the pedal is called for when the discs and pads are slightly warm, and the figures quoted in the performance data were taken in that condition.

R

The 2½-litre V-8 saloon

Daimler V-8 250 saloon

Reprinted from " The Motor ", April 17, 1963

Extended ROAD TEST No. 15/63

MAKE Daimler ● 2½-litre V8 Saloon
● MAKERS The Daimler Co. Ltd., Coventry, England ●

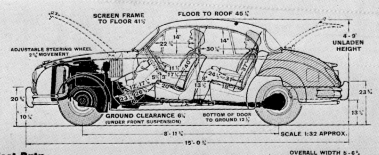

SCREEN FRAME TO FLOOR 41½
FLOOR TO ROOF 45½
ADJUSTABLE STEERING WHEEL 2¾" MOVEMENT
4'-9' UNLADEN HEIGHT
GROUND CLEARANCE 6¼ (UNDER FRONT SUSPENSION)
BOTTOM OF DOOR TO GROUND 12½
SCALE 1:32 APPROX.
8'-11¼"
15'-0½"

Test Data

Conditions : Weather : Mild and dry with light wind. (Temperature 45°—50° F., Barometer 29·8 in. Hg.) Surface : Dry tarmacadam. Fuel: Premium grade pump petrol (98 Octane by Research Method).

MAXIMUM SPEEDS
Flying Mile
Mean of four opposite runs	109·5 m.p.h.
Best one-way mile time equals	110·2 m.p.h.

"Maximile" Speed: (Timed quarter mile after one mile accelerating from rest)
Mean of four opposite runs	105·9 m.p.h.
Best one-way time equals	107·1 m.p.h.

Speed in gears (automatic control)
Max. speed in 2nd gear	64 m.p.h.
Max. speed in 1st gear	40 m.p.h.

ACCELERATION TIMES
from standstill
0-30 m.p.h.	4·8 sec.
0-40 m.p.h.	7·0 sec.
0-50 m.p.h.	9·6 sec.
0-60 m.p.h.	13·5 sec.
0-70 m.p.h.	18·4 sec.
0-80 m.p.h.	24·2 sec.
0-90 m.p.h.	31·8 sec.
0-100 m.p.h.	42·3 sec.

Standing quarter mile 19·8 sec.

on upper ratios
	Top gear	"kick down" range
10-30 m.p.h.	— sec.	3·6 sec.
20-40 m.p.h.	— sec.	3·9 sec.
30-50 m.p.h.	8·3 sec.	4·8 sec.
40-60 m.p.h.	8·8 sec.	6·5 sec.
50-70 m.p.h.	10·5 sec.	8·6 sec.
60-80 m.p.h.	11·5 sec.	10·7 sec.
70-90 m.p.h.	13·4 sec.	13·4 sec.
80-100 m.p.h.	18·1 sec.	18·1 sec.

Overtaking
Starting at 40 m.p.h. in direct top gear, distance required to gain 100 ft. on another car travelling at a steady 40 m.p.h. = 455 ft.

FUEL CONSUMPTION
Overall Fuel Consumption for 2,302 miles 140·5 gallons, equals 16·4 m.p.g. (17·25 litres/100 km.)

FUEL CONSUMPTION AT STEADY SPEEDS

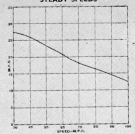

SPEED—M.P.H.

Touring Fuel Consumption (m.p.g. at steady speed midway between 30 m.p.h. and maximum, less 5% allowance for acceleration) 17·2 m.p.g.

Fuel tank capacity (maker's figure) 12 gallons

STEERING
Turning circle between kerbs :
Left	33 ft.
Right	34½ ft.

Turns of steering wheel from lock to lock 1·5 turns
Steering wheel deflection for 50 ft. diameter circle = 1·5 turns
Steering force (at rim of wheel) to move front wheels at rest = 15 lb.
Steering force to hold car on 100 ft. diameter circle at 15 m.p.h. (= 0·3 g approx.) = 4½ lb.

PARKABILITY Gap needed to clear a 6-ft obstruction.

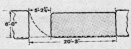

6'-0"
5'-2½"
20'-3"

OVERALL WIDTH 5-6¾.
16½
48
52½
54
56¾
20¾
57
26¼
57
12½
FRONT
REAR
FRONT TRACK 4'-7½
REAR TRACK 4'-6'

BRAKES
Deceleration and equivalent stopping distance from 30 m.p.h.
1·00 g with 110 lb. pedal pressure	(=30 ft.)
0·97 g with 100 lb. pedal pressure	(=31 ft.)
0·81 g with 75 lb. pedal pressure	(=37 ft.)
0·55 g with 50 lb. pedal pressure	(=55 ft.)
0·23 g with 25 lb. pedal pressure	(=130 ft.)

Handbrake
0·36 g deceleration from 30 m.p.h. (=83 ft.)

Brake Fade
TEST 1. 20 stops at ½ g deceleration at 1 min. intervals from a speed midway between 30 m.p.h. and maximum speed (=70 m.p.h.)
Pedal force at beginning	40 lb.
Pedal force for 10th stop	45 lb.
Pedal force for 20th stop	45 lb.

TEST 2. After top gear descent of steep hill falling approximately 600 ft. in half a mile increase in brake pedal force for ½ g stop from 30 m.p.h. = 0 lb.

Waterproofing
Increase in brake pedal force for ½ g stop from 30 m.p.h. after two runs through shallow watersplash at 30 m.p.h. = 15 lb.

INSTRUMENTS
Speedometer at 30 m.p.h.	accurate
Speedometer at 60 m.p.h.	1½% fast
Speedometer at 90 m.p.h.	2% fast
Distance recorder	1½% slow

WEIGHT
Kerb weight (unladen, but with oil, coolant and fuel for approximately 50 miles) 29 cwt.
Front/rear distribution of kerb weight 57/43
Weight laden as tested 32½ cwt.

Reprinted from "The Motor", April 17, 1963

DAIMLER V-8

Coachwork and Equipment

Starting handle .. .. .. None
Battery mounting .. .. Offside under bonnet
Jack .. .. Screw pillar type
Jacking points: Two each side adjacent to wheel arches.
Standard tool kit: Adjustable spanner, pliers, screwdriver, box spanner and tommy bar, 4 o.e. spanners, tyre pressure gauge, feeler gauge, distributor screwdriver, valve extractor, grease gun, wheelbrace, bleeder tube and jar, battery screwdriver.
Exterior lights: 2 headlamps, 2 foglamps, 2 sidelamps, 2 tail lights, 2 stop lights, reversing light, number plate lamp.
Number of electrical fuses 2
Direction indicators .. Self-cancelling flashers
Windscreen wipers: Two-speed, self-parking, electrical.

Windscreen washers .. .. .. Electric
Sun visors 2
Instruments: Speedometer, with total and trip distance recorders, rev. counter, with clock, ammeter, fuel, oil pressure and water temperature gauges.
Warning lights: Ignition, headlamp main beam, fuel level, direction indicators, mixture control, brake fluid level/handbrake.
Locks:
With ignition key .. .. Front door locks
With other keys .. Luggage boot and facia locker
Glove lockers .. 1, with locking lid, on facia
Map pockets: 1 in each door and 1 below instrument panel.
Parcel shelves .. .. .. 1 behind rear seat
Ashtrays: 1 below radio console and 1 in each rear door armrest.

Cigar lighters .. .. 1 in facia
Interior lights: 1 each side on door pillars, 1 above rear window, map light, cubby light.
Interior heater: Standard fresh air, heating and demisting system with two-speed fan.
Car radio: Optional extra, various Radiomobile models.
Extras available: Wire wheels, whitewall tyres, power steering, electrically heated rear window, laminated windscreen, radio, safety harness, Powr-Lok differential, reclining front seats.
Upholstery material: Leather on seating surfaces, P.V.C. for door panels, etc.
Floor covering .. .. Carpet with felt underlay
Exterior colours standardized 12
(others at extra cost)
Alternative body styles .. .. .. None

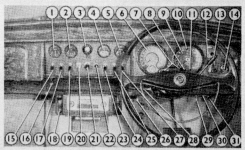

Key to photograph

1. Ammeter. 2. Fuel gauge. 3. Main lighting switch. 4. Oil pressure gauge. 5. Water thermometer. 6. Rev counter and electric clock. 7. Gear position indicator and flasher warning lights. 8. Ignition warning light. 9. Speedometer. 10. Main beam warning light. 11. Fuel warning light. 12. Mixture control and warning light. 13. Gear selector. 14. Hydraulic fluid level/handbrake warning light. 15. Interior lights. 16. Scuttle air vent control. 17. Panel light. 18. Heater temperature control. 19. Fan. 20. Ignition. 21. Cigarette lighter. 22. Starter. 23. Map light. 24. Heater air control. 25. Windscreen wipers. 26. Clock re-setting. 27. Windscreen washer. 28. Direction indicators and headlamp flasher. 29. Speedometer trip. 30. Bonnet release. 31. Aerial winder.

Specification

ENGINE
Cylinders V8
Bore .. .. 76.2 mm.
Stroke .. .. 69.85 mm.
Cubic capacity .. .. 2,548 c.c.
Piston area .. .. 50.2 sq. in.
Valves .. .. .. Overhead (pushrods)
Compression ratio 8.2/1
Carburetter .. .. .. Twin S.U. type HD6
Fuel pump .. .. S.U. electric
Ignition timing control Centrifugal and vacuum
Oil filter .. .. .. Tecalemit full flow
Maximum power (gross) .. .. 140 b.h.p.
at 5,800 r.p.m.
Maximum torque (gross) .. .. 155 lb. ft.
at 3,600 r.p.m.

Piston speed at maximum b.h.p. 2,660 ft./min.

TRANSMISSION
Borg-Warner model 35 automatic transmission with torque converter (giving torque multiplication up to factor of 2) and three speed epicyclic gearbox.
Top gear 4.55
2nd gear 6.60
1st gear 10.87
Reverse 9.51
Propeller shaft: Hardy Spicer divided shaft with centre bearing
Final drive .. .. Hypoid bevel
Top gear m.p.h. at 1,000 r.p.m. .. 16.6
Top gear m.p.h. at 1,000 ft./min. piston speed 36.3

CHASSIS
Brakes .. .. .. Dunlop discs all round
Brake dimensions: Front, 11 in. discs; rear, 11¼ in.
Friction areas: 31.8 sq. in. of pad area working on 495 sq. in. rubbed area of discs.
Suspension:
Front: Independent by transverse wishbones and coil springs with anti-roll bar.
Rear: Live axle suspended on cantilever leaf springs and located by torque arm and Panhard rod.
Shock absorbers:
Front and rear: Girling gas cell telescopic
Steering gear: Burman recirculating ball (power assistance as optional extra).
Tyres .. .. .. Dunlop RS5 6.40—15 tubed

Maintenance

Sump: 12 pints, S.A.E. 20 (winter), 30 (summer), 40 (tropical).
Automatic transmission: 14½ pints, automatic transmission fluid (no draining necessary).
Rear axle .. .. .. 3½ pints, S.A.E. 90 E.P.
Steering gear lubricant: Manual, S.A.E. 140 E.P.; Power, Automatic transmission fluid.
Cooling system capacity .. 24 pints (2 drain taps)
Chassis lubrication: By grease gun every 2,500 miles to 8 points and every 5,000 miles to 2 points.

Ignition timing .. .. .. 10° b.t.d.c.
Contact breaker gap .. .. .014-.016 in.
Sparking plug type .. .. .. Champion N7
Sparking plug gap .. .. .. .025 in.
Valve timing: Inlet opens 13° b.t.d.c. and closes 65° a.b.d.c. Exhaust opens 53° b.b.d.c. and closes 23° a.t.d.c.
Tappet clearances (cold) .. .. Inlet .011 in.
Exhaust .014 in.
Front wheel toe-in .. Parallel to ⅛ in. toe-in

Camber angle .. .. ⅛° × ¼°
Castor angle .. .. Zero ± ¼°
Steering swivel pin inclination .. .. 7¼°
Tyre pressures:
Normal {Front 28 lb. For town use {Front 25 lb. {Rear 24 lb. or bad roads {Rear 21 lb. (For full load increase rear pressures by 4 lb.)
Brake fluid .. .. To specification SAE 70 R3
Battery type and capacity .. 12 volt, 51 amp.-hour

Visibility 180° from the Driving seat. Shaded areas show one-eye visibility.

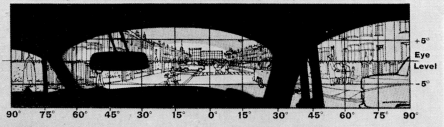

+5°
Eye Level
-5°

90° 75° 60° 45° 30° 15° 0° 15° 30° 45° 60° 75° 90°

Apart from having the seat adjustments already referred to, the driver can also set the steering wheel where he pleases on its telescopic column, and he looks through a zone-toughened screen. There are, of course, only two pedals, that for the brake being wide enough to be used by the left foot if preferred.

The Daimler has all the essentials and many luxuries of equipment usually listed as extras. The seven instruments include an electric clock and a tachometer; they have matt black faces free from reflections, and all give very steady readings. Lighting arrangements include two long-range headlamps with a flasher control, plus fog, spot and reversing lamps. There are little ruby tell-tales above each sidelamp, visible from the driving seat, and inside the car map-reading light and another in the fascia cubby hole. The screenwipers have a two-speed motor, and an electric screenwasher fitted.

Every door contains a map pocket; seat belt anchorages are provided front and rear, and there is a comprehensive heating and ventilating system with two-speed booster fan. A neat tool-kit in a proper box sits in the well of the spare wheel, which is kept beneath a metal panel forming part of the boot floor. A small but important point is that the push-button exterior door handles are said to resist freezing up in winter. There are 11 choices of exterior paintwork (of which six are metallic) as well as seven shades of leather trim.

Inevitably Jaguar adherents will be thinking of this car as very much one of their family, and weighing it in the same balance; it would be illogical, when describing it, to turn a blind eye to its true background. Nevertheless, the Daimler vee-8 engine is so fundamentally different from the familiar Jaguar units that the car has a true individuality. It feels good, sounds very quiet and behaves extremely well. . . .

A gold medal was awarded at the 1962 London show for the coachwork of the 2½-litre saloon exhibited there.

An important modification was effected in April 1964 from chassis 1A 3235 – in lieu of the model 35 Borg-Warner gearbox originally fitted there was installed a D1/D2 type of the same make effecting several improvements to the transmission. This type of gearbox was particularly well suited to the commendable torque characteristics of the 2½-litre V-8 engine. The new box offered fully automatic transmission with a dual driving range. With D2 on the steering column selector quadrant engaged, bottom gear was rendered inoperative. The car would then start from rest in second and would proceed automatically to change into top. In 'D1' all three ratios were employed and changes would occur in the usual manner according to road speeds and throttle openings. The overall gearing of the car was considered by many to be a little on the low side for really effortless high speed cruising but the exceptional smoothness and comparative silence, at all times, of the engine largely compensated for this. The engine's flexibility and excellent torque characteristics provided immediate and lively response to the accelerator without necessarily resorting to the 'kick-down' but if this device was employed the effect was instantaneous.

The Autocar road tested a later car equipped with D1/D2 transmission, in May 1966 and noted that a 4·27 to 1 final drive had been installed instead of the previous 4·55 to 1 axle. This obviated over-revving and although acceleration suffered somewhat, the higher ratio enabled a maximum speed of 115 mph to be attained and reduced petrol consumption to an average of 19·3 mpg through-out the test. The 1966 *Autocar* road test report contained some interesting remarks:

For balancing the reciprocating forces in an internal combustion engine, a vee-8 layout is the easiest giving outstanding smoothness. One so small as the 2½-litre Daimler engine, however, is rare and in terms of smoothness, refinement and silence it entirely lives up to expectations. At times in the past we may perhaps have been guilty of over-working the comparison of smooth engines with turbines, yet here is one which really justifies the claim. After a trip to Geneva in the Daimler earlier in the year, members of the staff admitted that if the car had been sent off with a sealed bonnet and instruc-tions that a new kind of turbine engine was installed, they would have been highly satisfied by its behaviour, and ready to sing the praises and advantages of the new form of power unit; the free-revving and high-speed smoothness are as impressive as that.

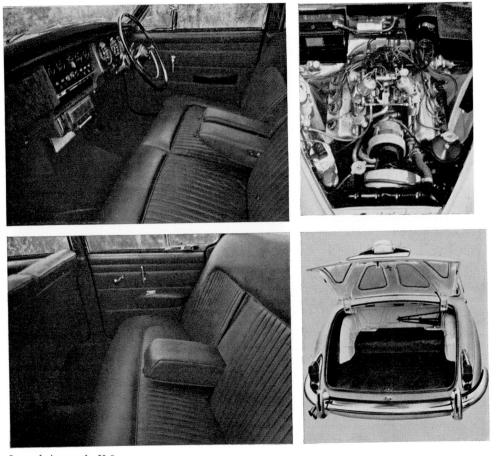

Internal views – the V-8 250

Apart from the axle ratio, other slight changes were incorporated from time to time and among the many optional extras there was now included a Powr-Lok differential and reclining front seats.

In keeping with Daimler traditions, the fascia and finishers were in polished figured walnut and the seats were upholstered in finest quality Vaumol leather hide over deep Dunlopillo foam cushions. The car was lavishly equipped with the appointments and refinements to which Daimler owners were accustomed. Official publicity literature said of the car:

– . . . here is the kind of Daimler which so many Daimler enthusiasts have long demanded and which truly provides prestige motoring in the modern manner.

In February 1967 a further innovation was introduced – the Daimler 2½-litre saloon was offered with a manual gearbox as an alternative. The SP 250 and then the 2½-litre saloon were the first Daimlers to be so equipped since the early 'thirties when the fluid flywheel with self change gearbox was standardized by the Company and the saloon was undoubtedly the first chassisless Daimler. Moreover, overdrive was offered as an extra and where fitted (in very few cases) it worked on top gear only to give a ratio of 0·78 to 1. The manual gearbox used, was the standard Jaguar 240 unit with unaltered ratios. The maximum speed obtained by *The Motor* testers with overdrive was 111·9 for a kilometre and an overall fuel consumption of 18·1 mpg was recorded. Incidentally where overdrive was specified a 4·55 to 1 rear axle was normally fitted.

The model was redesignated 'The Daimler V-8 250' from August 1967 and styling changes then introduced included 'slim-line' bumpers and overriders and interior improvements included padded screen rail and door cappings. A ventilated-type leather was used for the seats which in the front of the car were of the reclining type at no extra cost. Similarly there was included in the standard specification a heated rear window and an alternator in place of the dynamo and in consequence of the latter changes, a negative earth electrical system was provided.

Although a number of small mechanical changes were incorporated in the V-8 250, the basic specification and technical data remained unchanged.

The 2½-litre V-8 engine was the last Daimler power unit to survive the Jaguar takeover and it outlived its big brother – the 4½-litre V-8 as used in the 'Majestic Major' and DR 450 limousine. Production of the 2½-litre version continued up to October 1969. It is perhaps not generally known that specially adapted 2½-litre V-8 engines were sold for marine propulsion and a Simmonds Ski-boat driven by the record breaker Norman Buckley was very successfully run on Lake Windermere.

When introduced the total price of the car without extras but including tax was £1,568.19.7. The price rose to around £1,850 towards the end of production in 1969, to include the many items then provided within the standard specification.

293

The Majestic Major

The 4½-litre v-8 Majestic Major saloon (DQ 450/1) and the 4½-litre v-8 limousine (DR 450/1)

Type DQ 450 chassis numbers 136711–136890; 136916 137891
Type DQ 451 chassis numbers 136891–136915
Limousine – Prototypes 136001 and 136002
Type DR 450/1 chassis numbers 136011–136699; 139001–139176

Old-fashioned, yet able to 'play bears' with many sports cars. Spacious, yet looking compact, and simplicity to drive. A modern V8 disc-braked luxury car which is dignity personified, yet possesses qualities of handling, ride, braking acceleration and top speed that are as outstanding as they are unexpected. That sums up the Daimler Majestic Major saloon, and how anyone who can spare the purchase price of £2½ thousand can resist this fine car I find it difficult to comprehend. For it must surely be agreed that the aforesaid qualities in combination add up to all that is desirable in a motor car of any type. (W. Boddy – *Motor Sport* – June 1963)

THE DQ 450 chassis was a direct descendant from the pre-war 'New Fifteen' – 2,166 cc, introduced in August 1937. It was on the latter model that Daimler first introduced independent front suspension and although slight modifications and improvements were from time to time over the years made, the similarity between the design and layout of the chassis frame for the 1937 car and the 'Majestic Major' was unmistakable. The family resemblance was evident throughout the DB 18 range, the 3-litre, 3½-litre and 4½-litre 'Regencys' and their successors and variants including the 'One-O-Four' and 'Sportsman' and finally the 'Majestic' 3·8-litre. Even the wheelbase dimension of 9 feet 6 inches first introduced in August 1937 was retained for the models referred to and used for the 'Majestic Major'. However, the track measurement was of necessity, increased to accommodate the larger bodywork on the more recent cars.

The 'Major' closely resembled the 3·8-litre 'Majestic' which, in the assessment of some, was itself perhaps the best car Daimler had produced for several years. The 'Majestic' remained in production for some time notwithstanding the arrival of the newcomer. The outstanding feature of the new model, exhibited first at the 1959 London show, was its exceptional engine.

The v-8 'over-square' power unit was developed by Edward Turner, whose

295

earlier brainchild was of course, the $2\frac{1}{2}$-litre v-8 engine fitted to the s P 250. The enlarged engine – 95·25 × 80 mm (4,561 cc), had part-hemispherical combustion chambers, with short push rod operated valves worked from a single camshaft positioned centrally high up in the vee. The cylinder heads were of sand-cast aluminium alloy and light alloy was used for the valve covers, tappet blocks, sump and inlet manifolds. Cast iron was used for the block and the total dry weight of the engine was 498 lb. The sturdy crankshaft had five main bearings and a torsional vibration damper. Two semi-downdraught s U carburetters (type H D 8) were fitted. With a compression ratio of 8 to 1 the gross output was 220 bhp at 5,500 rpm. The power unit, like its $2\frac{1}{2}$-litre counterpart, was exceptionally smooth and efficient. Both the $2\frac{1}{2}$- and $4\frac{1}{2}$-litre v-8 engines were bench run at varying speeds for a total of approximately six hours before installation – reminiscent of pre-war Daimler practice.

Externally it was difficult to differentiate between the 6-cylinder 'Majestic' and the 8-cylinder 'Majestic Major'. On the larger car, a 'D' motif surmounted the bonnet and at the front – either side of the radiator, were circular apertures for the heater/demister intakes and the chromium plated grille coverings incorporated a 'v', indicative of the engine configuration. Another 6 inches was added to the length of the car resulting in an increase in luggage boot space to 20 cubic feet. Consequent upon this alteration the rear bumpers were given an extended return. Twin exhaust pipes also confirmed the presence of a 'v' engine. The instrumentation for the 'Majestic' did not include a tachometer but one was included in the layout of the 'Major's' comprehensive instrument board which was completely revised and in order to eliminate glare or reflection in driving at night, the dial surrounds were not generally chromium but matt finished in black.

As with the 3·8 'Majestic', so also with the 'Major' – disc brakes were fitted all round, their operation being servo assisted. A warning lamp in front of the driver served to indicate either that brake fluid was below the safety level or that the handbrake remained to be released.

Production of the 'Majestic Major' commenced in November 1960. At first power assisted steering was an optional extra at a cost of £66 but after October 1964 power assistance was included in the basic price and specification. This was of Girling manufacture and was of the transverse hydraulic ram type and the road testers for *The Autocar* were favourably impressed by the suitability of the assistance which made the steering at all times light and responsive without loss of 'feel'. They reported that at high speeds the 'Major' was very stable directionally and they also found that it could be cornered safely very fast for such a large car.

Notwithstanding the six-passenger accommodation of the 'Major', its performance was undoubtedly a salient feature and without exception the very flexible and powerful engine earned high praise from all the critics and journals. *Motor Sport* put a 'Major' through its paces on a track and using an electric speedometer, the acceleration figures shown on p. 299 were recorded.

ENGINE

4.5 litre V8 engine. Twin S.U. Type H.D.8 carburetters and double exhaust system. 95.25 mm. bore and 80.01 mm. stroke. Cubic capacity 4,561 c.c. (278.2 cu. ins.). Compression ratio 8 : 1. Develops 220 b.h.p. at 5,500 r.p.m. (and a maximum torque of 283 lbs./ft. at 3,200 r.p.m.). Overhead valves operated by short pushrods from chain driven central camshaft. Cooling by pump and fan with by-pass thermostat control. Forced lubrication by submerged pump system incorporating full flow filter. Chrome iron cylinder block. Cylinder head of high tensile aluminium alloy with hemispherical combustion chambers. Aluminium alloy pistons. Steel connecting rods. Large diameter counterweighted crankshaft carried in five (massive) bearings.

TRANSMISSION

Borg-Warner Automatic Transmission with driver controlled intermediate gear hold. Gear ratios: Low 17.4/8.701 ; Intermediate 10.8/5.418 ; Direct top 3.77. Gear selector lever on steering column.

SUSPENSION

Independent front suspension incorporating wishbones and coil springs with telescopic shock absorbers and transverse anti-roll bar. Rear suspension by semi-elliptic leaf springs and telescopic shock absorbers.

BRAKES

Dunlop bridge-type disc brakes on all four wheels. Vacuum servo assistance. 'Pull-up' handbrake mounted under facia actuates brake fluid level warning light.

STEERING

Power-assisted steering. 18" diameter adjustable three spoke steering wheel. Left or Right-hand steering optional. Turning circle 42 ft.

WHEELS AND TYRES

Pressed steel bolt-on disc wheels fitted with Dunlop 7.00 × 16 in. Road Speed Tyres. Spare wheel and tyre.

FUEL SUPPLY

By S.U. electric dual pump. 16 Imperial gallon tank capacity.

ELECTRICAL EQUIPMENT AND INSTRUMENTS

Lucas 12 volt battery. 72 amp./hr at 20 hr rate with current voltage control. Ventilated dynamo. Sidelamps with driver visible ruby glass inserts to warn of bulb failure faired into tops of front wings. Headlamps controlled by foot-operated dip-switch. Fog and pass lamps. Separate stop/tail direction and reversing lights. Number plate lamp and reflectors. Self-cancelling flashing direction indicators with warning light. Panel light. Two interior courtesy lamps, door-operated with independent switches for reading-lamp filaments. Cigar lighter with luminous socket. Twin blended note horns. Twin blade two-speed self-parking windscreen wipers. Electrically operated windscreen washers. Starter motor. Vacuum and centrifugal automatic ignition advance. Coil ignition. 5" diameter speedometer. 5" diameter revolution counter. Electrically operated ammeter, water temperature gauge, clock, fuel gauge with reserve switch, combined handbrake and brake fluid level warning light.

BODY

All steel four-door six-seater saloon. Separate cruciform braced boxed section chassis for rigidity and strength. Large windscreen with slim pillars and semi-wrap-round rear window for maximum visibility front and rear. Wide doors for ease of entry and exit. Panoramic rear view mirror. Chromium plated window frames on all doors. Push button door handles. Seats upholstered in finest quality Vaumol leather hide over deep Dunlopillo foam rubber cushions. Bench front seat (or optional individual seats) adjustable for reach. Folding centre armrests front and rear. Rear armrest incorporates storage compartment with hinged lid. Seats incorporate flush fitting tables in the back of the squabs. Polished figured walnut instrument panel features revolution counter, speedometer and separate instruments for water temperature, fuel gauge, ammeter and clock. Instrument panel also contains a large central ashtray and glove compartments either side. The locker on the passenger's side is fitted with a lockable lid. Provision for radio. Three spoke steering wheel and central horn button. Front and rear doors incorporate large pockets and armrests. Ashtray in rear of front seat squab. Universally pivoted sun vizors. Deep pile carpets over thick felt underlay. Nylon pile carpet at rear. Heavy duty wrapround bumpers with over-riders. Chromium plated door locks.

HEATING AND DEMISTING

New high output heating system incorporating windscreen demisting and de-frosting. Booster fan controlled by switch on instrument panel.

LUGGAGE ACCOMMODATION

Ample luggage accommodation is provided in a capacious rear locker with an automatic light. 20 cu. ft of luggage space available.

SPARE WHEEL AND TOOLS

The spare wheel is carried beneath the boot floor and is readily accessible. The tools, in a special container, are housed in the luggage compartment together with the jack and wheel brace.

JACKING

Jacking posts, front and rear, enable the car to be lifted with the minimum of effort by means of the jack provided.

PRINCIPAL DIMENSIONS

Wheelbase 9' 6", track front 4' 9", track rear 4' 9", overall length 16' 10", overall width 6' 1¼", overall height 5' 2¼", ground clearance 7".

297

The impressive interior of the Majestic Major

A special DR 450 landaulette built for the King of Thailand

0–30 mph – 3·4 seconds	0– 80 mph – 16·3 seconds
0–40 mph – 5·2 seconds	0– 90 mph – 22·0 seconds
0–50 mph – 7·0 seconds	0–100 mph – 28·7 seconds
0–60 mph – 9·6 seconds	
0–70 mph – 13·1 seconds	s.s. ¼ mile – 17·4 seconds

The claim made for the 'Major' – that it had a 'sports car performance' was, as the figures illustrate, fully justified. On the 12th May 1961, *The Autocar* reported a recorded maximum speed of 120 mph and made the remark –

In a category of its own, the Daimler Majestic Major has much to offer that is not easily found elsewhere. It appears almost as a sports saloon to the owner–driver with a large family; it may equally well be used as a chauffeur-driven limousine. With its powered steering it feels neither heavy nor cumbersome so it would be no embarrassment to a woman driver in a city. Without doubt it is dignified and distinctive in a traditional way yet the price is within the means of a great many people who favour a large car.

Speed and acceleration naturally had a marked effect on fuel consumption which could vary between 13 and 23 mpg but over a reasonable journey, an average of at least 18 mpg was easily obtained.

A single bench-type front seat could be had or alternatively, and more usually, single adjustable seats, but in either event veneered picnic tables were fitted. In fact the whole interior of the car was lavishly equipped and beautifully finished

Another view of the special landaulette

in best Vaumol leather and woodwork. Both front and back carpets were of high quality laid on underfelt and in the rear compartment there was in addition a thick silk pile rug. Where radio was installed this was normally equipped with twin speakers.

At the 1960 London show, the Company was awarded The Institute's bronze medal under Section X of the Coachwork competition – standard enclosed coachwork with four doors, retail list price of complete car exceeding £1,500 but less than £4,000 exclusive of purchase tax. That year no silver medal was awarded. In a similar category at the 1962 exhibition another bronze medal was gained for a 'Majestic Major' finished in two shades of grey.

In September 1961 a limousine version (chassis DR 450), was introduced. The vehicle was essentially the 'Majestic Major' with an additional 2 feet of structure interposed between front and rear and an interior partition, operated electrically or manually – according to customer's choice. Experimenting with such simple adaptations, manufacturers have often encountered body weaknesses and other problems but in this instance the result proved to be most satisfactory. Three Silver medals were awarded to the Company for the limousine – in the years 1964, 1967 and 1968.

The 'Major' and the limousine were the last Daimlers to have independent chassis. In both cases the bodies were of all steel construction and although zinc-phosphate rust-proofed they deteriorated rather more quickly than was normally expected of coachwork on a Daimler chassis. The total unladen weight of the eight-seater was 41·8 cwt and the distribution between front and rear was 51 per cent to 49 per cent. From a standing start to a quarter mile, the limousine was only 0·6 seconds slower than the saloon and about 5 mph slower on maximum speed. Comparatively speaking, the limousine's performance was even more impressive than that of the saloon. With the division raised passengers in the rear travelled in extreme comfort and could be quite unaware of the fact that for much of a journey they might have been proceeding at the rate of around 100 mph. Normally the front of the limousine was trimmed in leather and the rear compartment was finished with leather, West of England cloth or Bedford cord – according to customers' choice. At the time under review only three limousines were being produced in England, the Vanden Plas Austin 'Princess' selling for about £3,100, the Rolls Royce 'Phantom V' selling for around £10,700 and the Daimler DR 450 which sold complete for £3,557.14.0 – (all prices inclusive of tax and quoted for 1966). The DR 450 chassis could by arrangement be bought separately for £1,899. At the same time the total cost of a 'Majestic Major' saloon was £2,749. When first introduced the saloon cost £3,083 with purchase tax and although a year later the price dropped by a total of more than £500 the final price with tax, was £2,958 (March 1968). Late versions of both DQ and DR 450 chassis had limited slip differentials and alternators but these apart, very few changes were made in the specification throughout the production period, during which time an average of five 'Major' saloons and four or five limousines were

The 'DR 450' V-8 limousine

Rear interior of the DR 450

produced each working week compared to something like one hundred 2½-litre v-8 Daimler saloons per week.

The 'Major' was conceived before the Jaguar take over and it may seem rather a pity that the potential of both the 2½- and 4½-litre v-8 engines was not more fully explored in ensuing years. Both excelled from the viewpoint of design, construction and performance. Possibly if these units had emerged as immediate

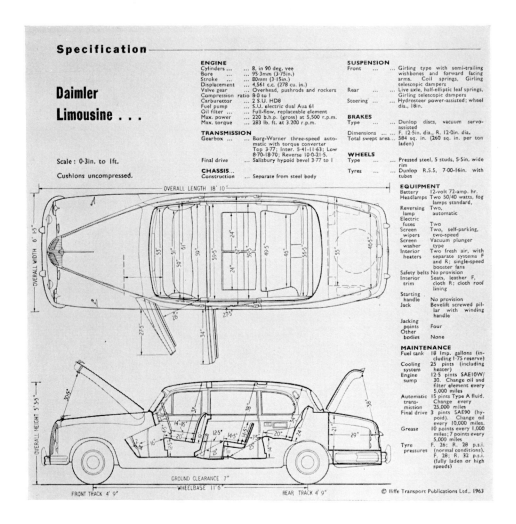

successors to the 'Straight-Eight', The Daimler Co, given also the right management, might have been in a more dominant position when it came in later years to takeovers!

The enthusiast may also lament over the passing of Hooper & Co in 1959 – a little too soon. A 450 v-8 chassis endowed with a Hooper product would really have been something. One enterprising owner did acquire an 'Empress' body no. 10013 removed from a 3½-litre chassis and had it fitted on DQ 450 chassis no. 137234. Although a number of modifications had to be made to accomplish the 'merger', the result was a unique 'Empress Major' painted in maroon with a tan interior and sunshine roof – a truly splendid vehicle.

Autocar road test · No. 1907

Make · DAIMLER   Type · Limousine

Manufacturer : The Daimler Co. Ltd., Coventry

Test Conditions
Weather...... Dry, overcast, with 10 m.p.h. wind
Temperature ... 6 deg. C. (43 deg. F.)   Barometer
29·3in. Hg.
Dry concrete and tarmac surfaces.

Weight
Kerb weight (with oil, water and half-full fuel tank)
41·8cwt (4,683lb-2,122kg)
Front-rear distribution, per cent F, 51; R, 49.
Laden as tested .... 44·8cwt (5,019lb-2,276kg)

Turning Circles
Between kerbs .... L, 53ft 7in.; R, 53ft 1in.
Between walls .... L, 55ft 2in.; R, 54ft 8in.
Turns of steering wheel lock to lock 4

Performance Data
Top gear m.p.h. per 1,000 r.p.m. .... 22·3
Mean piston speed at max. power ... 2,890ft/min.
Engine revs. at mean max. speed ...... 5,100 r.p.m.
B.h.p. per ton laden (gross) 98

FUEL AND OIL CONSUMPTION

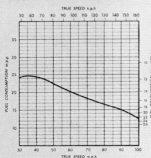

FUEL..............................Premium Grade
(97 octane RM)
Test Distance........................1,404 miles
Overall Consumption .... 14·7 m.p.g.
(19·2 litres/100 km.)
Normal Range ....12-18 m.p.g.
(23·5—15·7 litres/100 km.)
OIL: S.A.E. 10W/30...Consumption: 1,140
m.p.g.

HILL CLIMBING AT STEADY SPEEDS

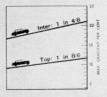

Inter: 1 in 4·8
Top: 1 in 8·6

GEAR PULL	Top	Inter
(lb per ton)	260	465
Speed Range (m.p.h.)	50-60	32-38

MAXIMUM SPEEDS AND ACCELERATION (mean) TIMES

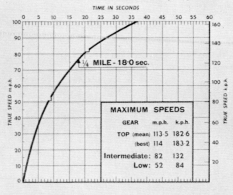

TIME IN SECONDS

¼ MILE - 18·0 sec.

MAXIMUM SPEEDS		
GEAR	m.p.h.	k.p.h.
TOP (mean)	113·5	182·6
(best)	114	183·2
Intermediate:	82	132
Low:	52	84

TIME IN SECONDS	3·9	5·8	8·2	11·3	15·2	19·8	26·9	37·0	56·9
TRUE SPEED m.p.h.	30	40	50	60	70	80	90	100	110
CAR SPEEDOMETER	30	40	52	63	73	83	94	104	114

m.p.h.	Top	Inter	Low
10—30	—	—	3·2
20—40	—	4·4	3·5
30—50	8·2	5·3	4·4
40—60	9·2	6·0	—
50—70	9·5	6·7	—
60—80	9·7	8·5	—
70—90	13·1	—	—
80—100	17·5	—	—
90—110	30·0	—	—

BRAKES (from 30 m.p.h.) in neutral	Pedal Load	Retardation	Equiv. distance
	25lb	0·18g	168ft
	50lb	0·41g	74ft
	75lb	0·63g	48ft
	100lb	0·72g	42ft
	125lb	0·86g	35·1ft
Handbrake		0·20g	151ft

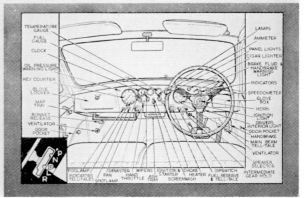

DR 450 limousines from the Daimler Hire fleet at St James's Palace, London on the occasion of the visit of the President of Italy, Summer 1969

CHAPTER 14

The Sovereigns

4·2 litre chassis numbers 1A 30001–1A 35476 (R.H.D.)
4·2 litre chassis numbers 1A 70001–1A 70355 (L.H.D.)
Suffix 'DN' denotes overdrive; Suffix 'BW' denotes automatic

XJ6-type – (Series XDM)
2·8 litre chassis numbers 1T 1001–   (R.H.D.)
2·8-litre chassis numbers 1T 50001– (L.H.D.)
4·2 litre chassis numbers 1U 1001–   (R.H.D.)
4·2-litre chassis numbers 1U 50001– (L.H.D.)

In October 1966, a new vehicle displaying a fluted grille appeared, but not only did this, like the 2½-litre v-8 look like a Jaguar – it was! Earlier Daimler practice of selecting model names alluding to Royalty – e.g., 'Consort', 'Regency', 'Regina' and 'Majestic' – was continued and the new model was christened the 'Sovereign'.

The 2½-litre and v-8 250 saloon cars although utilizing Jaguar bodies and other components, were at least powered by the highly esteemed Daimler engine. The 'Sovereign' on the other hand, was in essential respects all Jaguar but for name.

Back in 1948 Jaguar introduced their famous XK 120 Sports car – the first quantity produced British car to be fitted with a twin overhead camshaft engine. In 1949 one of the first production models was taken to Belgium and on the Ostend–Brussels highway, in a series of official runs, the XK 120 was timed at 132·596 mph for the flying mile. In ensuing years Jaguar XK's in various forms were immensely successful in rallies and races the world over and the power unit as fully developed has remained in production for more than twenty years.

Under the bonnet of the Daimler Sovereign was a Jaguar 6-cylinder overhead camshaft engine – 92·07 × 106 mm – 4,235 cc, fitted with twin HD 8 type SU carburetters and chrome iron cylinder block fitted with dry type cylinder liners. With the standard compression ratio of 8 to 1 the power output was 245 bhp at 5,500 rpm – about midway between the 265 bhp three carburetter engine used in the contemporary Jaguar E-type and 420 G and the 220 bhp produced by the 3·8-litre unit installed in the Jaguar 's' type.

The 'Sovereign' was the 'Daimlerized' version of the Jaguar 420 and distinguishing features on the Daimler were few – the fluted grille angled à la Jaguar, fluting over the rear number plate, the name 'Daimler' on each of the cam covers, and of course the stylized 'D' also appeared on the hub caps. Outwardly the 420 was otherwise little changed, except for the 'Sovereign' insignia on the boot lid, – first centrally and later to the side.

Included as standard equipment was Marles 'Varamatic' power-assisted steering, independent suspension and power assisted brakes all round, an electrically heated rear window, alternator and pre-engaged starter, reclining front seats and variable control interior heating for both back and front.

The car was offered with either fully automatic Borg-Warner (Model 8) transmission with D1/D2 dual drive range or conventional manual gearbox with the further option of de Normanville overdrive operating on top gear (giving an overdrive ratio of 0·78 to 1).

As a further alternative customers could specify compression ratios of 7 to 1 or 9 to 1 in place of the normal 8 to 1. The rear axle was of the hypoid type and incorporated a limited slip differential. For cars fitted with automatic transmission or with a synchromesh box without overdrive the axle ratio was 3·31 to 1 but a 3·77 to 1 axle was used where overdrive was added.

Twin fuel tanks – one in each rear wing were fitted and gave a total capacity of 14 gallons, which was hardly sufficient since both automatic and manual transmission models returned an average of only 18 mpg.

For some years Jaguars had dispensed with a separate chassis for their cars and accordingly the 'Sovereign' was of integral construction in all-steel and provided five passenger accommodation with maximum rigidity and minimum weight (approximately 32 cwt). Furthermore, Jaguars had for long held the reputation of providing real value for money. Whilst inevitably Daimler Purists were somewhat cynical about the new car, they could not have sustained any criticism levelled at the standard of finish of the 'Sovereign' – either outside or in.

The Daimler Sovereign (1966)

306

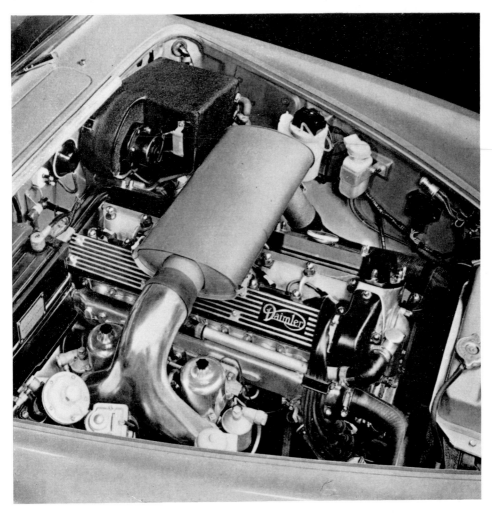

The works of the earlier Sovereign

The car was lavishly equipped and genuine leather and traditional woodwork were much in evidence.

The disparity between the performance figures for the automatic model and the stick-shift Sovereign was almost non-existent – both cars accelerated to 100 mph in just over 27 seconds and both had a top speed of around 118 mph.

After three years, production of the original 'Sovereign' was superseded by a new 'Sovereign' announced in October 1969. This was the fabulous XJ6 Jaguar with sufficient 'fluting' to ensure recognition as a Daimler. As the cars were

1966 Sovereign interior

mechanically identical, comments made by *The Autocar* (12th June 1969) concerning the Jaguar 4·2-litre, are equally referable to the Daimler:

The XJ6 has been built from the tyres up and it shows in the way it behaves on any road in any conditions. From our company chauffeur who merely took the test car through city streets to a drive-in car wash to our most blasé tester, everyone was impressed immediately with the completely out-of-its-class ride and silence. With certain qualifications we would say it is the smoothest and quietest car we have ever driven or been driven in. And that includes cars in the multi-thousand pound bracket like the Rolls-Royce and Mercedes 600. And after detailed discussion our test staff agreed that the handling was, if anything better than that of the E-type and certainly unmatched by anything in the saloon car class.

The XJ6 clearly portrayed its ancestry, for although it was an entirely new car in nearly all respects, it retained the 245 bhp twin-cam engine fitted to earlier Jaguars and installed in the original 'Sovereign'. The 4·2-litre unit was normally produced with 8 to 1 compression but 9 to 1 could be had to order. 17·5 seconds were required to cover a quarter mile from a standing start; from 0 to 60 mph took approximately 10 seconds and the car's maximum was almost exactly 120 mph. Specially designed tyres were produced by Dunlop and these provided

THE DAIMLER SOVEREIGN SPECIFICATION

ENGINE. 6 cylinder, twin overhead camshaft, 4·2 litre engine, 92·07 mm. bore × 106 mm. stroke (3·625 in. by 4·1732 in.). Cubic capacity 4235 c.c. (258·43 cu. in.). Compression ratio 8 : 1. Power output 245 b.h.p. at 5,500 r.p.m. Torque 282 ft./lb. at 3,750 r.p.m. Twin S.U. carburetters, type HD.8, with automatic starting control. Forced lubrication incorporating a full flow filter. Chrome iron cylinder block fitted with dry type cylinder liners. Special "straight port" cylinder head of high tensile aluminium alloy featuring hemispherical combustion chambers and twin overhead camshafts operating large valves of 70° included angle. Aluminium alloy pistons. Steel connecting rods fitted with lead indium big-end bearings. 2¾ in. diameter counterweighted crankshaft carried on seven large lead indium bearings. Pressurised cooling system with thermostatic control and viscous coupling fan.

TRANSMISSION. (Manually operated gearbox with overdrive.) Four-speed single helical all synchromesh gearbox with Laycock de Normanville overdrive. Gear change lever on floor between front seats. Overdrive controlled by a lever mounted on the steering column. Gear ratios; 1st, 11·46; 2nd, 7·44; 3rd, 5·00; Top, 3·77; Overdrive, 2·93; Reverse, 13·16. Borg and Beck diaphragm spring clutch with hydraulic operation. Needle bearing propeller shaft. Hypoid rear axle with limited slip differential.

TRANSMISSION. (Automatic Transmission model.) Borg Warner Model 8 automatic transmission with dual drive range D1/D2. Gear ratios; Top, 3·54/— with torque conversion 7·08; Intermediate, 5·16/10·32; Low, 8·5/17·0; Reverse, 7·08/14·16. Gear selector on steering column. Needle bearing propeller shaft. Hypoid rear axle with limited slip differential.

SUSPENSION—FRONT. Independent suspension incorporating semi-trailing wishbones and coil springs with telescopic dampers. Anti-roll bar between lower wishbones. Suspension assembly and steering gear are mounted on a separate subframe which is itself located in the body by rubber mountings.

SUSPENSION—REAR. Fully independent rear suspension incorporating on each side a lower transverse tubular link pivoted at the wheel carrier and sub-frame adjacent to the differential case and, above this, a half shaft universally jointed at each end. These serve to locate the wheel in a transverse plane. Longitudinal location is provided by the rubber mountings locating the sub-assembly in the body structure and by a radius arm between the lower link and a mounting point on the body structure. Twin coil springs, each enclosing a telescopic hydraulic damper, provide the suspension medium. The whole assembly together with the differential unit is carried in an easily detachable sub-frame which is located in the body structure by rubber mountings.

BRAKES. Disc brakes, featuring quick change pads, are fitted to all four wheels. Front brakes fitted on wheel hubs, rear brakes fitted inboard of half shafts adjacent to differential unit. System is divided into two entirely independent hydraulic circuits to front and rear brakes. Operation is by suspended vacuum tandem type servo operated by a master cylinder and reaction valve. Handbrake with automatic adjustment operates on rear wheels only. Combined handbrake "on" and brake fluid level warning light.

STEERING. "Varamatic" power-assisted steering. Ratio 21·5 : 1 in straight ahead position varying to 13 : 1 at full lock. 2·75 turns lock to lock. Power supplied by vane pump, incorporating its own fluid reservoir, and driven from front of crankshaft by separate belt. 17 in. diameter two-spoke steering wheel adjustable for reach. Left or right hand steering optional. Turning circle 33½ ft.

WHEELS AND TYRES. Pressed steel bolt-on disc wheels fitted with Dunlop SP41 tyres and tubes. Wire spoke wheels available as an optional extra. Spare wheel and tyre.

FUEL SUPPLY. Two separate tanks—one in each rear wing—total capacity 14 gallons. Two electrically operated S.U. fuel pumps (one for each tank) controlled by change-over switch on instrument panel. The separate fillers to each tank are concealed beneath individual covers.

ELECTRICAL EQUIPMENT AND INSTRUMENTS. Lucas alternator 12-volt battery with negative earth system. 60 amp./hour at 10 hour rate with current voltage control. Sidelamps. Four headlamps controlled by foot-operated dip-switch. Separate lever for actuating headlamp flashing. Separate stop/tail, direction and reflector units mounted in a single assembly. Twin reversing lamps. Self-cancelling flashing direction indicators with warning lights. Instruments and labelled switches illuminated by internal lighting controlled by a two-position dimmer switch. Concealed map-reading lamp beneath screen rail in front compartment. Courtesy lights above the centre door pillar and above rear window, operated either manually by switch on the instrument panel or automatically by any of the four doors. Luggage boot illumination controlled by automatic switch. Cigar lighter with luminous socket. Twin-blended windtone horns. Twin blade, two-speed, self-parking windscreen wipers. Electrically operated windscreen washers. Electrically heated back light. Pre-engaged starter motor. Vacuum and centrifugal automatic ignition advance. Oil coil ignition. 5 in. diameter speedometer incorporating total trip and distance recorder. 5 in. diameter impulse driven revolution counter. Separate transistorised time clock centrally mounted in padded screen rail. Ammeter, electrically operated oil pressure gauge, water temperature gauge, fuel gauge, combined handbrake "on" and brake fluid level warning light.

BODY. All steel, four-door, five-seater saloon. Integral body-chassis construction providing maximum rigidity with minimum weight. Large zone-toughened windscreen with slim pillars and semi-wrapround rear window for maximum visibility front and rear. The semi-wrapround windscreen does not interfere with ease of entry or exit. Wide view rear mirror incorporating dimmed image position. Chromium-plated window frames to all doors. Chrome finishers on rain guttering and top of door waist rail. Seats upholstered in finest quality leather hide over deep foam rubber cushions. Front seats have combined height and reach adjustment and reclining squabs. Central folding armrests front and rear. Padded safety screen rail with centrally mounted transistorised time clock. Polished figured walnut instrument panel with heavily padded surround features revolution counter and speedometer positioned directly in front of driver, and separate instruments for oil pressure, water temperature, fuel gauge and ammeter. The panel also contains, on the passenger's side, a glove compartment with interior light and lockable lid. A large padded parcel shelf runs the full width of the car beneath the instrument panel and houses the heater temperature control in its forward edge. A separate housing beneath the instrument panel contains a radio and speaker (optional extra) together with a large ashtray. When no radio is fitted, the speaker grille is retained and the radio control panel aperture is blanked off with an escutcheon. Two-spoke steering wheel and semi-circular horn ring. Front and rear doors incorporate large pockets and armrests, whilst the rear doors also contain ashtrays. Sun visors. Deep pile carpets over thick felt underlay. Heavy duty wrapround bumpers with over-riders. "Zero-torque" door locks enable doors to be closed easily and quietly. Seat belt anchorage points are incorporated for both front and rear seats.

HEATING AND DEMISTING. High efficiency fresh air heating system capable of high temperature and volume supply to front and rear compartments. Separate control regulates supply to rear compartment. Air intake vents and heater valves are vacuum servo assisted. Two-speed fan controlled by switch on instrument panel.

LUGGAGE ACCOMMODATION. Ample luggage accommodation is provided in a capacious compartment of 19 cu. ft. capacity. The lid is counter-balanced for ease of operation. Interior of compartment illuminated by night by a separate lamp. Compartment fully trimmed to protect luggage.

SPARE WHEEL AND TOOLS. The spare wheel is carried beneath the luggage compartment floor in a separate compartment and is readily accessible. The tools, in a special fitted and lined container, are housed in the spare wheel compartment. Jack and wheel brace (or wheel hammer on wire wheel models) housed in luggage compartment.

JACKING. Exterior jacking points, front and rear, enable car to be lifted with the minimum of effort by means of the jack provided.

PRINCIPAL DIMENSIONS. Wheel base 8 ft. 11¾ in., track front 4 ft. 7¼ in., track rear 4 ft. 6¼ in., overall length 15 ft. 7¾ in., overall width 5 ft. 6¾ in. Dry weight 3463 lb.

Specification 1966–1969.

incredible grip and contributed to the lightness and accuracy of the rack and pinion power assisted steering.

At the front of the car there were double wishbones and coil springs with separate dampers and a rubber mounted sub-frame which also served the purpose of supporting the engine. Independent suspension was also employed for the rear and this followed usual Jaguar practice of using transverse lower links, radius arms and twin coil-springs and damper units each side with the half shafts acting as the upper links.

The first class appearance of the Jaguar xj6 was altered and improved by the Daimler additions: notably the broad new style fluted radiator grille. The 'fluted' theme was repeated at the rear for the number plate housing and side-view identification was assisted by the traditional 'D' centred nave plates. Inside too there were differences. Wider pleats appeared in the leather seating and at the front the armrests were extended to provide a handle-grip and to form a cover for the door pocket. In keeping with the tradition, the equipment of the 'Sovereign' was indeed lavish and included twin swivelling fascia ventilators, voltmeter, transistorized clock, dipping mirror, hazard warning lights, map and interior lights, brake-warning lights, steering adjustment and lock, rear window demister and all other necessary and usual instruments and controls. The front door quarter lights were operated by rotating an adjacent knob. In addition to the normal range of optional extras, there was included from the end of 1970 a

The New Daimler Sovereign – 1969

The New Daimler Sovereign – 1969

1970 Sovereign interior

push button radio which had stereo-audio output and a cassette recorder with stereo playback. A microphone was also included with the installation together with four loudspeakers, an electrically operated aerial, and a miniature control box. Electric windows could also be had for another £56·25. From September 1970, the door tread plates incorporated 'Daimler' and the instrument bezels were in black matt instead of chrome.

With identical appearance and finish, the 'Sovereign' was offered with an alternative 2·8-litre engine. This too was a Jaguar unit and had all the design

311

THE NEW
DAIMLER SOVEREIGN SPECIFICATION (1969)

ENGINE – 2·8 LITRE In-line six cylinder, twin overhead camshaft engine with straight port type cylinder head. Twin S.U. H.D.8 carburetters with automatic enrichment for cold starting, and dual exhaust system. 83 mm bore × 86 mm stroke. Cubic capacity 2792 c.c. developing 180 b.h.p. at 6,000 r.p.m. and 182 lb/ft torque at 3,750 r.p.m. Compression ratio 9 : 1.

ENGINE – 4·2 LITRE In-line six cylinder, twin overhead camshaft engine with straight port type cylinder head. Twin S.U. H.D.8 carburetters with automatic enrichment control, and dual exhaust system. 92·07 mm bore × 106 mm stroke. Cubic capacity 4235 c.c. developing 245 b.h.p. at 5,500 r.p.m. and 283 lb/ft torque at 3,750 r.p.m. Compression ratio 8 : 1.

COOLING SYSTEM Two-row tube-and-fin, cross-flow radiator. 12-bladed fan driven by viscous coupling for reduced power absorption, improved cooling at low engine speeds, and minimum noise at high speeds.

OVERDRIVE MODELS 4-speed all-synchromesh gearbox with addition of Laycock overdrive unit – hydraulically operated, and electrically controlled by sliding switch in the gear lever knob. **2·8 Model** – Overall ratios: 1st 13·32 : 1, 2nd 8·67 : 1, 3rd 6·33 : 1, 4th 4·55 : 1, Overdrive 3·54 : 1, Reverse 15·35 : 1, Rear axle ratio 4·55 : 1. **4·2 Model** – Overall ratios: 1st 10·53 : 1, 2nd 6·75 : 1, 3rd 4·49 : 1, 4th 3·54 : 1, Overdrive 2·76 : 1, Reverse 11·92 : 1, Rear axle ratio 3·54 : 1.

AUTOMATIC TRANSMISSION MODELS 2·8 version Borg Warner Type 35 unit with D·2·1 control system. Overall ratios: Top 4·09, with torque conversion 8·18; Intermediate 5·93/11·86; Low 9·82/19·64; Reverse 8·5/17·10; Rear axle ratio 4·09 : 1.

4·2 version – Borg Warner unit. Overall ratios: Top 3·31, with torque conversion 6·62; Intermediate 4·8/9·6; Low 7·9/15·8; Reverse 6·82/13·24; Rear axle ratio 3·31 : 1. The gear selector lever, on both models, is mounted between the front seats and operates in a slide-gate.

SUSPENSION Fully independent suspension, front and rear, on sub-frames located in body by rubber mountings. 'Anti-dive' geometry on front suspension of completely new design, incorporating coil springs and separate dampers with expanded polyurethane damper mountings. The whole system is designed to provide new standards in roadholding and handling. At the same time, transmission of road noise and vibration have been reduced to an exceptionally low level.

WHEELS AND TYRES Pressed steel bolt-on wheels, fitted with chrome plated wheel trims. 6 in. wide rims. Dunlop low profile. S.P. Sport radial ply. E70 VR 15 tyres featuring an 'anti-aquaplaning' tread pattern.

BRAKES Disc braking of all four wheels. Vacuum servo-assisted hydraulic system with independent circuits to front and rear brakes. Automatic adjustment for wear. 'Pistol-grip', self-adjusting handbrake operates on rear wheels, combined handbrake 'on' and brake fluid 'low level' warning light on instrument panel.

STEERING Rack and pinion steering, with power assistance for precision and sensitivity combined with low effort. 16 in. diameter two-spoke steering wheel. 3¼ turns lock to lock. Turning circle approx. 36 ft. Left or right hand steering optional. Telescopically adjustable steering column. Steering column lock incorporating ignition switch.

FUEL SUPPLY Twin fuel tanks, enclosed in steel compartments, one in each wing. Twin filler caps, recessed into bodywork, have spring tensioned flush-fitting levers with locks. Electrically operated pumps controlled by changeover switch on instrument panel. Total fuel capacity 23 gallons.

ELECTRICAL EQUIPMENT AND INSTRUMENTS Lucas alternator and generator. 12-volt battery with negative earth system. Sidelamps. Four headlamp system. Foot operated dipswitch. Steering column lever for flashing headlamps. Stop/tail and direction lights mounted in single assembly. Twin reversing lights and reflectors. Self-cancelling flashing direction indicators. All four direction indicators operated as hazard warning lights when required. Instruments and labelled switches illuminated by internal lighting with two-position dimmer switch. Map reading light. Courtesy lights operated by switch on facia or automatically by opening doors. Luggage boot illumination. Cigar lighter with luminous socket. Twin-blended windtone horns. High pressure electrically operated windscreen washer. Twin blade, two-speed, self parking windscreen wipers. Automatic ignition advance. Ballast coil ignition. Speedometer with total trip and distance recorder. Revolution counter. Separate transistorised time clock. Battery condition indicator. Electrically operated oil gauge, water temperature gauge, fuel gauge, combined handbrake 'on' and brake fluid 'low level' warning light. Electrically heated rear window.

BODY All-steel, four-door, four/five seater body of integral construction, extensively proofed against sound and rust. Large semi-wraround, deep windscreen and rear window, both with slim pillars, giving maximum visibility front and rear. Wide view rear mirror incorporating dipping mechanism. Chromium-plated window frames to all doors. Chrome rain gutter finishers. Pleated upholstery and safety padding. Floors fully carpeted over thick felt underlay. Front seats have combined height and reach adjustment and reclining squabs with provision for fitting head-rests. Rear seat has central folding armrest. Front seat occupants have combined armrest/grab-handle on front doors. Polished figured walnut instrument panel, with heavily padded surround, incorporates lockable glove box with self-aligning internal vanity mirror. Padded central shelf beneath facia, rear door combined pocket/armrests and wide rear window shelf, provide generous space for maps and personal effects. Central console contains heating and ventilating controls, space for optional radio, gear lever mounting and twin ashtrays. Padded sun visors. Burst-proof locks to all four doors and concealed child-proof safety catches on rear doors. Heavy duty wraparound bumpers with over-riders. Seat belt anchorage points incorporated for front and rear seats.

HEATING AND VENTILATION The comprehensive heating and ventilation system features face level directional air ducts and separate rear compartment ducts, a heat-sensing unit for automatic control of air input temperature, two-speed flow fans, adjustable screen demister vents, and 'Posivent' air extraction for rapid and quiet change of air. Individual volume controls for left and right hand front compartment and for rear compartment.

LUGGAGE ACCOMMODATION Ample luggage accommodation is provided in a capacious compartment of 17 cu. ft. capacity. Counter-balanced lid for ease of operation. Interior lamp operated by automatic switch. Compartment fully trimmed to protect luggage.

SPARE WHEEL AND TOOLS Spare wheel carried beneath luggage compartment floor. Tool kit, jack and wheel brace, contained in spare-wheel compartment.

JACKING Four point jacking allows individual wheels to be raised. Special location studs adjacent to each wheel fit into forked lifting pad on screw type, manually operated, easy lift jack.

PRINCIPAL DIMENSIONS Wheel base 108·8 in: Track front 58 in. Track rear 58·6 in. Overall length 189·5 in. Overall width 69·6 in. Overall height 52·8 in. Ground clearance (mid-laden) 6 in. Dry weight: 2·8 litre, 30¼ cwt.: 4·2 litre, 30¾ cwt.

characteristics of its big brother. The engine (83×86 mm – 2,792 cc), developed 180 bhp at 6,000 rpm with a standard compression ratio of 9 to 1 (8 to 1 alternative). Although obviously no equal for the 4·2 version in terms of optimum performance, the smaller 'Sovereign' lost nothing in its handling qualities and refined character. Only seventeen years earlier the 'Regency' 3-litre weighing about the same, was regarded as quite something with its 'new' engine producing 90 bhp – exactly half of the 2·8 'Sovereign'. Such is progress!

At the time of introduction (October 1969) the prices for the New Sovereigns were: 2·8 version with overdrive £2,356.4.2 including £553.4.2 purchase tax (automatic transmission £61.7.3 extra), and for the 4·2 car with overdrive – £2,713.18.7 including £636.18.7 purchase tax (automatic transmission £91.8.10 extra). In January 1972, following further price increases, the automatic 2·8 cost a total of £2,878 and the automatic 4·2 £3,213.

The original Sovereign was a very good car but the later version was quite outstanding. Both types were produced in considerable numbers and for quite some while demand for the xj6 types was such that second-hand examples were able to command a handsome premium over the list price for a new car.

Competing with cars many times its price, the 4·2 'Sovereign' for the second successive year, won the Gold Medal for bodywork in the 'no price limit saloon category' at the 1971 motor show. Thereafter, advertisements in the press were captioned – 'maybe Daimler should call it the "Golden Sovereign" now'. No mechanical changes were made but the exhaust tail pipes were re-shaped and the door locking mechanisms slightly modified.

DAIMLER OF COVENTRY

have always been associated with quality, refinement and advanced engineering in the manufacture of sophisticated motor cars for its discerning audience.

All the skill of the craftsmen, all the science of the technicians, have retained for Daimler a leading position in the progressive and competitive world of luxury.

Today, that position is epitomised by the finest cars ever to carry the famous name of Daimler . . . . . . the Daimler Sovereign and the Daimler Limousine.

(*Daimler brochure 1970*)

The new Limousine (Type DS 420)

The limousine 'cockpit'

CHAPTER 15

The new Daimler Limousine – (Type DS 420)

Chassis numbers IM 1001–   ; (R.H.D.)
Chassis numbers IM 20001–   ; (L.H.D.)

V ANDEN PLAS (England) 1923 Ltd had for many years, been producing the highly successful Austin 'Princess' limousine and they and their parent Company, The British Motor Corporation had by the mid-'sixties plans for a successor: Daimler engineers and designers had been busy too, planning a replacement for the DR 450 V-8 limousine. When in July 1966 the Jaguar Group was integrated into British Motor Holdings, it was manifestly obvious that both the new projects could not be nurtured and in the result it was decided that the new model should be a Daimler and that Vanden Plas should be responsible for the coachwork. The combination of resources talent and tradition within the combine in this way was a prudent and economically necessary move.

Both the Daimler 'DR 450' and the 'Princess' limousines were by 1968, a bit old fashioned – the 'Princess' especially, as this was still powered by the Austin 4-litre engine (120 bhp at 4,000 rpm) dating from the late 'forties. Both cars were built on to separate chassis and both retained semi-elliptics for the rear springs.

By comparison with these, the new Daimler, revealed in April 1968, was quite radical. Rolls-Royce had dispensed with a conventional chassis frame for 'T' series Rolls and Bentley cars and Park Ward, Mulliner Ltd (a subsidiary of Rolls-Royce Ltd) had accepted the necessary transition from coachbuilding to body engineering. Only the Rolls 'Phantom V' limousine and a few special-to-order ceremonial cars were still built on to a conventional chassis and according to traditional coachbuilding practices. The new Daimler limousine, in common with the 'Sovereign' saloons, had no separate frame.

By cleverly utilizing as many body components as was practicable from the Jaguar '420 G' saloon, a base structure was contrived for the limousine. In this way the new model inherited from the race bred Jaguar a sophisticated modern all round independent suspension system providing excellent ride and handling characteristics of the highest order.

'420 G' pressings were used for the front inner wing and main scuttle structure, the main floor pressings with certain modifications, the double sills from the scuttle to the central door pillars and part of the rear seat and transverse

315

The New limousine supplied to Queen Elizabeth the Queen Mother – 1970

The rear compartment of the '420' limousine

structure and luggage compartment base. In the floor a 20 inches wide section was inserted to increase the wheelbase to 11 feet 9 inches.

Incidentally, during the embryonic stage, it was envisaged that a close-coupled saloon version might possibly emanate from the design, but the idea did not materialize beyond the prototype stage.

Optional extra equipment

Radio, front and/or rear compartment

Electrically operated aerial

Electrically operated front door windows

Electrically operated rear door windows

Electrically operated rear quarter-windows

Electrically operated division glasses

Chrome flag mast

Electrical time clock (rear compartment)

Adjustable reading lamp (rear compartment)

Nylon rug (rear compartment)

Rubber mats (front compartment)

Wing mirrors

Fire extinguishers

Fog lamps

Seat belts

Electrically heated backlight

Laminated windscreen

Rear compartment footrest

THE DAIMLER COMPANY LIMITED

The issue of this catalogue does not constitute an offer. The specification described in this brochure varies for different countries and The Daimler Company Limited reserves the right to amend specifications at any time without notice

317

The Daimler Limousine Specification

ENGINE—4·2 LITRE. Six-cylinder, twin overhead camshaft engine. 92·07 mm bore × 106 mm stroke (3·625 in. × 4·173 in.). Cubic capacity 4235 cc (258·43 cu. in.). Compression ratio 8·0 : 1. Power output 245 bhp at 5,500 rpm. Torque 282 lb/ft at 3,750 rpm. Twin S.U. carburetters, with automatic mixture enrichment for cold starting.

TRANSMISSION. Automatic transmission with dual drive range. Gear ratios: Top, 3·54—with torque conversion 7·08; Intermediate, 5·16/10·32; Low, 8·5/17·0; Reverse, 7·08/14·16. Gear selector on steering column. Needle bearing propeller shaft.

SUSPENSION—FRONT. Independent suspension incorporating semi-trailing wishbones and coil springs with telescopic dampers. Anti-roll bar between lower wishbones. Suspension assembly and steering gear are mounted on a separate subframe which is itself located in the body by rubber mountings.

SUSPENSION—REAR. Fully independent rear suspension incorporating, on either side, a lower transverse tubular link pivoted at the wheel carrier and subframe adjacent to the differential case and, above this, a half shaft universally jointed at each end. These serve to locate the wheel in a transverse plane. Longitudinal location is provided by the rubber mountings locating the sub-assembly in the body structure and by a radius arm between the lower link and a mounting point on the body structure. Twin coil springs, each enclosing a telescopic hydraulic damper, provide the suspension medium. The whole assembly, together with the differential unit, is carried in an easily detachable subframe which is located in the body structure by rubber mountings.

BRAKES. Servo-assisted disc brakes, featuring quick change pads, are fitted to all four wheels. System divided into two entirely independent hydraulic circuits to front and rear brakes. Handbrake with automatic adjustment operates on rear wheels only. Combined handbrake "on" and "low" brake fluid level warning light.

STEERING. Varying ratio power-assisted steering. Ratio 21·6 : 1 in a straight ahead position varying to 13 : 1 at full lock. 2·75 turns lock to lock. 17 in. diameter steering wheel adjustable for reach. Turning circle 46 ft.

WHEELS AND TYRES. Pressed steel bolt-on wheels fitted with 225 × 15 radial ply tyres and tubes. Spare wheel and tyre.

FUEL SUPPLY. Two separate tanks—one in each rear wing—total capacity 20 gallons. Two electrically operated S.U. fuel pumps (one for each tank) controlled by changeover switch on instrument panel. The filler to each tank is concealed beneath a lockable cover.

ELECTRICAL EQUIPMENT AND INSTRUMENTS. Lucas alternator. 12-volt battery with negative earth system. 60 amp/hour at 10 hour rate with current voltage control. Four-headlamp system with foot-operated dip switch. Separate lever for actuating headlamp flashing. Sidelamps. Separate stop/tail, direction and reflector units mounted in a single assembly. Twin reversing lamps. Self-cancelling flashing direction indicators with warning lights. Instruments and labelled switches illuminated by internal floodlighting with two-position dimmer switch. Overhead map reading lamp in front compartment operated automatically by front doors and manually by switch on fascia. Twin overhead courtesy lamps and twin door sill lamps in rear compartment operated automatically by rear doors and manually by switch incorporated in armrest. Luggage boot illumination controlled by automatic switch. Cigar lighters in front and rear compartment. Twin-blended windtone horns. Twin blade, two-speed, self-parking windscreen wipers. Electrically operated windscreen washers. Oil

coil ignition. 5 in. diameter speedometer incorporating total trip and distance recorder. 5 in. diameter impulse-driven revolution counter, ammeter, electrically operated oil pressure gauge, water temperature gauge, fuel gauge, combined handbrake "on" and "low" brake fluid level warning light. Separate transistorised time clock in front compartment.

BODY. All-steel four-door eight-seater limousine body, rustproofed and treated for maximum sound deadening characteristics. All doors forward hinged on concealed hinges. Accommodation for two persons, including driver, on bench type front seat, facing foldaway occasional seats. A fixed division between compartments incorporates sliding glasses and a flush-fitting ashtray. Front seats are finished in high-quality upholstery. Rear seats and occasional seats are upholstered in West of England cloth or finest quality leather. Rear seat squab incorporates folding central armrest. Side armrests in rear compartment each incorporate ashtray, cigar lighter, courtesy light switch and, on one side only, the heater controls. Floors in both compartments have fitted carpets over thick felt underlay. Roof and door fascias are padded and fully trimmed to match. Instrument panel, waist rails and wooden trim pieces in polished figured walnut. Screen rail and waist mouldings are safety padded and leather trimmed. Padded bulkhead in front compartment incorporates large map pocket. Window frames, door sill cappings and rain gutter finishers are chromium plated. The instruments and lockable glove box are neatly arranged in the main fascia panel, below which are located the heating and ventilating controls. Front doors have pivoted quarter-lights and windows down windows, in the rear compartment both door windows and side panel windows wind down. Sun visors. Chromed grab handles in front compartment. Leather straps in rear. Seat belt anchorages front and rear. Heavy-duty bumpers and overriders. "Zero torque" door locks enable doors to be closed easily and quietly. Overhead map reading lamp in front compartment operated automatically by front doors and manually by switch on fascia. Twin overhead courtesy lamps and twin door sill lamps in rear compartment operated automatically by rear doors and manually by switch incorporated in armrest.

HEATING AND DEMISTING. Fresh air dual heater unit capable of delivering a large volume of air at high or ambient temperature. Separate heating to rear compartment and separate supply controls. Air outlets, for through ventilation, are incorporated in the rear parcels shelf.

LUGGAGE ACCOMMODATION. Ample luggage accommodation is provided in the very large boot, which is fully trimmed to protect luggage. Illumination is provided by an automatically controlled interior light operated by opening the counterbalanced boot lid.

SPARE WHEEL AND TOOLS. The spare wheel is carried vertically in the luggage compartment and is readily accessible. A comprehensive set of tools is supplied in a special container, and this, together with the wheel-changing equipment, is fitted behind the spare wheel, which is supplied with a protective cover.

JACKING. Jacking posts on each side enable the car to be lifted with the minimum of effort by means of the jack provided.

PRINCIPAL DIMENSIONS. Wheelbase 11 ft 9 in., track front and rear 4 ft 10 in., overall length 18 ft. 10 in., overall width 6 ft 5¼ in., overall height 5 ft 3¼ in., ground clearance 7 in., turning circle 46 ft (approx.) dry weight 42 cwt.

Daimler limousine general dimensions

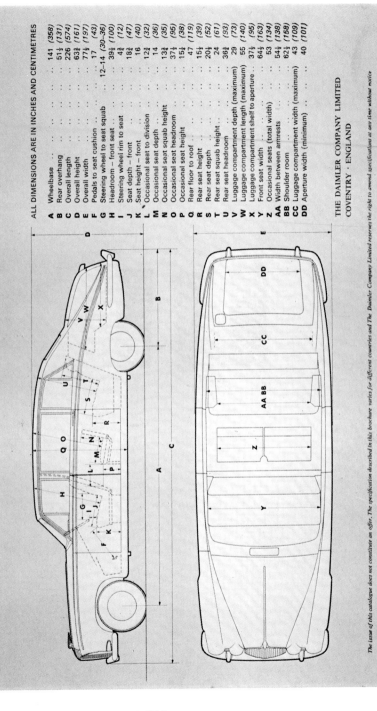

ALL DIMENSIONS ARE IN INCHES AND CENTIMETRES

A	Wheelbase	141 (358)
B	Rear overhang	51½ (131)
C	Overall length	226 (574)
D	Overall height	63½ (161)
E	Overall width	77½ (197)
F	Pedals to seat cushion	17 (43)
G	Steering wheel to seat squab	12–14 (30–36)
H	Headroom – front seat	39½ (100)
I	Steering wheel rim to seat	4½ (12)
J	Seat depth – front	18½ (47)
K	Seat height – front	16 (40)
L	Occasional seat to division	12½ (32)
M	Occasional seat depth	14 (36)
N	Occasional seat squab height	13½ (35)
O	Occasional seat headroom	37½ (95)
P	Occasional seat height	15½ (38)
Q	Rear floor to roof	47 (119)
R	Rear seat height	15½ (39)
S	Rear seat depth	20½ (52)
T	Rear seat squab height	24 (61)
U	Rear seat headroom	36½ (93)
V	Luggage compartment depth (maximum)	29 (73)
W	Luggage compartment length (maximum)	55 (140)
X	Luggage compartment shelf to aperture	37½ (95)
Y	Front seat width	64½ (163)
Z	Occasional seats (total width)	53 (134)
AA	Width between armrests	54½ (138)
BB	Shoulder room	62½ (158)
CC	Luggage compartment width (maximum)	43 (109)
DD	Aperture width (minimum)	40 (101)

THE DAIMLER COMPANY LIMITED
COVENTRY · ENGLAND

The issue of this catalogue does not constitute an offer. The specification described in this brochure varies for different countries and The Daimler Company Limited reserves the right to amend specifications at any time without notice

The 'DS 420' design was such as to permit assembly in 'chassis' form so that specialist hearse bodies could be mounted.

The engine was the standard twin overhead camshaft 6-cylinder 4·2-litre unit as used in the 'Sovereigns' with a Borg Warner automatic gearbox as standard. A two-piece needle bearing propeller shaft carried the drive to the Salisbury hypoid axle, via a centre bearing.

In yet another new form the Daimler fluted radiator focused attention on the pleasing frontal aspect of the car and the modern mildly-hooded four head-lamps blended well into the bold and stately good overall looks of the model. With so much of the car being Jaguar in origin, it was perhaps quite remarkable how traditionally Daimler the final product looked. There was a strong 'Hooper' look about the line and if compared with the 'Gold Daimler', the 'Empresses', and the special Hooper bodied 'DK 400's', the striking resemblance in part will be appreciated.

The body shells in bare metal were delivered to Vanden Plas at their Kings-bury, London works where they were phosphate-coated, bituminous-sealed, baked, primed, painted and trimmed. The assembled engine and other components were also sent from Coventry to Vanden Plas ready for installation or assembly. The entire car was an excellent example of the high class coachwork for which both Daimler and Vanden Plas were justly renowned.

Standard body colours were black or Carlton grey. Alternative colours listed at extra cost were maroon, dark green, light grey, or dark blue and to special order, certain other colours and combinations could be had. For upholstery, purchasers had a wide range of colours from which to select and there was also a choice of West of England cloth or leather.

The fascia board followed the familiar Jaguar layout with a cubby hole on the passenger side, the large speedometer and tachometer immediately ahead of the driver, with a centrally placed clock (just above the steering column). The smaller dials and switches were positioned in the middle of the fascia in an orderly and convenient fashion. As with the majority of limousines, the front seats were fixed but some variation in driving position could be obtained by adjustment of the telescopic steering.

Two occasional seats were normally fitted and so placed that three passengers could be seated thereon in reasonable comfort and of course the back seat would accommodate a further three. The division was normally fitted with sliding glass but an electrically operated partition was among the many optional extras. Others included:

Cocktail cabinet in the rear compartment fitted between narrower occasional seats.
A cocktail cabinet also enclosing a portable television set.
Dark glass all round the rear compartment for privacy.
Twin radio sets (one in front and one in back compartment) with twin electrically operated aerials.
Fluorescent lights in rear compartment.
Detachable blanking panels fitted to the quarter windows to provide additional privacy.

Special Plessey radio fitted to rear centre folding armrest (as fitted in the car supplied in 1970 to HM The Queen Mother).

Vanity box to rear centre armrest.

Radio/tape player fitted to rear side armrest with provision for storing tape cassettes in special compartment in rear centre folding armrest.

Eight-track stereo tape players.

Blue police light to front centre of roof for Royal cars only.

Provision for the fitting of Royal Insignia and Standard to roof.

Opera light to roof.

Relocation of spare wheel under a special flat floor in boot, which could also accommodate a radio telephone equipment.

Internal two-way telephone to enable conversation between chauffeur and rear compartment passengers.

Short-wave transmitter/receiver to front or rear compartment.

Special shaped seating to suit customers' requirements.

Concealed armour plating and special glass.

Vanden Plas limousine for the Congolese Ambassador in London – Reg. No. 1 CGO

Consistent with expectations for this modern Daimler, its performance was most commendable: 0 to 50 mph in 9·2 seconds; 0 to 100 mph in 43·5 seconds, and a standing start quarter of mile in 19·5 seconds with a top speed of around 110 mph. The original basic price was £3,461 (purchase tax an additional £963.9.5) and the drive-away 'chassis' was listed at £2,369 (exempt from tax). Inevitably price increases took effect and by January 1972 the figures were £4,531 plus £1,134·63 – purchase tax for the standard limousine and £3,020 in respect of the 'chassis'. There was nothing produced in the United Kingdom to compete with the Daimler and demand was always ahead of production. To date (January 1972) over one thousand limousines have been produced and more than 150 'chassis' have been turned out for mounting with hearse bodies by other specialists.

In 1968, – the year of its introduction, the model earned a Silver award for coachwork at Earls Court. The Gold medal went to the Rolls-Royce limousine costing more than double the price of the Daimler. The same position obtained in 1969, in 1970 and again in 1971. The limousine was supplied to many distinguished personages; the following among them:

	Body no.	Chassis no.
Her Majesty The Queen Mother	12493	1M 1559
King Hussein of Jordan	12300	1M 2008
King Frederick of Denmark	12351	1M 2009
Prince Rainier of Monaco	12668	1M 20033
The Ruler of Bahrain	12050	1M 1063
Prince Bismark	12175	1M 20005
Crown Prince of Luxembourg	12771	1M 20042
The Prime Minister of Mauritius	12418	1M 1454
The Prime Minister of Malawi	12386	1M 1418
The President of Nauri	12661	1M 1716
	12662	1M 1718
The President of Guyana	12759	1M 1813
King of Morocco	12770	1M 20043
The Sultan of Oman	12916	1M 20051
	12917	1M 20052

Daimler Hire Ltd have replaced their former 'DR 450' limousines with a fleet of the new 'DS 420's'. Increasingly the Daimler is sought after by many of the foreign embassies in London, the British Consulates in many parts of the world, by municipal corporations and the heads of large industrial and commercial concerns.

Vanden Plas have received enquiries for Daimler landaulettes and although there has been some experimentation, to date no such vehicle has been produced. The coachbuilders have, however, exhibited their ability to execute special orders. For the Congolese Ambassador in London (registration no. '1 CGO' – chassis IM 1655) Vanden Plas installed television, a cocktail cabinet, ice-box and cut-glass set.

In another limousine, a luxurious reclining seat with head rest and folding arm-rests was located in the centre of the rear compartment – with the primary object of enabling the owner to sit as near as possible midway between the axles and on the centre line of the car to reduce the effect of pitch and roll. This single seat was adjustable fore and aft and on the rear face of the division there was fitted a picnic table, ash tray, grab handle and in addition a radio/tape – player/ recorder.

The main back seat was itself modified and beneath a detachable cushion, there was provided a commode and in the centre portion of the seat there was a cubby box containing glasses and a water container together with two detachable picnic tables. Blinds were fitted to the windows and division.

The lower chromium waist strip was omitted from cars produced after January 1971 and in its place there was added coachlining. 'Mark II' would be an in-appropriate designation for examples produced from around chassis IM 2180

The above-mentioned limousine with special equipment

(RHD) onwards but from that time (early in 1972), further modifications were incorporated. The original two-piece drop-type rear quarter lights were replaced with one-piece swivel windows and inside an illusion of greater space and light was created by dispensing with the division top frame piece so that the glass extended up to the roof.

'those of us who grew up associating a Daimler radiator with important occasions are likely to see the association continued for at least another two decades with this new model'

(The Motor – 15th June 1968)

CHAPTER 16

The new Daimler 'Double Six'

For some considerable time rumour implied that Jaguar were working on a vee engine to supplement or succeed their illustrious twin-cam XK six-cylinder power unit. It was not at first known whether this would be a V8 or a V12, but the truth is out – the new engine is a 5·3-litre V12 with two (not twin) o.h. camshafts, for installation alongside the famous XK six in a revised E-type and ultimately, but not necessarily this year, in the fast-selling XJ saloons – one hesitates to say it at the present time, but a 12-cylinder XJ Jaguar, if sold at Sir William Lyons traditional competitive price, might well constitute a tough rival for the V8 Rolls-Royce Silver Shadow. However, that is for the future . . .   (*Motor Sport*, April 1971)

In the early 1960's an experimental Jaguar V12 engine was designed and built for racing purposes. After only modest development the 5-litre unit (87·5 × 70 mm) with two cams per bank and with fuel injection was at 8,000 rpm producing something in excess of 500 bhp.

From this experimental racing Jaguar engine was evolved a single overhead camshaft per bank V12 unit which was ultimately adopted for production and which was disclosed to the public on the 29th March 1971.

This new 60° vee engine has a capacity of 5,343 cc (90 × 70 mm) and produces 314 bhp at 6,200 rpm on a 9 to 1 compression. Single overhead chain driven camshafts serve each bank of cylinders; carburation is provided by four Zenith–Stromberg instruments; in place of a conventional contact breaker there is (for the first time on an engine intended to be produced in quantity) a Lucas Opus mark 2 electronic ignition system; in the construction of the engine, extensive use has been made of light alloys – the cylinder block, heads, tappet blocks, crown-recessed pistons, inlet manifolds, sump and many other parts are constructed from aluminium alloy – and in the result the engine complete with exhaust emission equipment and all ancillaries, weighs only 680 lb; the 3-plane forged steel crankshaft runs in seven main bearings; and the lubrication system incorporates an oil heat exchanger, also of cast aluminium and an oil pump of the 'crescent' gear type.

The foregoing hardly does justice to the design team of Walter Hassan, Harry Mundy, Claude Baily and their leader Bill Heynes, but it may serve to indicate that the product of their labours is a significant and very advanced piece of automobile engineering. Constructional methods at Radford, Coventry are equally advanced. At a cost of around £3 million a new production line equipped with

The Jaguar V-12 (the new Daimler Double-Six power unit)

the very latest machinery has been installed and this has an optimum output of approximately one thousand units per week.

It is therefore unlikely that the v12 will for long be confined to the 'ᴇ'-type – a logical and indeed expected progression will be to endow the xᴊ saloons with the new unit.

The Daimler 'Double-Six' represents the finest achievement that has ever been made in engine construction . . .

– that assertion was made in 1927 but it may not be without relevance in 1972. The history of the marque is still in the making and the announcement of a New Daimler 'Double-Six' (utilizing the existing Sovereign body) is eagerly awaited.

As befits the longest-established of all British marques, Daimler today worthily upholds its fine tradition in the production of the top prestige models in the vast British Leyland range. As a matter of conjecture, thoughts of a Vanden Plas v12 limousine may not be out of place. Of this at least we can be certain – The Daimler Tradition is a living tradition!

Appendix

The Daimler and Lanchester Owners' Club was inaugurated on the 6th June 1964 and since 1969 it has incorporated The Lanchester Register.

The principal objects of the Club are to preserve as many examples of the marques as may be possible and to maintain them in roadworthy condition. To this end a spares register is kept, a monthly magazine is issued and technical and general advice is proffered. The cars command respect on the road – so should their drivers and through diverse activities the Club seeks to promote skill in driving and courtesy on the road. There are several active branches of the Club and a special section caters specifically for SP 250 owners. Social and other functions and events are held throughout the year.

Full membership is open to the owner of any Daimler or Lanchester car and to owners of certain BSA cars.

Patrons: Sir William Lyons and Mrs G. Lanchester

President: F. W. Hutton-Stott

General Secretary: H. D. Saunders, Eastgate House, Top Street, Appleby Magna, Burton-on-Trent, Staffs.

Members' Secretary: I. Venables, 1 Lullington Road, Overseal, Derby

Chairman and Technical Adviser: C. B. Bromfield, 38 Clayton Road, Coundon, Coventry

Registrar and Historian: B. E. Smith, 81 Lake Rise, Romford, Essex

Index

Page numbers in italics refer to illustrations

Turner, E., 269, 276, 285, 295
Twenty, *83*; Light introduced, 101, *105–6*
Twenty-Four introduced, 98, *116–8*
Twenty-Five introduced, 71, *72–3*, 80
Twenty-Seven introduced, 147, *148*, *150–4*
Tyres, 8, 9, 11, 48, 203, 225, *229*, 246, 271, 284, 308

Vacuum booster, 245
Valves (*and see* sleeve), 2, 15, 20, 22, 82, 84, 88, 90, *91*, 131, 152, 190, 189, 220, 221
Vanden Plas, vi, 98, *110*, *156*, 157, 259, 300, 315, 320, *321*, 322, 323, 326
Vaumol hide, 164, 293, 300
Vauxhall Cresta, 285
Venables, I. 327
Ventilation, 50, 115, 164, 195, 216, *233*, 233, 246, 248, 257, 258, 291
Victoria, Queen, 260
Visco-static, 273

Walker, C. M., 49
Walter, Martin, *57*, *92*, *110*
War, World I, *32*, *34*, *35*, *37*, 39

War, World II, 98, 119, *124*, 241
Warners, 179
Water jacket, 219
Water pump, 132, 149, 190
Westbury, P., 282
Weymann, 56
Weymouth, 76
Wheels, 8, 139, 196, 200, 271, 276, 277, 284
Wheelbase, 27, 40, 50, 62, 68, 71, 81, 89, 92, 100, 147, 160, 245, 249, 250, 295
Wilson, Captain, 75, 241
Windermere, Lake, 293
Windovers, vi, 101, *111*, 120, 153, *154*, 155, 160, 162
Wisdom, Tommy, 183
Wolverhampton, 127
Wood & Piggott Ltd, vi
Worm drive, 20, 22, 24–7, 44, 80, 140

Young, J., 87, *94*, 102

Zenith, 221
Zenith-Stromberg, 325